The **OCEAN** *in the* **SCHOOL**

Duke University Press · Durham and London · 2020

The OCEAN
in the SCHOOL

PACIFIC ISLANDER
STUDENTS TRANSFORMING
THEIR UNIVERSITY

RICK BONUS

Library of Congress Cataloging-in-Publication Data
Names: Bonus, Rick, [date] author.
Title: The ocean in the school : Pacific Islander students transforming their
university / Rick Bonus.
Description: Durham : Duke University Press, 2020. |
Includes bibliographical references and index.
Identifiers: LCCN 2019016286 (print)
LCCN 2019980922 (ebook)
ISBN 9781478006046 (hardcover)
ISBN 9781478006725 (paperback)
ISBN 9781478007425 (ebook)
Subjects: LCSH: Pacific Islanders—Education (Higher)—Washington (State)
| Pacific Islander American students—Washington (State) |
Education, Higher—Social aspects—United States. | Educational
equalization—United States. | Academic achievement—United States.
Classification: LCC LC3501.P33 B66 2020 (print) | LCC LC3501.P33 (ebook) |
DDC 378.1/982909797—dc23
LC record available at https://lccn.loc.gov/2019016286
LC ebook record available at https://lccn.loc.gov/2019980922

Cover art: *Hina kakau ki Nukuseaveave*, 2017. © Va'eomatoka Valu. Courtesy
of the artist.

FOR MY STUDENTS,

FOR OUR OCEAN.

The Ocean in the School presents a set of ethnographic tales and analyses about Pacific Islander students and their allies who attempted to transform a university that they thought did not value their presence on campus. It is an account of the struggles that underrepresented and nontraditional students faced in light of educational programs that attempted to promote "diversity" without much structural change, and the ways in which such struggles were generative of alternative attitudes and practices that enabled college "success" for them. It is a story of how students turned to their indigenous and evolving conception of the "ocean" to understand their world, their school, and themselves, as much as it is a chronicle of how the students' "ocean" became a site of unlimited possibilities in their quest for meaningful schooling.

All of the students mentioned in this book have been or are still mentees of mine, and it is to them that I express my fullest gratitude for being part of my work. They are the reason why this book project began, they were my partners when this ethnography proceeded, and they became my primary motivators for writing and finishing this manuscript. For those who know them, you will probably recognize David G. Palaita and Michael Tuncap in this book, as you will Nestor Enguerra Jr., Brukab Sisay, Deborah Tugaga, Staliedaniel Uele, Taylor Ahana-Jamile, Benjamin Lealofi, Toka Valu, Hork Chay Do, and so many others. Research protocol forbids me to name them directly in the book, but I have no qualms about thanking them profusely out in the open. They, and a whole array of students that I have closely worked with over the course of doing this ethnography—more than sixty-five in number, and growing—have shown me how loving and caring for each other in a school environment is *constitutive* of meaningful schooling, not decorative or supplementary to all the learning that takes place within and outside of our campuses. I am forever indebted to all of you, and this book is but one expression of my desire to always keep you close in our ocean.

Martin Manalansan IV and Ileana Rodriguez-Silva have been my daily companions in working on this book. I am grateful for your deep generosity in sharing your intellect and time with me, and I am truly blessed and honored to count you as my lifelong friends. I thank the rest of our *juju* study table members—Chandan Reddy, Kiko Benitez, Stephanie Smallwood, Gillian Marshall, Maria Oropeza—and my esteemed colleagues at the University of Washington (UW): Moon Ho Jung, Michelle Habell-Pallan, Angela Ginorio, Juan Guerra, Sonnet Retman, Connie So, Richard Atienza, Kell Juan, Jacque Waita, Carolyn Pinedo-Turnovsky, LaShawnDa Pittman, La TaSha Levy, Devon Peña, Lauro Flores, Jang Wook Huh, Linh Nguyen, Alina Mendez, Dian Million, Christopher Mena, Gail Nomura, Steve Sumida, Anjelica Hernandez-Cordero, Lorna Hamill, Ellen Palms, Harry Murphy, and Tekea Tesfaldet. In so many ways, you have all supported my work with unparalleled understanding and kindness. Miriam Bartha, Priti Ramamurthy, Shirley Yee, Jim and Cherry McGee Banks, Holly Barker, Mimi Khan, Gene Edgar, Ana Mari Cauce, Shirley Hune, Susan Kemp, Vince Rafael, Suhanthie Motha, Sasha Welland, and Habiba Ibrahim are colleagues who help me find meaning in my work and in our work within collectives; thank you for building community with me.

Myron Apilado, Rusty Barcelo, Rickey Hall, Gabriel Gallardo, Linda Ando, Ink Aleaga, Cynthia Del Rosario, Raul Anaya, Gene Kim, Sheila Edwards Lang, Betty Schmitz, Keoke Silvano, Tey Thach, Cicero Delfin, and Muhamed Manhsour have always supported my work with students in their own ways; I am most grateful for your warm sustenance over the years. I want to honor the guidance and friendship of people I worked with from my "other offices" at the Southeast Asia Center, the Diversity Minor Program, and the Oceania and Pacific Islander Studies Minor Program: Laurie Sears, Sara Van Fleet, Tikka Sears, Judith Henchy, McKay Caruthers, Celia Lowe, Jenna Grant, Shannon Bush, Christina Sunardi, Luoth Yin, Marc Robinson, Derek White, Eric Hamilton, Sarah Ledbetter, Jamie Barnhorst, and Kai Wise. I am grateful for all the support of my work provided to me by several UW units: the Office of Minority Affairs and Diversity; the Royalty Research Fund (grant no. 3409); the President's Diversity Appraisal Implementation Fund; the Jeff and Susan Brotman Diversity Award; the Simpson Center for the Humanities, especially Kathy Woodward; and the dean's office in the College of Arts and Sciences, particularly Bob Stacey, Susan Jeffords, Judy Howard, and George Lovell. My participation in "The Politics of Storytelling in Island Imperial Formations," a Simpson Center–funded conference organized by Laurie Sears and Ileana Rodriguez-Silva, helped me tremendously in getting through my final thoughts on this book project and resulted in an essay version of it; thank you for inviting me!

Outside the university, I am indebted to the members and leaders of the Northwest Association of Pacific Americans, the Filipino American Educators of Washington, the Association for Asian American Studies, the American Studies Association, the Japanese Association for American Studies, the Association for the Study of Higher Education, the National Conference on Race and Ethnicity in Higher Education, the American Educational Research Association, the Asian American and Native American Pacific Islander-Serving Institutions program, the City College of San Francisco, and the Philippine Women's University for their generosity in supporting and funding parts of my research and for encouraging me to present my work in their meetings.

My research assistants have helped me immensely in this project, so I thank them profusely: Exekiel Arañez, Third Andresen, Nestor Enguerra Jr., Niño Guzman, Myra Aquino, and, most significantly, Thaomi Michelle Dinh. I have also benefited from, and am therefore grateful to, the more informal assistance, deep connection, and selfless guidance provided by the following students and mentees of mine: Brady Angeles, Reuben Deleon, Michael Schulze-Oechtering, Cheryll Alipio, Helen Enguerra, Donna Enguerra, Isaac Simpson, Alina Aleaga, Ryan Javier, Jonny Esparza, Kefu Puloka, Tui Tausinga, Joseph Mose, Manu Fifita, Timothy Nguyen, Patrick Pineda, Tina Arañez, Rachel Aleaga, Apa'auletalalelei Talalemotu, Malaelupe Kiunga Samifua, Christina Pelesasa, Natalie Santos, Matthew Vaeena, Harrison Togia, Kiana Fuega, Kapiolani Laronal, Vake Mafi, Junior Coffin, Tusi Sa'au, Andrew Acob, Tino Camacho, Mario Teulilo, Vanessa Matautia, Trenton Tuiasosopo, Mark Palaita, Chasmon Tarimel, Stephen Martir, Stephen Selam, Daniel Tugaga, Sione Potoa'e, Kyle Chow, Michael Otaguro, Daya Mortel, Maile Kaneko, Antonio Manalo, Edgar Flores, Angelita Chavez, Renato Mendoza, Alex Cuevas, Andy Garza, Victor Diaz, Osvaldo Guel, Priscilla Donkor, Ethiopia Berta, Arthur Sepulveda, Michael Peralta, Heinz Henry Togafau, Clarissa Sugatan-Santiago, Adrienne Ines, Ane Phillips, Jedidiah Enguerra, Theresa Enguerra, Jonas Nocom, Tulili Tuiteleleapaga-Howard, Nuki Makasini, Raymond Westerlund, Grace Tuato'o, Kat Punzalan, Jason Nocom, Dalya Perez, Edward Nadurata, and Benze Deraco. My mentors, colleagues, and friends George Lipsitz, Lisa Lowe, Yen Le Espiritu, Dina Maramba, Tony Tiongson, Linda Trinh Vo, Shirley Hune, Mary Yu Danico, Gary Colmenar, Theo Gonzalves, Leo Pangelinan, Joseph Ruanto-Ramirez, Allan Isaac, Anna Gonzalez, Robyn Rodriguez, Nerissa Balce, Lucy M. Burns, Dylan Rodriguez, Emily Ignacio, Rudy Guevarra Jr., E. San Juan Jr., Keith Camacho, Anita Morales, Ed and Vicky Villacorta, Cindy Domingo, Frank Irigon, Gloria Adams, Lauren Divina, and Akira Kinoshita have always understood the politics of my work, so I am most appreciative of their warmth, encouragement, and abiding intellectual input. Ken Wissoker of Duke University Press, thank you so much for your remarkable sustenance of and faith in my project. And to Nancy Abelmann, thank you for your work on race and schooling; I am forever inspired by your amazing scholarship on students of color.

The enduring love and kindhearted nourishment provided by my family and friends are stuff I won't survive without, so I am immensely grateful to all of you: Marie Nanette Bonus, Bobby and Rosanna Bonus, Maritel and Manny Naguit, Vida Bonus Anderson, Emma Bonus and Laurence Foster; Noelle, Kat and Justin, Matthew and Marie, Paulo and Abby, Jay and Claire, Mya Anne, Michelle and Rommel, Monica and John, Victoria Bonus Cecilio, Chloe, Cayson, Romeo, and Sera; Bebigel Valenzuela; Joji and Billy Guzman, Armin and Maria Guzman, Niño and Lei Guzman, Anne and Noynoy Castillo, Madelynn, Alivia, Sophia, Preston, Noah, and Rylee; Dondi and Fay Dizon, Cristina, Anton, Mel, and Andru; Digos, Glo, Pearlie, Jerry, Marilu, and Jeremy Caudal; and Veronica and Gilby Cabrera. I especially honor the memory of Eddie and Miren Bonus, Lucy and Isio Tiongco, Cely Dizon, and Lita Andrade. And, of course, I can't miss mentioning my lifelong friends David Ria Vera Cruz, Bobby Abastillas, Manolo Tanquilut, Bebon Gatuslao, Ariel Reyes, and Mariole Alberto. *Maraming marami pong salamat sa inyo!*

INTRODUCTION
What Does It Mean to Transform Schooling?

Going to this campus introduced me to many people and definitely changed my life. But me and my friends . . . we also changed this campus.

. . .

I dropped out of college because I couldn't take it anymore. I was ditching class, I was angry at my teachers, I was not havin' a good time. But hey, I didn't drop out because I failed. I didn't fail, you know. School failed me.

. . .

On the eve of her graduation from college, a young Pacific Islander woman told me how excited she was that, at last, her school was graduating with a degree *from her*. I did a double take and responded, "Say what?" "Yup," she said. "It's not just me who's really graduating, you know. It's the school too! I taught [this school] what our culture is, I taught it how to respect us, I taught it how to practice it. So yeah, I'm giving it a diploma, ha-ha, even though it's barely passing, you know. Congratulations!"

That same year, during the summer school session right after graduation, I was cleaning up my office when a young man, a Filipino who also identified as Pacific Islander, came knocking unexpectedly. I was surprised. I hadn't seen him for a while. And I wasn't sure if he was still a student, or had left school, or was somewhere in between. I wondered quietly, but I didn't want to ask him about school right away. So, after our usual hugs and how-are-yous, as well as brief social updates, I half seriously asked, "So where are you now? Are you gonna be back sometime soon? Or have you finally given up on school?" "Ha-ha," he replied. "You're funny. I haven't given up on school. School gave up on me!"

I begin with the two epigraphs above, and the parallel anecdotes after them, to frame a set of ethnographic tales about the multilevel meanings and critiques of schooling for select groups of students of color in a major research university in the U.S. Pacific Northwest—the Seattle campus of the University of Washington (UW). These were students I taught, mentored, advised, and interacted with as a professor and academic program director in this university. I offer these narratives, along with my framing and analysis of them, as an engagement with ideas and practices of transforming schools—making them more meaningful to the cultures and experiences of all their students so that they can thrive in them—by proposing that we consider seriously how students themselves define and make meaning out of their own schooling experiences.[1] Transforming schools entails reworking places of learning in a structural sense, instead of focusing solely on making students individually conform or change in order to do better in them. I propose that in this affirmation of student meaning making, we make antiracism and the larger struggles toward social justice be the central practices of changing schools, from those that emphasize the subjugation and control of students' minds and communities into those that value meaningfulness, respect, and critical thinking of everyone who participates in them. In this regard, I present the specific university experiences of mainly Pacific Islanders, including their allies at the UW—students who also identified as Filipina/o Americans, African and African Americans, Native Americans, Southeast Asian Americans, and Chicanas/Chicanos/Latinas/Latinos—to provide a glimpse of how such meaning making looks from the perspectives of selected members of these underrepresented groups and within the context of a large urban university that has expressed a strong commitment to the well-being of its increasingly diverse student body.[2] This is a study, then, of some members of a higher educational institution—about sixty-five of them[3]—and what they thought about their university and their experiences in it, including especially how they attempted to change or transform it. It is not a formal study of the school per se, although one major part of this work looked into a university-supported student retention program, and a chapter touches on a study abroad program offered as a university course.[4]

Through ethnographic fieldwork conducted from 2004 to 2009, and continuing informally until 2018, I offer a set of student voices that fundamentally critiques certain schooling practices that ignore or devalue racial difference and consequently impede meaningful college education. Such a critique, I argue, can be most adequately understood not when it is just seen as responding to local school-specific occurrences that appear isolated and decontextualized, but only when it is placed constitutively within the larger historical conditions of racism and other forms of school inequity in the United States. These conditions are principally mediated within long-standing arguments and debates about the presence of nonwhite bodies in schools and the power that these bodies hold (or not) in relationship to dominant school cultures.[5] Hence, we can imagine these student voices as coming from those whose underrepresentation does not merely emanate from a position that denotes their on-campus marginality or powerlessness; they are expressions of what contemporary university schooling looks like in a moment when more and more nonwhite students are entering our schools, while many of our ways of teaching all of our increasingly diverse students have remained quite unchanged.[6]

Contemporaneously, and most critically, we may also begin to limn how the experiences of such an ignored and "underrepresented presence" on many campuses signify the realities of U.S. schooling within imperial, global, and transnational frameworks. These optics allow us to recognize, for example, how the university in the United States was and has been a central defining apparatus for the disciplining and constructing of "American citizens" and workers, especially of nonwhite populations in places here and abroad, and through circuits of power and control over the resources and destinies of those who are subjected to it.[7] So, to say that the college experiences of Pacific Islander students and those who are similarly situated are merely the mirror consequences of their perceived outsider or even "foreigner" status is to discount their colonial relationship to the U.S. state and their parallel histories with others who have been enslaved, exploited, and dominated under the aegis of U.S. global imperialism.[8] To wit, many of these students and their parents may have come from places outside of the United States and the U.S. mainland, but all of the students' historical and continuing encounters with U.S. society—whether through formal and informal colonization or within global circuits of economic exploitation and cultural domination—had most assuredly already begun long before they arrived on the mainland and enrolled in its educational institutions.[9] To assume, then, that all these students unwittingly enter our schools as ignorant and empty vessels ready and willing to be filled with Western knowledge and skills that they have no prior critique of is to undervalue the impact and critique of U.S. imperialism, settler colonialism, and white supremacy here and abroad.[10] Such omissions of historical and sociopolitical contextualization often drive many of our school engines to run at idle despite the increased presence of these students on U.S. campuses.

In so many ways, then, the student critiques that I represent in this book are informed by the contexts I mentioned above—a consciousness of both the historical and continuing effects of racism and social inequality, as well as imperialism and neoliberalism,[11] in several forms and locations that students were already well aware of before entering college, but that they learned to think about in more complex and sometimes unsure or contradictory ways during my conversations with them. In varying forms and intensities, then, the students in this book, like many students in general, belonged to off-campus and on-campus communities that defined and gave meaning to their lives. But what set them apart from most other students were their experiences of realizing, once they set foot on campus, that their prior communities, backgrounds, and histories had little or no value in relationship to their college education. These, they connected most directly with racism and imperialism. And then, yoked with this set of experiences were the multiple strands of student and community devaluation that explained why their people's histories were not taught, why most of their teachers and classmates did not know anything about them (or knew them only in demeaning ways), and why most everyone made them feel that they did not belong in a campus that ironically acknowledged them loudly, but only when their nominal value needed to be proclaimed.[12] They felt that they were struggling to succeed, or at least exist, in a place that did not know, value, or truly care for them. This was at the heart of their critique.

In considering both the students' specific historical and contemporary contexts, along with their critiques of the educational institution that they became a part of, I place this study within the academic literature of educational research that has been concerned with minorities in schools. This subject encompasses such a wide range of interests—from studies that assess the impact of institutional desegregation all the way to policy recommendations regarding culturally sensitive teacher training—so I wish to train our attention to a more specific research focus here, which is the study of college-level school transformation from the perspectives of underrepresented students. Numerous studies point to students' identities and their personal and social development as keys to understanding their higher education experiences and, to a great extent, their performance as students—something that I interrogate centrally in this book.[13] But fewer studies consider at the same time, or with equal attention, the "identities" of schools themselves, particularly in the ways they are made manifest to minority students, as principal variables that significantly shape student and school performance. These, in daily transaction with the collective identities of underrepresented students, are what I more substantively focus on here. By school identities, I mean to say that similar to how students comprehend and "develop" their own personal and social identities, they also observe, experience, and question how their school is racialized, classed, gendered, sexualized, and differentiated through other interrelated forms of social categorization.[14] Despite appearing to most others as neutral, unremarkable, or simply possessing innocuous institutional "character," the university, as the students reveal here, has everything else but those qualities.[15] It has a culture of a dominant and dominating kind, a set of practices that privilege some over others, and a smug attitude of exclusivity and elitism that is oftentimes regarded as "the way things work" or something that has very little connection with inequity. The individuals in this study lived with and through these university identities, so much so that their experiences as students and, for many, as student activists were most definitively influenced by the critical attention they directed at figuring out how such institutional identities mattered to them and affected them so. Later on, students would realize the extent to which their efforts at school identity transformation—with the angle of intervention pointed most directly at their university, along with their relationship to it—would butt heads with emerging pressures for their school to cut costs, increase class sizes and tuition fees, and rely on other free market approaches to education in a neoliberal moment of decreasing state support for all levels of schooling.[16]

How, then, did school transformation occur? As minority students, Pacific Islanders and their allies felt the deep hold of their institution upon their on-campus lives, adversely affecting their motivation to succeed or limiting their opportunities to do better even when they or their teachers thought they were being successful. But simultaneously, these experiences and school conditions were also generative of a set of proactive gestures and attitudes that altogether comprise what I consider to be a cultural politics of transformative schooling for youth of color, a set of practices that students and I would collectively and metaphorically connect with conceiving "the ocean in the school." We attribute the intellectual and cultural/community source of this conception fundamentally to Epeli Hauʻofa, a Fijian anthropologist, essayist, storyteller, and poet of Tongan ancestry, whose writings about Oceania as an alternative episteme for those who inhabit it, or have a deep relationship with it, were an important source of knowledge and inspiration for students who have traveled far away from their ancestors' homes.[17] Looking to the ocean, as Hauʻofa writes, not only as the referent for many Pacific Islanders' sacred ancestral space, but as a repository of values, conditions, and resources that are specific to those who are connected with it, was something that students found meaningful in making sense of their struggles on campus.[18]

The ocean, or at least the imagination of its presence in everything they did in the university, represented to the students a most highly regarded aspect of their social lives that somehow extended the reach of their relationships to distant ancestral locations—since the ocean connected, not separated, them—and deepened the recognition of their current fates.[19] In reference to their particular situations, then, to regard the ocean in the school was to name the students' strategic resolution of their alienation as a consequence of their physical sensory distance from what they regarded as home, as much as it was to signify the compendium of struggles and strategies that students had to go through given their political and cultural distance from the power to determine their schooling process. It meant grappling with the realities of imperialism, underrepresentation, and minoritization while devising creative ideas and actions to mitigate, circumscribe, or transform such realities through and within the contexts of oceanic sensibilities. It drew from what they knew by heart about what it meant to be related to one another, the importance of respecting nature, ancestry, and religious belief, and how paramount it was to care for the community above the self—almost everything that they thought their university did not care much about. It was through these imaginations and practices of "the ocean" that these students were able to find clarity and clarification in figuring out the complications of their historical and cultural locations, especially for those whose comprehension of indigenous culture was something wedded to native land set amid a vast ocean. And, as participants in an elite university, it also became the students' wellspring of critical thinking and source of alternative practice against color-blind discourse, ignorance, and understandings of "diversity"—a term that was so much in vogue during the conduct of this study—that were shallow, empty, and toothless.[20] Such strategies derived from what students understood as their communities' cultural practices, indigenous traditions, and moral values, in tandem with their homegrown and transplanted experiences of family and social upbringing.[21]

As such, *The Ocean in the School* presents a most historically fraught, collectively inflected, but site-specific set of conditions that students experienced, which effectively generated particular practices that students and their teachers and mentors devised, tested, applied, and promoted. These advocacies included building and sustaining on-campus communities that valued students' cultures and histories, supporting off-campus networks that mitigated the separation between student lives within and outside of campus, and reimagining specific nondominant cultures not just as practiced within the space of the "extracurricular" but as cultures and conditions that were justifiably integral to overall university learning. These were advocacies that recognized and appreciated the crucial connections between notions and practices of cultural identities and experiences—mostly imagined as racial in these cases—and school performance, connections that are pursued by a subfield of education studies that this work is in conversation with. Scholars of multicultural education, principally trailblazed by James A. Banks, Cherry A. McGee Banks, and Sonia Nieto, have made numerous claims about how schools perpetuate racism and other forms of injustice, which, in turn, cause profound harm to all its students, especially those coming from minority backgrounds. Critical of pursuing antiracism in campuses by merely celebrating "heroes and holidays" or by simply offering courses in native languages and cultures in order to foster tolerance and "good feelings" among students, such scholars call for more direct and purposeful challenges to racism and all forms of discrimination in schools and the larger society. These challenges may take the form of culturally conscious pedagogy, multicultural and socially critical curricula, and schooling opportunities that promote reflections on and actions against institutional and systemic forms of discrimination, white privilege, and white supremacy, including the disempowerment of minority groups. In all of these, the educational goals are directed toward the attainment of social justice through a critique of and set of actions against different forms of oppression within and outside of schools.[22]

For this ethnography, I extend the discussion of these critiques and advocacies by calculating their specific significance within long-standing debates regarding postsecondary student performance in particular. Many of our preoccupations about how students fare in college, especially in a period of radical changes in student demographics in most urban universities, as well as the increasing prominence of neoliberal ideologies in running educational institutions in general, enable us to think more deeply about why we run our schools the way we do and ultimately behoove us to ruminate on the overall significance of university schooling in our society.[23] In this book, I will build and sustain these interests regarding the logic between student performance and school significance as thematic hooks that will run across each and every ethnographic portrait. Why do our students perform in particular ways? And how are these performances linked to our thinking regarding the role of schools in society? I will use this logic to frame and inform my arguments regarding the students' quest for change and transformation in our schools. In the following section, then, I will introduce you to a good part of the world that students in this book inhabited, as a way to familiarize us with a specific set of academic frameworks and attitudes within which we gauge their college performance.

FAILURE AND SUCCESS

Why do certain students fail in college, while the seeming vast majority of students succeed? When such students fail, how do we understand their failure and to what do we attribute such failure? Or when they succeed, besides asking what enabled them to succeed, how do we define and measure their accomplishments? What accounts of failure and success get privileged in the discourse and practice of university schooling, and which ones get submerged or excluded especially when calls for repairing student failure or for applauding student success are voiced? I focus on these questions to highlight the principal thematic aspects of this ethnography. In truth, I began this work, over ten years ago, with a different set of questions that poked at the reasons why certain students who are usually thought of as "high risk" were surprisingly doing well in school. They were earning grades in the high Bs and As, and they were graduating on time, in six years or less, rounding up our conventional ways of referencing "college success." I was interested in finding out what was motivating them to succeed; what strategies for success were they alternatively, if not inventively, deploying; and what impact did they have on others. I was on my way to preparing what I envisioned to be a blueprint for college achievement.[24] But as I got to know the students more deeply, both those who were flourishing and some who were leaving school (as a way to perform a comparison), I began to ruminate about what I thought was a more profound set of questions that plumbed deeper than what my original interest in student achievement could potentially reveal.

What changed? I was, first of all, struck by my subjects' extraordinary levels of academic engagement both as students in the classrooms *and* as campus activists who demanded what many would call "school reform" right in the offices of our university administration. Their acute sense of the ways in which schools deprived them of what they thought of as meaningful and culturally relevant education, their firm grasp of the historical depth of social injustice within which their demands were contextualized, and their insistence that they be heard and valued even though their numbers were small, all gave me a vivid impression that something much greater than highly engaged school performance was afoot here. These students were bright, accomplished, and high achieving. They entered and were enduring the university with the so-called right tools to enable them to succeed, and their successes were both envied by other students and lauded by their teachers, including me. Yet they were also demanding that the very place that was giving them academic accolades left and right be changed. They were challenging their university to treat them and others like them differently, not similarly. They were daring their teachers to be educated on who they were and why their histories and communities mattered. They wanted their school to be transformed.

These college students, the first batch of those I observed and interviewed, identified themselves collectively as Pacific Islanders. They were troubled by the historical failure of their university to recruit, retain, and graduate substantial numbers of Pacific Islander and other underrepresented students and were poignantly appealing for greater inclusion of minorities in all levels of the university and a more diversified curriculum from their location as straight-A students, but it took me a while to figure out the logic of their claims.[25] One would assume, say, that these high achievers should not have been having problems with racial isolation and white-exclusive curricula precisely because they were succeeding despite such conditions.[26] Why would they bite the hand that was enabling them to succeed? And why would they want to change the terms and conditions that were allowing them to flourish? These incoherencies and contradictions captured my interest in exploring how particular kinds of students who are not the majority on their campus experience uniquely the realities of underrepresentation, a telling reminder that minority status does not translate neatly into predictions and expectations of (low) student performance. I was also awed at how these realities coincided with or, in fact, generated a specific narrative of advocacy that demanded a transformation of how we understand student achievement and student failure or, even larger, the meanings of a university education as a whole. As we will see in the rest of the narrative of this ethnography, the subjects in it draw eloquent distinctions between school success that can only be narrowly defined as assimilative or conservative and school success and *failure* that can both be powerfully marshaled toward, dare we say, revolutionary change in our schools.

To a similar degree that these students were advocating for an enriching experience in their school via a counterintuitive internal politics of transformation, another group of students—in particular, a less vocal group who identified individually as Pacific Islanders, Filipino Americans, and Chicanos—were reckoning with their struggles in schooling as an effect of their exclusion from it. These students stopped going to school at different periods in their lives, and because I knew them as mentees when they were still attending college, we maintained close contact with each other even after they left. I should venture to say right from the outset that these students withdrew themselves from school not because they were not intelligent. They were not students who could no longer afford college, nor were they unprepared to do well in college, as most explanations for dropping out of or stopping college would offer.[27] Our typical and intuitive understandings of why certain students fail almost always imagine failure as something that is located within and produced by the students themselves.[28] They are the only ones at fault. But in this case, we will have to imagine these students differently, for they quit school not because they were failing in it. They left school because university schooling had lost its appeal for them. They could not find the reason for staying on as college students; their university held no significant meaning for them anymore; and to them, the school did not make attempts to lure them back, anyway. These students represent a break from our usual understanding of student failure as personal or family or community failure, to instead comprehend student failure alternatively as *school* failure. And it is through their testimonies that I also pursue a set of related claims about schools as they are critiqued not only from the outside but from the purviews of the continuing experiences of those who are excluded from them.

These twin poles of failure and success—of not passing classes and obtaining the highest grades, or eventually graduating—that are embedded within opposite ends of a continuum of student performance indicators have the ability to tell us much about the consequences of ways of teaching as well as ways of learning, studying, and taking tests on the part of students. But they can also tell us very little. When I asked students if studying hard and getting As were things that made them feel successful in school, many of them shrugged their shoulders. Sure, nice grades would make you feel successful. But is that all there is to a really successful college experience for them? Education scholars overwhelmingly agree that grades and the ability to graduate on time are just two of the many markers of worthwhile schooling, in a diverse list that can include a host of other variables such as having effective teachers, a recognized athletic record, and an accessible team of counselors, as well as a focus on beyond-the-classroom social activities and relationships.[29] And yet many students in this study thought that their teachers' and classmates' preoccupation with and valorization of grades, and their counselors' (and parents') relentless fixation on urging them to graduate on time, dominated so negatively the campus environment they inhabited.

Furthermore, and without a doubt more pressing for all of the students in this study, a most palpable sense of their collective identity and subjectivity— the ways in which they thought they were being looked at and treated—as students of color mattered in all aspects of their lives on campus.[30] All angles and analyses of their school performance, they felt, were drawn from lenses and categories of race, gender, class, and other kinds of social differentiation that deterministically judged them narrowly, erroneously, or unfairly. They constantly wondered anxiously about other people's expectations and assumptions about who they were and what they could or could not do, they themselves oftentimes felt unsure or conflicted about their own abilities or lack thereof, and they also could not find clear and neat answers all the time when their beneficial presence as minorities in their school or if their school was the right place for them as minorities was questioned. Many students found the heavy weight of such anxieties about their presence as brown bodies terribly distracting and unnecessary, but a good number of them also found ways to make their unique status itself the reason for and the engine of their attempts at school transformation. Of course, they experienced success as well as disappointment, for even when the students and I turned to education scholarship for solutions, we found no guaranteed answers.[31] Struggling to be represented while resisting forced assimilation, wanting inclusion without saying yes to exploitation, and desiring recognition within an institution that was organized to discipline and control them—all of these conjointly made up their daily lives as students and thoroughly complicated the usual expectations everyone had about how they should behave and perform in college.

EXTRAORDINARY STUDENTS

I really wanted to stay and keep goin' at it, at UW. That's where my friends were at, that's my community . . . of love, of care, you know. That's my community too. But other than that, school meant nothing else to me. It was like I wanted to go to school to be with friends, not really to go to school and go to class and all that.

. . .

I'm a part owner of this school. It's a public school . . . for the public of our state and our country. As part owner, I have a right to change it . . . to make it better.

. . .

I got to know many of the students in this study, almost all of them from working- or lower-middle-class statuses and many of them first-generation college students, even before they were in my classes and academic programs. Many of them were born and raised in the United States but had significant ties with their homeland nations, states, and cultures (American and Western [or independent] Sāmoa, Tonga, Guam, Hawai'i, Palau, New Zealand, the

Philippines, Mexico, Ethiopia, Cambodia, Duwamish, Nooksack, Quinault, Yakama, and Klamath), so much so that they had either full or practical proficiency in several non-English languages. With the exception of Native Americans, all of the students had parents who either immigrated into the United States or migrated into the U.S. mainland. These parents came into the state of Washington to become skilled and unskilled workers, as military recruits or refugees, and with less educational attainment than most immigrants. They all mirrored a national statistic regarding the preponderance of working- and lower-to-middle-class statuses in these population groups. It was, therefore, common for almost all of the students' parents to have multiple low-paying and low-status jobs, become unemployed or underemployed at least once in their lifetimes, and have children who work while attending school.[32]

Of the sixty-five individuals who were part of this study up close, thirty-eight identified as Pacific Islander, nine as Filipino, six as Chicana/o/Latina/o, four as black, four as Southeast Asian (Vietnamese and Cambodian), and four as Native. At the time of the study, these students ranged in age from eighteen to twenty-five years old, forty-two were male and twenty-three were female, all were single (although a few were married later), and almost all were working full- or part-time in the school and its neighborhoods. About twenty-nine of these students were on full-scholarship status, and a good number of them, close to thirty-six, were receiving some form of financial aid. Half of them were daily commuters (usually from working-class neighborhoods south of Seattle), a quarter rented apartments within the vicinity of the campus, and the rest lived in the university dorms. They were students majoring in different areas and disciplines, from American ethnic studies to biology.

I underscore the category "Pacific Islander" in this study to echo the signifier of choice for the majority of the respondents who were involved in the conduct of my ethnography. They were mostly Sāmoan, Chamorro, Tongan, and Hawaiian, including some Filipinos and Filipinas who identified as Pacific Islander or who were products of both Filipino and Pacific Islander unions. Although they had a common understanding of "Pacific Islander" as a collective name for themselves, and given their awareness of shared histories, social practices and statuses, heritage, and language usage, they were heterogeneous in other ways. They were not all from the same religious groups, they had varying family migration patterns, and some of them did not identify as working-class, first-generation college attendees, single-raced, and straight. Like all U.S. racial groups, then, this category had traces of commonalities as well as heterogeneities within its nominal designation, indicators of both the complexity and fluidity of race construction in American society.[33] Concurrently, I have also added the phrase "and their allies" to mark the certainty that there were indeed other students in the ethnography, besides those mentioned above, who associated themselves with Pacific Islanders and allied with them socially and politically. These students were careful not to recklessly claim a shared "identity" with their Pacific Islander classmates and friends, an identity that is usually bound up in strict definitions of blood or heritage connections. Instead, they discovered how the appellation "Pacific Islander," along with those who identified as such, provided them with a most vivid account of shared histories and contemporary realities they did not know existed outside of their own racial and ethnic groups. Hence, they were drawn to such an affiliation—a tight relationship, actually—with another category over a process that was organic, thoughtful, and respectful. I welcomed them into my study, just as I was prodded to do so by the Pacific Islander students on campus who embraced them and me into their group's culture and politics.

Some of my early student subjects were directly involved in the recruitment process for a faculty position on the UW Seattle campus that I was applying for. So, when I was eventually hired in the Department of American Ethnic Studies, they were among the first to welcome me into their university. I was touched by their gesture because I did not know beforehand their involvement, and I was even more gratified when they welcomed me, a Filipino American from Manila and Southern California, into their circle of Pacific Islanders and allies who were thinking seriously about the university, particularly its relationship to their racial identities and race-related experiences. I thereafter cultivated multidimensional teacher-student relationships with many of them, especially those who were recruited to be a part of this study. Two students who stood out in this group were Migetu and Tavita, who, at that time, were emerging campus leaders bent on making more visible the presence of Pacific Islanders on the UW campus despite and because of their small numbers.[34] They were engaged in establishing their own race- and ethnic-based student organizations, disentangling their groups from their forced and unwanted assignment into the Asian American category, and educating students, staff, and faculty on their otherwise unknown, misunderstood, or devalued cultures and histories. And they were relentless in seeking out any opportunities, rare as they were, in making the university work for them instead of the other way around almost all of the time.

I helped establish a peer mentorship program with Migetu, Tavita, and other Pacific Islander students, the story of which I detail in chapter 2, along with a similar program formed later on, specifically targeting Chicano and

Chicana students, which student organizers fondly and formally named Adelante, Spanish for "forward" or "ahead." Angelica and Eduardo were my principal informants for this program. Their college tales mirrored to a great extent the experiences of their Pacific Islander schoolmates, including the Filipino Americans who allied with them, and whose narratives I present here as well. Two other programs, Yəhaẁali and Ubuntu, geared for Native American and African diasporic and African American students, respectively, were formed later.[35] My protracted conversations with them usually began with me asking them how they were doing in school, evolved into discussions about how school was treating them and how they were treating their school in turn, and eventually progressed into how their schooling experiences, including their own school as a whole, could be proactively transformed or changed for the better. The mentorship programs—mainly our "study tables"—became the principal setting of and context for many of our conversations and activities.

From the early years, when I was hired as a regular faculty member at UW in 2000, and up to the present, my interactions with youth of color on campus, especially with Pacific Islanders like Migetu, Tavita, and their college mates, flourished into deep and lasting relationships that occurred on many levels: inside and outside of classrooms, within formal and informal mentorship environments, in family and community settings, and in larger contexts of activism and advocacy both on and off campus. During these years from when I informally started talking with the students and all the way until the end of data gathering for this project, I developed significant friendships with them that continue to this day, in ways that have made me regard them as more than mere subjects of analysis for this ethnography. I have since called them extraordinary students in the sense that they were quite different from most of the students I have known—mostly in terms of the deep passion with which they regarded their schooling—and because of the powerful ways they have had a positive impact on my work and my life, and the lives of the many campus communities we have touched. Many of them have graduated, and some of them are now academics like me. I enter this conversation about the meanings of schooling with all of them as my partners and allies in the struggle for change and transformation in our schools. And I recognize and acknowledge that the work that all of us do, principally in operation through and as an expression of our identities as activists of color, is part of a larger set of struggles against social injustice that find recognition here in collective forms and are now represented through the accumulated student testimonies that I have organized and opened to analysis.

On the other end of the thematic logic that *The Ocean in the School* is engirded by, one that transacts with ideas and practices regarding measuring student performance, is the attention students paid to evaluating *school* performance. The research work that I detail here is fundamentally an account of people who do not fit into a predetermined mold of university education. It is about students who enter college almost always already prefigured as outsiders primarily by virtue of their nonwhite and nonelite status—and relatedly, on account of the lack of the legacies of former students like them that these current students should have stood to inherit once they came in—and on the basis of a numerically insignificant number of students counted as part of their groups who are already in the university. This latter reason is usually invoked as an ideal illustration of their outsider status, as a cause and effect of their distance from centers of power, and as evidence of their alleged unpreparedness for college (and, therefore, their unsuitability for retention and graduation, despite being admitted), a kind of circular argument that explains low enrollment numbers as indications of deficiencies that are internal to the students and the communities they come from.[36] But how do we expect outsiders to fit in an environment that is designed to not make them fit in the first place? What are the conditions that generate and sustain expectations of fitting, and what happens when these expectations are not met? More importantly, how are these incommensurabilities directly experienced by those who inhabit such spaces of otherness? How do they comprehend their unfit status, and how do they work through their conditions of domination not as outsiders or marginal players, but in their position as insiders and stakeholders in the university system?

In many ways, then, this project engages with a desire to transform how schools may deal with extraordinary students by offering alternatives to the ways they conventionally deal with student failure and success and by using the perspectives of those who themselves experience unfitness and nonrecognition. Education scholars Angela Valenzuela and Marcos Pizarro ask parallel questions and provide unconventional answers in their work, arguing about the critical necessity of understanding student failure not as a consequence of laziness, indifference, or lack of intelligence "displayed" by the students, but as something that ought to make us question at least two things: how such "displays" may actually be representative symptoms of a larger systemic failure of schooling and, more specifically, how these "displays" may be the very same ones that mirror the ways in which schools treat such students.[37] Students' indifference and laziness, in both studies conducted by Valenzuela and

Pizarro, are but the effects of schooling indifference and laziness toward students, notwithstanding the schools' inability to provide access to resources, high-quality and culturally competent teaching, and environments that are nontoxic especially to particular groups of marginalized students, including campus spaces that respect their voices. And to address student failure, they say, the angle of intervention must be recalibrated to focus on schooling practice and resource allocation instead, accompanied by changes in attitudes that uphold racism against students of color. Valenzuela reveals in her ethnography the myriad ways in which schooling "divests youth of important social and cultural resources, leaving them progressively vulnerable to academic failure," hence her use of the term "subtractive schooling" to emphasize (as a negative critique) how students' cultural assets can instead be harnessed for productive use on campus.[38] And for Pizarro, it is the pursuit of social justice itself that will require the understanding of "Chicana/o experiences in conjunction with communities, under the direction of these communities, and *with a recognition of the unique knowledge systems and knowledge bases in these communities*" in order to make a difference.[39]

Schools and universities constantly undergo change. But the students and I believe that the conditions we face in our universities these days demand a specific and deeper account of what to do with change and, even before that, how to recognize and define change—beyond one version that celebrates how the "face" of schools has changed because of demographic diversity, for example, while ignoring how schools have themselves not changed in providing the kind of education that is appropriately designed for such a different and diverse demographic. When our schools' criteria for teaching courses and evaluating students worked well for a good majority of students all these years, how do we expect the same criteria to work well this time for a good newer crop of minority students? This question pokes at the core of how we define education and schooling especially in American society and, in particular, at how we define and interrogate the relationships between race and schooling as indexes for determining student performance. What does it mean to attend a university for someone who has never known any family member who has been to a university? What is the experience like for students who take a lot of courses in school that have nothing to do, or are not made to be connected, with their culture and history? How significant is it for nonwhite students to go to a university where very few students and faculty look like or understand them and where the conditions are such that their histories are ignored, misrepresented, devalued, or, worse, not known? How do these combined conditions affect the ways in which students fail, succeed, and make meaning out of their schooling?

ONGOING AND UNFINISHED STRUGGLES

I'm always seen here as someone who represents diversity, as someone who was given a chance because she's different and comes from somewhere not usual. So the pressure is always there for me to do well. I make this university look good. But I do most of the hard work for it.

. . .

I don't represent diversity. I represent inequality! Just take a look at people around us. Very few people look like me.

. . .

I argue in this book that Pacific Islander, Filipino, Chicana/Chicano, Latina/Latino, African American, Southeast Asian American, and Native American students, including those students who are similarly situated, provide us with a glimpse of contemporary college experiences that enlighten us about the inadequacies of many of our attempts to address diversity in our schools. These attempts range from those that ignore the specific historical conditions faced by newer, emerging, or minoritized student populations to those that forget the impact of an unrelenting set of institutional forces that resist change despite the influx of different presences of bodies in academia.[40] Through the perceptive voices of my student interviewees, I propose that the struggle to make diversity advocacy real and effective on a college campus must include a direct challenge to reimagine a more nonalienating environment for students so that classrooms are transformed as places for meaningful learning and so that students get better equipped to transform their worlds. And in this transformation, we strongly suggest that knowledges of and critiques against the continuing realities and impact of imperialism, settler colonialism, white supremacy, and identity-based discrimination—everything that structurally shapes and determines the life chances of all students—be placed at the center, not at the margins, of all schooling practice.[41]

I began the explanation for these arguments by contextualizing them within conventional frameworks of student assessment that assume a universal and, therefore, problematic set of definitions regarding success and failure. This is a bipolar set of standards that is difficult to escape because the alternatives to it are hard to configure. Students, for example, are evaluated on the basis of the degrees of success or failure by which they comprehend course material. What happens if the course material is not presented to them as relevant to or connected with their lives? Who gets to be blamed when a student ends up failing to comprehend course materials or when a student does not utilize the appropriate language to express a connection between course material and culture? And what needs to be done instead? Our suggestions are outlined in this book.

In chapter 1, I open with a large picture of the contemporary university within the context of race relations in American society, as drawn by the students I interacted with. We will see how students experienced the space of the university as dauntingly majestic and replete with the trappings of elite cultures that are not theirs. Yet they will also show us how they mitigated their anxieties and feelings of loneliness about such a forbidding place by simultaneously constructing it as a space of desire, pleasure, and possibility, especially within the seemingly boundless parameters of the ways in which they imagined "the ocean in the school." In these senses, I attempt to explain how schooling may be understood as a site in which contemporary politics of diversity and the dynamics of power relationships are played out especially from the point of view of students of color and against the backdrop of the changing and increasingly diverse demographics of students, teachers, and communities who turn to history and culture as sites of transformative struggle.

Chapter 2 names and narrates the activities of two mentorship programs, the Pacific Islander Partnerships in Education (PIPE) project and Adelante, as sites for configuring how a cultural politics of a transformative college education looks as they are originated and sustained by students. These programs are the principal sites where we will meet the students in closer view, where we will understand their struggles from the ground and within the context of their underrepresentation in school and in society, and where we will consider how their collective meaning-making and practices of community building converse with larger questions regarding college success and failure, and to a good extent, in relationship to social injustice.

In chapter 3, we will meet those students who have left school, either temporarily or permanently. We will hear the reasons why they decided to leave college, and, as we do so, they will reveal to us how they framed such a departure not as a simplistic and unfair calculation of their individual deficiency but largely as a critique of ideas and practices of uniform schooling. We will see how their notions of school as a place of discovery, family and community sustenance, and collective resource building ran in contrast to dominant attitudes regarding how to behave and succeed in college. Along with citing some students who stayed in and graduated from the university but had something to say about student departures, I will attempt to cohere the sentiments of these students who left by way of an argument about building and sustaining meaningfulness in school in order for students to succeed in it.

Chapter 4 pays attention to certain site-specific schooling activities— student organization meetings, cultural events, recruitment projects, and the experiences of being in a study abroad program—to see the breadth as well as depth of students' engagement with school and life transformation inside but also outside of the confines of typical classrooms. All of these sites were sustained by, as well as generative of, alternative thinking and practice with respect to culturally relevant curricula, an acute sense of the historical and ongoing struggles regarding the measurement of academic performance, and critical questions regarding the value of schooling for nondominant cultures. I eventually culminate this chapter with a visit to a classroom where a Pacific Islander historical and contemporary cultures course was offered and taught by one of my mentees who eventually became a professor like me.

I offer a concluding chapter to ruminate on the connections between trans-formative schooling and the notion of schooling that is not afraid of bound-aries and change.[42] In determining bases for measuring those who succeed and those who fail, in designing curricula that are meant to comprise and produce various understandings of human existence, and in deciding who and what counts in addressing unequal relationships of power in our schools, we tend to enforce distinctions drawn according to received assumptions regarding the values of competing group identities, particularly racialized and gendered ones. We are also often hampered by conventions and universal notions of education, we almost always assume that schools are bounded spaces discrete from larger society, and we tend to forget that schools are not meant to simply reproduce and disseminate knowledge. My students and I believe that schools are also sites for resisting and transforming knowledge, that schools are and should not be disconnected from the communities outside of them, and that schools are places where we can find meaning and where we can have imagina-tive and pleasurable ways of knowing and acting. On grander levels, we under-stand schools as oceans of real lives, real struggles, and real destinies. They are sites of rich resources as much as they are sites of fantastic possibilities. They are sites of unfinished business, simultaneous to and parallel with thinking of and reckoning with racism and other forms of social inequality as incomplete, imperfect, and ongoing struggles.

STUDYING STUDENTS

Professor Bonus, you and me, and all of us, we are the ocean. We are vast, we are complex, we are profound. Most of all, we are connected and our love for one another is boundless.

. . .

May our ancestors guide you well, Bonus, in writing this book.

. . .

This book of ethnographic tales, complemented by my analysis and supplemented also by my individual narratives, emanates from a position of collective interest and inspiration.[43] I became initially interested in documenting student lives because they largely mirrored my own and they reminded me of my struggles particularly in attending graduate school as an underrepresented minority student myself. I experienced and continue to experience out-of-placeness in the several schools I attended and at UW, where I work. I felt and continue to feel a disjunction between my cultures and the mainstream cultures of schooling. And I am constantly negotiating my underrepresented status between a politics of nominal representation and a politics of meaningful recognition; between my obligations to my institution and my ethical responsibilities to my students, colleagues, and communities; and between my identity as an individual and my membership in and belonging to larger collectives. I admire and am inspired by my students not only because I see myself in them, but especially because they decided to include me as a partner in the struggle to transform our schooling and, consequently, our lives. They are the source of my strength and wisdom, and the reason for my daily perseverance as a university professor.

My research on education and race speaks to the conditions of racial underrepresentation and discrimination in schools—about going to school, staying in school, and graduating from school as political acts and sites of creative yet conflicting struggles for meaningfulness and social mobility for minority youth. I want to invite readers of this book to consider these ethnographic narratives as sites for imagining these conflicting struggles, not so much to present a set of foolproof recipes or models for successful undergraduate education, but to put out in the open parts of an ongoing conversation about what some of our students experience in college, why certain students stay or drop out of college, and what it means for our students to have a meaningful college education, or at least attempt to have one. These, to me, are the most important pieces in the set of conversations regarding race and education that I participate in.

As I write this introduction, and as I reflect on the specific aspects and the cumulative picture of what I paint in this book, I want to alert the reader of yet another underlying theme that has informed and propelled this ethnographic project. Simultaneous with thinking about this ethnography as a critique of racism and imperialism, of conventional models of student assessment, and of schooling ideologies and practices in general, this work expresses a struggle with identifying, sorting, documenting, and explaining social phenomena— represented here as student voices and activities—in ways that honor the spirit, intent, and integrity of its subjects. In my disciplinary training in the social sciences and, in particular, in my training and experience in ethnographic work, there is always the compulsion, indeed a requirement, that its practitioners make good sense of their subjects' realities as they are observed and written.[44] It is the scholar's task to "capture" what they decide as interesting and important, to select and organize from a universe of data what is logically (or disciplinarily) possible and sensible, and to analyze the chosen narratives as they resonate with larger contexts and previous theories of social living. My struggle with performing all of these is not about whether or not I have fulfilled these tasks sufficiently. It is, rather, the opposite. It is about whether or not I have presented the students' tales only as they are partially, provisionally, and incompletely observable, narratable, and analyzable to me.

Subjects' truths have interesting ways of creeping up on the ethnographer, and, in my experience, I oftentimes got flustered when my student subjects revealed significant parts of their lives to me in moments when I was not paying close attention, when I got the point of their jokes days after they told me, and when the intent of their actions sometimes produced what seemed to be harmful consequences to our communities. I have also had moments of doubt, fear, and uncertainty about the ways in which I have affected my students'/subjects' lives—how some of my comedic acts, for example, seemed to distract others, or how my frequent dramatic moments of hyper-mentorship overwhelmed them. My disciplinary imperatives to organize what amounted to seventeen or so variables that I wrote on index cards to help me begin my writing seemed, many times, to be so inadequate to and inappropriate in producing a veritable account of my subjects, simply because I wanted everything to make sense to me and to my discipline. All throughout this work, then, I wrestled with these academic imperatives as I searched for and experimented with other ways of understanding and cohering on top of and in resistance to such obligatory modalities and formations.

So, in the spirit of studying "what does not fit," I present this book's collection of accounts as a representation of my struggles to make sense of my subjects' truths as they are engaged both within the analytical models pre-scribed by my intellectual training (formally in communication, ethnic stud-ies, and, tangentially, in education) and in consideration of those alternative ways of thinking and doing that my discipline and fields of study have yet to codify or have simply comprehended as "not making sense." My editorial se-lection of narratives and specification of analytical points are strung together only to the degree that they can be regarded not so much as an amalgamation of intellectual insights that speak to large theories of education and society but as a collection of nodes of engagement enunciated principally by my eth-nographic subjects about their school, their communities, themselves. In these engagements, they have oftentimes spoken, remained silent, or acted in defi-ance of expectations or without careful attention to an assumed logic, stuff that I am careful not to dismiss. But what I have found provocative, and what has introspectively defined my work on this project on all levels, is that stu-dents have also done such actions so prophetically, imagining the impossible, performing the unscripted, anticipating what can be inconceivable, and prac-ticing what is yet to be named.[45] I hope that my attempts at representing these remarkable engagements and constituting my work in the form and spirit of these engagements do justice to my subjects.

I am thoroughly convinced that my student subjects were my best teachers in performing and writing this ethnography, and they did so while "thinking outside of the box" and "through the ocean," so to speak.[46] They taught, and continue to teach me, what they know from their collective experiences and from the books they read—how to simultaneously respect and defy tradition, how to be open-minded about untested ways of doing things, how to not be always afraid of failure or be overwhelmingly held down by fear in the act of disobeying rules or not following protocol. These are attitudes and actions that no social science project intent on proposing reproducible social axioms can fully account for without losing the dignity and nuance of its subjects and their actions. This work, on the contrary, is an account of fissures and snip-pets of activities arranged in a logic that makes sense, hopefully, as a set of ac-counts that selectively express the imaginative, creative, and innovative ways of understanding how some of our students experience their schooling and how we can try to make our schools more understanding of and respectful to all of their students. To a great extent, this is what transformative schooling looks like to the students here—the imagination and building of communities within and across sites of schooling where learning is meaningful only to the degree that it is defined by all of those who care about these communities.

The STUDENTS, *the* SCHOOL, *the* OCEAN

Tracking Students' Lives on Campus

"Just to be honest with you," Tavita tells me, "I didn't even know where UW *[the University of Washington] was before I came here. I thought it was where the capital of the U.S. is! . . . So I was flying in from Hawai'i . . . and I noticed that . . . wow . . . this plane ride is so short! I was expecting, you know, to fly across the mainland and see all of these states from above. That would have been tight. And then, yeah, oh my God, we were suddenly about to land? That was kinda unexpected. Welcome to Seattle, Washington! I knew about Washington, but honestly, I thought we were going to D.C.! Man, I was so weirded out, I was so* FOB *[fresh off the boat]!" We both roll our eyes and chuckle.*

. . .

When I met Tavita for the first time, he was introduced to me as some kind of a well-known and respected leader of Sāmoan and other Pacific Islander students on campus. We saw each other at the campus's Husky Union Building, otherwise known as "the HUB," where many student activities took place. It was also the location of the school's main cafeteria, and it housed many student organization offices. Tavita graciously stood up and shook my hand, like he was pleased to meet me, repeating the word "Filipino" when he asked me about my background and I told him what I identified as. Two months later, he would confess to me that he thought then that I was a custodian, not a professor, for he could not imagine connecting the words "Filipino" and "professor" in one person at that time. We will talk about this identity mismatch of his at length later. Tavita's seeming ignorance about the university and its professors of color belied his firm grasp of his own academic know-how, potentials, and direction. As I got to know him more, I was able to observe that he was not only a quick learner; he was also a deep thinker of social phenomena, always prepared to explain his occasional lack of practical or everyday knowledge as perhaps the result of his devotion to serious academic studying, like reading too much. He claimed to "not know so much about regular things," but then it was interesting that he did come out at the top of his high school class in Hawai'i. I do not completely understand this logic either, so I will also get back to this later with more rumination.

Migetu, on the other hand, already knew about the University of Washington way before he became a student in it. Born and raised in a suburb within the vicinity of Tacoma, Washington, about thirty miles south of Seattle, he carried through most of his young adult life a vision of someday attending the so-called big school. "But in high school," Migetu clarified, "no one bothered to encourage me. No one recruited me for college. No teacher came and said to me, 'You should apply.' I just kept some kind of a dream inside of me to go to college." And he persisted. He did not know yet what he wanted to become, but he and his parents were just as happy he got into what they thought was a very competitive, exclusive, and elite school. Soon, Migetu would be heavily involved in campus politics, something he was not seriously prepared for but, like Tavita, he very quickly picked up on. He was one of those students who sought me out the very first week I reported for my new job as an assistant professor at UW, fresh out of graduate school in California. He welcomed me as a "Pacific Islander professor" and told me that I was the first one of such kind that he had actually met in person. I was touched by his gesture. Migetu was a first one for me too, the very first Chamorro student I got to know at UW, and over the years, he has been one of those many students who have kept in touch with me even beyond their college graduation.

Tavita and Migetu represent two of the more than forty-seven subjects I regularly interviewed and heavily interacted with for this particular section of my ethnography, and I use selected accounts of their experience of college education to open the doors a little bit into their world of schooling so that we can glean how different such an experience is for certain students who come from nondominant cultures with nontraditional college preparation and background. I probe into their experiences to ascertain how these particular accounts of minority college student life reveal to us the damaging consequences of a kind of schooling that is perceived as and practiced to be uniform, universal, and configured for homogeneous groups.[1] One size fits all. But more critically, I employ these narratives as pathways for understanding the complexities and contradictions of managing a "diverse student body" (as most college institutions would declare), while curricula remain white-centered, where dominant-culture-thinking and dominant-culture-acting faculty and administration continue to hold power, and where teaching strategies as well as research training that benefit only the majority of those in school endure.[2] On another end, I also highlight aspects of those nontraditional student narratives here that educate us about the risks and potentials of resistance to universal schooling and other kinds of proactive engagement with struggle that these students deployed.[3] To a good extent, much of the advocacy work that students found themselves busy with constituted a set of responses to the disadvantageous conditions that they faced. This is, of course, reminiscent of the student movements that coalesced in the 1960s and 1970s, especially those that demanded school reforms connected with ethnic studies curricula, minority student admission, and minority faculty-staff recruitment.[4] Students were thoroughly familiar and conversant with these histories. But, inspired by these, I would like to proffer that in this ethnography, transformative schooling "from below," whether it was a kind of labor that was self-generated, historically motivated, or serendipitous, also became the site from which a deeper and contemporary understanding of the connections across schooling, diversity, and histories of colonization and their aftermath were enabled. Students educated themselves in various ways, and over a span of time that extended even beyond college, to excavate and obtain a better grasp of these connections. This chapter traces parts of their educational journeys that taught them the ways in which their minority status was directly a product of unequal race relations that were already in place long before they were admitted and which they proactively connected with and beyond the colonized lives and lived spaces of their ancestors.

Underpinning, then, the students' descriptions of the conditions they faced as underrepresented bodies on their campus was their unfolding sense of the palpable contradictions within which they existed.[5] Their school routinely told them that they added "diversity" to their campus, that they helped enable better education for all, and that they were free (and expected) to overcome whatever it was that had kept them from succeeding. At the same time, they also felt ignored or undervalued, even exploited or ridiculed, especially when they were seen to privilege collective practice over liberal individualistic behavior, when they were critical of their own schooling or, generally, when their actions simply did not correspond strictly to what they were expected to do.

They understood these contradictions as things that were borne out of a colonized history whose comprehension and opposition required engaging with a struggle to reckon with the ravaging effects of U.S. empire in their past and present lives, which now have found their way into their educational experiences. It was in their school where they began to learn all these things that were larger than them, and it was within their communities inside and outside of their classrooms where they started to think about what to do with such conditions they were being confronted with.

The overarching strategy deployed by the students that I document here, one that protractedly unfolded to me as they started talking about it and practicing and refining it through the years, was the practice of regarding the school as an *ocean*—a kind of alternative or creative process of experiencing and transforming schooling. This strategy, for sure built upon the historical contexts of colonial subjugation of Pacific islands and peoples, as well as the cultures of indigenous societies that fought against such intrusions, enabled students to comprehend their experiences of racism, devaluing, and invisibility, and their varied reactions to them, as intimately parallel to ongoing conditions and consequences of U.S. control of their lives writ large and their people's resistance to it. Even more tightly configured, regarding the school as an ocean, for the students, made them understand how conditions of colonization, as historically experienced by their ancestors, have not ended spatially and temporally, and did not merely occur on the islands. Rather, their lived realities as minority students signaled to them the enveloping scope and depth of U.S. empire right on their campus, but profoundly connected with—although far from—the islands and oceans of their ancestors.[6] Therefore, the ocean in the school historically and spatially linked students not only with the distant locations of their ancestors and communities; it reassuringly brought together mainland islanders in a sense of common history as it braided their present spaces and times of struggles with those who have struggled elsewhere and before them in intellectual, political, and spiritual contours.[7]

These students' particular experiences of attending college, in these instances and through these conditions, enabled them to connect, configure, or integrate antiracist/anticolonial and survival practices with traditional Pacific Islander cultural traditions, indigenous maritime navigation, collective rowing, and the overall maintenance of a set of "oceanic" sensibilities, which, in many ways, defined and nurtured both their personal and social lives on campus. These sensibilities encouraged the appreciation and respect of their relationships to nature (including their relationships with their spiritual beliefs and with their ancestors), confirmed and strengthened the parameters of their relationships with others as profoundly familial by making them constitutively connected through and by the ocean, and brought to the forefront their sensitivity to the primary needs and desires of the communities they created and made themselves a part of.[8]

Vasa, the word for "ocean" in the Sāmoan indigenous language, was something taught to me mainly by Tavita as a deeply meaningful expression that students used and primarily referred to a geographical and metaphorical location of an ancestral or primordial home, a space that surrounded and connected multiple locations, and a place of comfort, sacredness, and sustenance, where one was loved and nurtured. To speak of being in the vasa was to exist in a place of reassuring familiarity and connection, so that one felt secure, knowledgeable, and respected in such a place. For these students, vasa was place, process, and relationships. And to be able to find and sustain community in a place that was alien or alienating to them, they invoked the holistic and evocative spirit of the vasa. To understand and engage with their surroundings and the conditions they faced as underrepresented minority students, they looked to the vasa as a repository of meaningful traditions, teachings, and valuable practices of resilience, respect, and illumination from as well as reverence for sacred beings and ancestors. And by regarding school or aspects of school as if they were parts of a living ocean, the vasa, these students were able to treat and infuse meaning into their school as if it were one's place of love, respect, and belonging. In other words, for students, to transact school as vasa was to render it as if it were one's indigenous and sacred home.[9]

The ocean in the school was structurally organized so that everything else that was practiced before and then, and everything that was yet to be done, both off and on campus, emanated from the logic of its existence in one's inner self or heart and then radiated into one's "outside self," or one's community.[10] For certain, this logic did not always proceed in one direction, as if oceanic cultures were simply transported intact into the mainland; it instead undulated back and forth between selves and others in the ways conversations and negotiations flowed between being a cause and being an effect. The vasa also did not exist as if it was separate, apart, or immune from the dominant European American cultures in school. Nor was it not interactive with other nondominant cultures around it. It lived within and through numerous and intersecting formations, conditions, and spaces.[11] In these ways, the students' ocean was a product of a process as much as it was something that produced other things. For one, parts of the process of finding the ocean in their school gave students reason and ability to make their school seem smaller and more familiar. To navigate this ocean, they had to know more about it, how it treats them, and how it can better serve their needs and promote their interests. Naming the school as their ocean empowered students to treat their school as if they had some measure of access to it or, at the least, that access to specific resources in their school was possible for them. Moreover, this ocean had to be imagined also as a source of great knowledge that was oftentimes yet to be known and appreciated; it was a school, a place of learning, after all. But somehow, for these students, thinking of their school as an ocean made searching for knowledge more logical, bearable, and pleasurable and, therefore, meaningful. Students directed their attention to searching for knowledge about their culture in the school where they rowed and navigated, something they mostly treated as akin to looking for a pearl in a deep dark sea. This gesture stood both as a critique of the lack of scholarly and social attention paid to their people and as a proactive move to generate what was lacking in their school.

In addition, students' imagination and practice of the vasa necessitated the imagination and practice of school as a site for generating and sustaining community.[12] There was this popular saying among many of the students who echoed what their parents and ancestors had told them over and over: that you are never all by yourself; you are always part of something bigger than you. *You are never alone. You are always a part of a family, a community.*[13] In the middle of doing this ethnographic project, I often wondered if community making among students was something that was simply done by everybody, so much so that I did not have to write about it. Many times, I thought to myself that this was such a natural and logical thing to do when faced with loneliness or alienation, as almost all of my students experienced. But I would like to submit some nuance of community building here that was uniquely practiced within the context of institutional invisibility with a view to rendering it as a powerful act of not only student transformation but, to a good extent, school transformation. In other words, for these students, serving the community or serving one another fundamentally meant serving the vasa, the ocean, the school.

Learning how to find the ocean in the school, therefore, meant approximating its size and dimensions relative to what the community needed and what the students desired. Making the school feel familiar, regarding it as a source of great knowledge, and acting upon it as the location and emanation of communities in an ocean of social relationships depended on a host of factors, and on this list, the necessity of having the desire and will to "oceanize" the school was at the very top. To explicate the full context and particularity of this process, I organize the rest of this chapter into three sections. First, we get to know a bit more about the students who were part of this ethnography. The intent in constructing this extended, though succinct, profile is to provide a deeper sense of where they came from, including their personal and social backgrounds, vis-à-vis the conditions they faced as a collective in their school. These students may appear to us simply as individuals, but they were also seen and treated by their school, their teachers, and classmates, in particular ways, as members of larger social categories that were themselves products and productive of social and individual values that students may or may not have agreed with. Students will tell us how they understood themselves as UW students who were racialized and what they thought about their school in relationship to this understanding. In this section, then, we both profile the students *and* their school from their vantage points.

Second, we look into how these underserved students experienced their schooling specifically as a collective critique of their nontraditional status or, more precisely, as an expression of their recognition as members of an undervalued and historically colonized and racialized group. I focus on two broad but specific aspects of their experiences in this regard: uncertainty and the combined or coexistent emanations of historical invisibility and misrecognition. Third, we peer into the students' responses to the conditions they encountered. We ascertain the extent to which the turn to "culture," or more specifically the vasa/ocean, as a site of repair and recovery, as a source of profound knowledge, and as some kind of a glue that fastened their communities together, became a viable and critically important practice for students who intended not only to transform themselves but, indeed, to transform their school.

THE STUDENTS AND THEIR OCEAN

Pacific Islanders who attended the UW during the period in which I started and then formally finished this ethnographic project (2004–9) came from different places. About three-quarters of those I knew were local, working-class, and the first in their family to attend a U.S. or mainland university. A few of them were from out of state and the rest were of upper-middle-class status, and there were equal numbers of males and females. Two self-defined as gay and queer. Most of them attended elementary and high schools in the state of Washington. There were small pockets of Hawaiian, Sāmoan, Chamorro, Tongan, and other Pacific Island communities scattered throughout the Puget Sound area during these years, but their settlement in Seattle and its vicinity had been going on since even before and was mostly made possible as a consequence of U.S. military recruitment from the Pacific beginning around the 1970s.[14] The McChord Air Force Base (now known as the Joint Base Lewis-McChord) located near Tacoma, for example, has drawn and continues to attract military workers from

places such as Guam and American Sāmoa. When the Boeing aircraft manu-
facturing facilities in Everett and Renton were still booming, a good number of
islanders found employment there as well.[15] But the presence of such available
skilled and technical jobs for islander workers has not brought enough gains
in terms of UW visibility for their offspring. Rather, there has been a low-scale
and irregular trickling of Pacific Islanders into the UW because the significant
majority of college-bound youth in these communities usually ended up in
community or junior colleges (for eventual transfer into the larger universities if or when it was possible), in teaching-focused state universities (where
it was assumed that admissions requirements were not as competitive), or not
attending college at all (in order to work full-time and help support their families). Very few islanders bothered with the private colleges in the state even
though they were desired, presumably because they found these schools unaf-
fordable. Pacific Islanders were also not heavily and proactively recruited by
many of the schools in the area, most probably because their identity groups
were not known or regularly acknowledged or they were perceived as just
too small to be numerically significant for a proactive recruitment program.
This is what many Pacific Islander students have told me.[16] In the years that
I interacted with those who attended the UW, Pacific Islanders numbered no
more than two hundred students per year, less than 1 percent of the student
body population (compared to an average of 65 percent white students and
20 percent Asian students).[17] In this ethnography, they comprise the majority
of the students I observed and conversed with. And, to protect their privacy
and to heed their preference to be anonymous, all their names, and the names
of all the subjects in this ethnography, are aliases.[18]

The Filipino American students in this study, in contrast, mostly came from
middle-class and upper-middle-class families whose members immigrated into
the United States as recruits to fill professional job openings in the medical
or health care fields as well as in engineering and business.[19] On average, they
were financially better-off than the Pacific Islanders, there were more female
than male students, two students referred to themselves as sexual minorities,
and one student identified as disabled.[20] In general, Filipino households and
communities in Seattle and its surrounding suburbs were numerous, genera-
tionally heterogeneous, and scattered. I remember being new to the Seattle
area and expecting to find descendants of the Filipino farmworkers recruited
during the early part of the twentieth century. I did not find many of them
at UW, owing to their small numbers in Washington State in general. Moreover, Filipino farmworkers were mostly bachelors, had low birthrates, and were
subject to antimiscegenation laws in many states, hence, the low numbers of

offspring from their generation.[21] Instead, I found a good number of Filipino students from the post-1965 professional immigration era. "They're found everywhere!," some Filipino students told me, "and they make sure their kids go to college!" Indeed, there was a strong value and pride, and pressure, attached to college attendance and completion that many parents from other groups, including Pacific Islanders, wished their children would imbibe, too. Some of the Filipino Americans, like Sāmoans, Tongans, and Chamorros, worked for the military, and a good number of their children, again mostly female, and about 790 every year from 2004 to 2009—close to 2 percent of the student population on average—were UW students.[22] For many parts of this study, we will encounter many Filipino American students who identified also as "Pacific Islander." And we will get to know the reasons for this later on.

I got to know a good number of Chicana and Chicano students, and some Latinas and Latinos, as deeply as I did Pacific Islander and Filipino students. "Aren't Filipinos Chicanos too?" one of them once half jested to me, and, of course, I smiled back approvingly, acknowledging the profound historical connections with Spanish and American colonization experiences among Filipinos and Chicanos, as well as with Pacific Islanders, now finding appreciation and recognition in our campus encounters.[23] These students shared similar backgrounds with the rest—immigrant (although not as recent), working-class (but more rural and farm-based), militarily connected, equal numbers of females and males, and with a solid commitment to schooling as a pathway for social mobility. One of them identified as a gay man. On campus, Chicanos and Latinos averaged about one thousand, which was about 3 percent of the UW student population.[24] In equal numbers of males and females, they did not formally identify as Pacific Islanders, but when prodded by others and me about their close interactions with their islander friends, they usually said they were allies of, or connected with, Pacific Islanders.

The other one-quarter of the students I interacted with—other Pacific Islanders and a smaller number of students coming from African, African American, Southeast Asian American, and Native American racial groups that were part of this ethnography who were also self-proclaimed allies of Pacific Islanders—were a mix of out-of-state youth, mostly male, who had family connections in Washington and Oregon; those who came in by way of a scholarship offer (need-based or merit-based, or both); and those who were recruited to play for the school's football team, the Huskies.[25] Just like everyone else in this study, every student in this subgroup was considered underrepresented. African American students as a whole comprised about 3 percent of the entire student population at UW, while Native Americans were less than 2 percent on average.[26] All of them were of working-class backgrounds. Except for the Native Americans, the rest of them came from families who were either recent immigrants or non-U.S.-mainland-based. Some of them also called themselves sexual minorities. These students easily blended with their local underrepresented counterparts, mostly out of a necessity and desire to find or create smaller communities within a large school just as the rest did. And their aspiration to do well in college equaled, if not occasionally exceeded, in deeper ways, the rest of their cohort, most palpably as a response to the pressures of being an outsider, of having to carry alone the family name and honor, and of fulfilling scholarship obligations. Like me or any other newcomer and outsider, they initially found Seattle to be strange and uninviting, but many of us relished the discovery of existing communities that were small yet seemingly ready and excited to embrace us.

If I were to paint an academic portrait of all of these underrepresented students of color I interacted with, that picture would be dotted with diverse elements across the board. They were mostly high-achieving students in both their coursework and extracurricular activity. By this, I mean that they had successfully met the academic qualifications that the institution required of them in order to be admitted. Many of them were bilingual or multilingual, had outstanding grades out of high school, and were accepted into a variety of competitive and popular majors and programs. As undergraduates, they frequently thought of professional careers after college, and so they tried as much as they could to do well in their classes by studying after school and, oftentimes, together in small groups. Many of them had difficulty in keeping up with their academics: we realized later that their high schools did not prepare them well enough for rigorous and demanding academic work in a big university; they spent too much time and energy working in order to cover family obligations and expenses way beyond what their financial aid or scholarship funds could cover; plus they were heavily involved in on-campus and community organizations, mostly student-based associations, churches, and other religion-centered institutions. Almost all of them occupied leadership positions in these on-campus organizations, which made them all the more busy with all sorts of extra responsibilities and commitments. In many cases, I thought they were much too involved in these organizations—the Polynesian Student Alliance (PSA), the Filipino American Student Association (FASA), the Micronesian Islands Club (MIC), MEChA (Movimiento Estudiantil Chican@s de Aztlan), the Omega Delta Phi (a fraternity), the Khmer Student Association, First Nations (a Native American undergraduate student group), the African Student Association, and the Black Student Union, as examples—because they ended up devoting more time to organizing than studying. This is a view I would change later on.

I opened this section with a partial profile of my ethnographic subjects not to imply that these are the only pieces of information we need to know about them, but to begin to know them briefly for now, as a collective representation of the youth of color I followed, who have come to the university not merely as individuals but as members of specific groups and social categories. I do not wish to disrespectfully and arbitrarily lump this mix of students into one collective group, for we already know that they are, at the very least, racially and ethnically, and in gendered and sexualized ways, distinct from one another. Indeed, they were different from as well as similar to one another, so I will invoke the specificity of their race or sex/gender/sexuality group experiences (or other categories of social difference) whenever it becomes necessary. To a good extent, though, the majority of students whom I will focus on here were Pacific Islanders, including, at different times, those students who called themselves "allies" of Pacific Islanders or those who identified as "Pacific Islanders" even though they were not conventionally defined by others as such. My observations with the students, then, will oftentimes illustrate the porous boundaries of their race-group definitions, the instabilities of singular race and other social identifications, the shared similarities of experiences they have as students of color, and the wide extent of their cross-category alliances that I attribute to be the result of intersecting social affinities they discovered on the basis of race, working- and middle-class statuses, gender, sexuality, religion, and especially their identities as underrepresented nontraditional UW students. I will continue with more details of who they are throughout the rest of this chapter, but for this moment, I will concentrate next on how they themselves have profiled their school as a computation of both their experiences of being students in it and how they thought their school responded to their presence.

Two initial observations regarding the students' school stand out here. On one end is a picture of the campus as an empty slate, represented by Tavita's humorous story in the beginning of this chapter. This is somewhat of a ruse because, as we will find out later, Tavita and many other students like him will demonstrate how this seeming ignorance or limited knowledge of college life can turn into an occasion for crafting fresh, bold, and serious ideas for transforming schooling. It is like turning or channeling ignorance into a potential asset, or being bold about change because one is not necessarily trapped in too much familiarity with location and condition. This means that even though such students came in with some kind of unfamiliarity with their school in specific, or they learned about schooling only through books, as Tavita did, they did initially possess a form of social capital or knowledge about schooling in general as a place to learn skills, to make good use of time (while playing sports or meeting new friends), and, finally, to obtain a piece of paper called the college diploma. They also already had many clues beforehand that school was going to be a difficult place to be in, that they would not see many people like themselves, and that they would have a hard time adjusting to it. That a school can also be a place to radically change lives or potentially be a site for some kind of progressive politics was something they would get to discover and reckon with later. But in the beginning, schooling for these kinds of students was not a big deal. Students who were the first in their family to go to college typically did not have the college experience memories of those who came before them to draw on. Instead, they had images and imaginations of university life culled from popular culture or anecdotes from acquaintances. These made them qualitatively different students in an elite university, and thus their school's treatment of them and their responses to school conditions were understandably unique as well.[27]

On the other end were students like Migetu, who arrived in the university already having some formed thoughts about its elite and elitist status (and, therefore, its assumed inaccessibility to students like him) and certain criticisms regarding what the university was all about, chiefly its legacy of reinforcing social inequalities and domination over others. They had a strong inkling that they were coming into a battlefield of sorts. And although these students may not necessarily have come into campus with set ideas about what specific tasks were needed to accomplish in view of these criticisms, they had already imagined their school as a place of challenge and struggle beforehand. They were already convinced that it was going to be daunting and difficult to be successful in it. And they were surely expecting that, at some point, they would have to come to grips with an environment that was designed for students who were not like them.[28] Given what they knew or heard from high school teachers as well as family and community members, they were already cognizant of the university's prestige and high rank among the world's best. But as much as they were excited, proud, or even pleasantly (but nervously) surprised that they had been accepted into it, they were simultaneously anxious and skeptical. They had already heard other stories about students who dropped out, gave up, or were forced to leave. They had known others who had struggled and a few who were actually still in the midst of struggle. Eventually, certain events, encounters, and experiences while in school would mobilize them into action, propel them into advocacy, and dare them to think and act differently.[29]

Whether school was profiled as a space to test out new ventures or to participate in ongoing confrontations and struggles, all of these students already knew or imagined themselves as *minorities* right from the very start of their college education. They already anticipated that their school would not regard them as regular students, even though they would be surprised later how historically persistent, deep, and extensive this regard would be. They knew, as they had experienced in elementary and high school, that they would be treated differently and that they would arrive learning swiftly about this, in a much larger and complex environment. Beyond their classrooms and labs, then, they ascertained how to strategize in balancing their attitudes and actions as students of color between at least two things: how their schoolmates, teachers, and school officials would treat them and how they, in turn, would mobilize whatever resources in kind and in attitude they possessed as individuals and collectives to respond to such treatment. We can consider the narration of this calculus not simply as an account of difference of, say, conflicting values or unequal treatment among groups, and how such a difference is experienced by those who are less powerful or minoritized. We will for sure read those kinds of accounts here. But more than these, we will also see a narration of a particular set of encounters between the students and their school in which discoveries will be made about what it means to be a student of color in a moment of "diversity" and how to respond when those who are made to fit in a system that they perceive is unfit for them are forced to endure what they deem as false promises of social mobility or individual gain through uniform assimilation, acceptance, and compliance. These encounters and responses expressed fields and spaces of competing relationships of power that were unevenly contested yet almost universally experienced by students from dominant groups as "natural" or irrelevant, as opposed to "forbidding" and infuriating for the nontraditional students I interacted with.[30] We will eventually find out, then, why and how students turned to a reimagination of their school as an "ocean," and we will understand why the most important lesson here was learning how that "ocean" navigated them.

What my students called the ocean that is the University of Washington was founded more than 150 years ago, in 1861, on Native American Coast Salish land, through a private gift that has now expanded into three campuses in the cities of Seattle, Tacoma, and Bothell.[31] This ethnography focused on students who were attending just the UW Seattle campus, the public university system's urban flagship school situated on a sprawling 703-acre prime property north of downtown Seattle. Students popularly referred to it as "U-Dub" and called themselves "Huskies" in reference to the school's mascot. And, between 2004 and 2011, they numbered annually from forty thousand to about forty-nine thousand as undergraduate, graduate, and professional school students. The UW is an "R-1" research university, consistently rated as one of the top in the nation and the world, and known as the country's largest recipient of federal research funding since the 1970s.[32] In the years of this study, about five thousand professors, researchers, and lecturers worked on campus full-time, and about sixteen thousand administrative staff members were employed to support them. This school was one of the city's and the state's largest employers and contributors to their economies, it was top-rated in many sports leagues and athletic conferences, and it was highly regarded in many disciplines, fields of study, and research arenas.[33] Given this self-promotion-sounding description, and notwithstanding the mixed attitudes of my students regarding their school's treatment of them, to say the least, there was a profound sense of pride at being a member (and later, product) of such a prestigious university that was palpable, yet not frequently spoken aloud, within all of them. Being a "Husky" was a big deal.

I was just like one of my students in this regard. I do not clearly remember if I said it as often or as occasionally as others did, but I, indeed, have been generally proud of the school for all the reasons above, but also for its willingness to pursue "diversity" efforts that I have been interested in and for supporting related programs and other various opportunities that my students and co-faculty and I have availed of. Of course, I strongly think as well that it has not been a perfect school, but my deeper observations and analysis of it belong to another project.[34] With a view toward briefly narrating the school from my perspective as a professor and mentor in it, and in relationship to what is relevant here, and that is the lives of its underrepresented students, let me give you a sample.

In the beginning of this ethnographic project in 2002, UW Seattle was already in the midst of intensifying its efforts to diversify its student population and professoriate as one response to the promulgation and enforcement of Initiative 200. Passed in 1998 and otherwise known as I-200, this Washington State initiative called for the prohibition of race and gender preferences by state institutions, including the University of Washington, in their hiring procedures.[35] So, as a newly hired employee at that time, I felt very anxious to be in a place that, for me, seemed to not want me or, at least, was in doubt about how I, a person of color, ended up as a professor at the top university in Washington State. But I was pleasantly and unexpectedly surprised when I learned at that time that the school was already actively thinking about and acting upon ways to combat whatever negative effects had resulted from I-200, from decreasing admission rates of underrepresented students all the way to the low morale experienced by persons of color and women already at UW.[36] I was soon drawn to and volunteered to help out in several outreach and recruitment programs of the university's Office of Minority Affairs and Diversity, particularly those that targeted Pacific Islander students, and I became more and more committed, as the years went by, to several projects that addressed possibilities for transforming curricula, pedagogy, faculty hiring and retention policies, and institutional attitudes toward difference and power. All of these activities directly influenced my interactions with students involved in this project, and oftentimes I proactively used my position in the university to advocate for and realize our collective goals. Some of these attempts were successful, some of them were not, but many of them have continued. As many of my students told me more than a handful of times, especially in moments of our collective despair, "The ocean . . . it has no limits, no boundaries."

WHAT IS THIS OCEAN LIKE?

(With gratitude to Epeli Hau'ofa, 1939–2009)

"So, Kato, how was it like for you to come to UW on the first day? What happened to you?"

"Oh," Kato replied, so softly and slowly. "First day of school. (*Sighing.*) I was so nervous. I was so afraid. I was crying inside."

Kato, a Tongan American, had never felt "at home" at UW.[37] Right from day one, as soon as he got here from Puyallup, about thirty-five miles south of Seattle, he felt homesick, not because he missed home. He actually wanted to leave Puyallup and "explore the world." It was just that he wished the campus were more welcoming and not as unfriendly and cold to people like him, so unlike "home" for him. It helped that he had been to campus before and had known other Pacific Islander UW students, who assisted in recruiting him to apply. This was rare and not really intense at that time, but the recruiters who worked with him persevered, and their efforts paid off. So by the time Kato set foot on the campus, he had a small university students' community already formed and ready to accommodate him in their circle. But the reality of having to go to school with about forty thousand other students who were racially different from him, and also indifferent to him, coupled with the sheer absence of any part of the school curriculum that was even remotely connected with his Pacific Islander culture, was quite overwhelming. School, to Kato, was like going to another country—an extremely large, white, and uncaring country.

Kato thought that his first impression of UW was going to be just a fleeting occurrence. But after about two years of attending school here, he realized it was going to be a permanent and constant impression. School would always be alienating and impersonal for him; he was not ever going to get rid of that feeling, he thought. I could multiply Kato by as many as fifty or more students like him, I thought, as I perused the volumes of field notes I collected, which detailed similar observations of my fieldwork subjects. School was an imposing and forbidding place—a campus so grand, majestic, commanding, and well kept. "It is like going to paradise," Debbie, another Sāmoan American student, remarked. "A paradise that's beautiful, and green, and clean, but intimidating, and scary [al]together, like I'm not meant to be here, or [that] I'm just a guest here. I'm not [supposed to] . . . stay here and finish."

From my field notes, I list here what almost every student said or wrote:

Fearful.
Afraid.
Afraid but excited.
So nervous!
Scared.
Scared shit!
Fearful.
Worried sick, but yeah, afraid too.

I asked them, "But so were other students, right?" "No," Debbie said, "a lot of these other students were afraid because they were also new like me. But me, I was not only new. This is the first time someone from my family ever stepped into UW, or ever stepped into a freakin' college campus. Do you see what I mean?" Tavita, Migetu, and Kato said the same thing. To them, coming to college for the first time overwhelmingly sucked them into a place of despair because they were the first generation in their families to do this and, as a result, they possessed no road maps to guide them, no family college tradition to rely on, not even anyone else besides family who could have given them some tips or, at the very least, could have been visible to them as some kind of "I've been to college" model.[38] Of course, these feelings produced a great deal of uncertainty, of not possessing the required social capital to properly attend school, or of not knowing what to do, what to be, and how everything and anything was to be accomplished. "All I heard from my mom was 'Be good, Son,'" Tavita whispered, and then he continued: "Yeah, you know what I mean. People assume we come here knowing all the rules already, that all of this has been talked about at the dinner table many times. Not really. Not for my family. My mom wanted me to go to college. But I don't think she knew what that meant exactly. Or what it meant to do that."

Debbie added:

Going to college, for me, meant going to a place that has existed for so long, but now knowing what it really is. I just knew that UW was a very good school, and my dad told me that only very smart people go there. He was so proud of me. So, yeah, I was proud of myself too and excited at first, but when first day [of school] came, and even for the next weeks and months, I was kinda living in fear. Very intimidated. I thought that everyone else was smarter than me. And that I was going to fail . . . sooner . . . than later.

"But I'm not one to complain," Kato clarified. "This is what I have dreamed of, and I'm lucky to be here. There are so many people like me who want to come here, and they're not here. I'm so lucky to be one of the few. I just wish that now that I'm here, I wish that UW should feel lucky too that they have one of my kind here." "You're right," I said, "we [at UW] very rarely think about how lucky we are that we have students like you here. We don't make our students feel that way. We always think students owe us something." Kato gazed at me intently, as if I said something that he needed to think about some more. But I felt that I had also said something that made him sad. I thought later on that Kato's words were powerful enough to convince me that in the battle of conflicting cultures, in instances when members of dominant and minority groups mix, we tend to forget that every person from every culture has a capacity to bring in something enriching to a group. But those who are different from the rest of the majority in the group are usually expected to be enriched only by those in the majority, as if their presence and potential contribution to the mix do not matter at all. "So true," Kato said after a long pause. "I always feel like I owe this school a lot for giving me a chance." Up until the time he graduated, and continuing until he actually found work on campus, this powerful sense of indebtedness would stay with him.

In Kato's estimation, when students like him take in a strong feeling of indebtedness, they lose their sense of ownership of their "public" school. It is like the feeling of always being a guest. Or, it is like receiving a gift for which exchange or return is expected but never completely or amply satisfied, so that the feeling of obligation becomes constant and endless, and quite burdensome or shackling.[39] "I hate to feel like I owe. And I owe a lot," said Junior, a Sāmoan-Filipino student. This debt relationship between students and their school had a tendency to produce anxiety and alienation, of course, as students assumed that the gift giver was always someone more powerful than they were, someone they could not level with. True, this gift giver was technically an "institution," but this institution was almost always perceived as "the white man"—the one who sat in the school's administrative offices and boardrooms. To a good extent, this white man was imagined as the munificent and merciful benefactor, the venerable distributor of goods, the powerful holder of resources who dispensed valuable university spots with singular authority and heavy-handed decision-making.[40] No one was allowed to touch him. In one conversation I had with several students, no one even claimed to have seen him—the president who sat in an old, dark, and cold building. "Is that where the person we owe is?" Junior rhetorically asked me once while we were walking on campus with Kato, motioning his head toward the building where the UW president's office was. "So should we say thank you to him?"

"Why do you feel this way?" I sadly mused and glanced toward Junior. "Where is this coming from?" He then spoke in a slow, thinking way:

Do you want the short or the long answer?

Well, the short thing is that we're just visitors here. As in, visitors to America, yeah? We are told that we are given a chance to improve ourselves here. So now that we are here, we have to pay back. The long answer? Well, a different answer. We should not be treated like visitors here. Why are we just made to feel that way? School is for everybody. It's that . . . many people do not think we are a part of everybody. That's because we're brown and we're not the majority, and we're not the people in power. We are different. But being different also means not being the ones in a power position thing-y. You know what I mean? It's okay to be different, they always say. But it's not okay when you're different and then you get treated differently. It's not okay, right? Tell me. What do they say? I will respect you, but I will still be in power. That sucks for us, ya?

The two of us, including Kato, paused.

"You can continue, Junior," I said, only half seriously, for I was more focused at that time on getting to the place where we wanted to go. But I quickly sensed his apprehension, so I looked back at him, as he continued to talk.

Wait, do you see what I'm saying? Listen. This thing-y makes us different from all the rest of the students here. Not only are we made to feel like strangers here, we are also told that we have to [be] good and behave, and achieve, because we owe them. Didn't you say this in class? You said this is all part of colonization, ya? See? I'm learning from your class! Ha-ha-ha. Or maybe I'm wrong. You think so? You tell me.

All right, let me carefully unpack some of these for a moment. Students like Debbie, Junior, and Kato, including many of the other students of color I interacted with, embarked on a college education at UW filled with fear, awe, and anxiety because of uncertainty. As I wrote earlier, for many of them, they were the first ones to step into college, either ever or on the U.S. mainland, at least. This was definitely the major reason for their anxiety. They have had no history or legacy of family members being in a so-called big school before them. Their history was instead sourced from the knowledge they have had regarding what others have told them, or what they have heard or seen in popular media. This knowledge is quite specific and, evidently, unquestioned or simply taken for granted. These students understand right from the moment of even thinking about going to college, which in itself is already a rare and unexpected privilege, that college will be like going to the white man's space. Yes, it will be like paradise, as we heard earlier from Debbie, but it will also be a counter-paradise of fear, intimidation, uncertainty, indebtedness, and disempowerment. All of these were both produced by and productive of a school environment that was alienating, and it should not shock us to hear how students narrated these experiences of alienation as similar to or indicative of colonization, which they all knew too well as a familiar history of their people.

In schooling environments like these, as specifically defined by certain students as spaces where one exists as "colonized," social hierarchies were oftentimes distinct and clear. Students felt as if they inhabited and exhibited some form of a colonized status in which social differences across race, class, and gender, for example, were never neutral, harmless, or innocent. These differences were played out in the open—from the looks they got from others (as if they should not be where they were) to the bold verbal questioning of their intelligence (as if they were not smart people, or as if they were not smart enough to be in college). To be sure, these experiences produced ways of damaging them personally, for these instances made apparent to them how students' race and gender, and sexuality, mattered greatly in practically determining who obtained access to resources and opportunities, who got better treatment, and who was left alone. For many of these students who took courses with me in American ethnic studies, this was lesson number one right on the first day of class. They learned early on how calls for "respecting other people's cultures" and "tolerating differences" tended to mask the ways in which inequality operated structurally and how such propositions frequently reinforced the invisibility of unearned privilege enjoyed by dominant groups. Relatedly, they found out how the concept and practice of difference as it was constituted by and productive of unequal relationships of power can be thought about differently, not merely as simplistic accounts of unintentional ignorance, personal hatred, or individual prejudice. These differential treatments were themselves manifestations of structural arrangements that produced inequalities among different individuals and groups. In time, these students also comprehended how such practices, gleaned from certain institutional levels, can be uncloaked, resisted, and even changed.

"I get it," Kato suddenly jumped in, with a half smile. "Wow, that was quite a leap, Bonus. We went from feeling lucky, to feeling bad, to owing someone, to alienation, to colonization! And now, resistance! And change. Let's go!"

"I guess this is what we're up against, huh," I said slowly but trying to sound excited, for his sake.

The academic literature on the topic of alienation or social isolation for minority students in every level of the American educational system is vast and deep.[41] It is routinely listed as a quintessential minority experience in schooling as much as it is regularly mentioned as an indicator of or reason for these students' inability to flourish and succeed in academic settings. It is also deeply historical, as it is connected to working- and middle-class anxieties about gaining greater access to once thought of as thoroughly exclusionary postsecondary education sites beginning in the 1940s, and the more familiar, yet profoundly misunderstood, antiracist and anti-imperialist student protest movements that led to the creation of African American and other ethnic studies programs in the 1960s and 1970s. I say misunderstood because some educators tend to think of these movements as those that narrowly advocated for mere inclusion into the university, not its transformation. Expressed often through collected stories of being "strangers in the academy," coupled with its widespread persistence within climates of anti-affirmative action in many campuses later on, alienation has not been an unexpected theme in the lives of students who are different.[42] In this light, I do not want to shove aside the prolific accounts of students who mused about their experiences of campus alienation, so I will explore further a particular iteration of alienation that, to my students and me, is a little bit more nuanced and multifaceted.

School alienation appeared to many of the students here by way of the contradictory forms of fear of and desire for school. School, as "paradise," was both daunting and unrelenting in its power to tempt and scare at the same time, so that it was both and *simultaneously* a place of want and horror. It was something they were scared of, yet it was something they also yearned for. When Junior said that his school was a school of both desire and fear, that fear came from his realization that he was now part of something that he neither was comfortable to be a part of nor desired to be a member of—an elite class or group of students from high social and intellectual status who have been selected to become members of an exclusive school. Therefore, now, and in a seemingly absolute sense for him, he felt he became subject to the fulfillment of that school's high standards and expectations. Junior knew that he could not easily subvert these standards even if he wanted to; these standards were steeped in historical and long-standing practices of prestige maintenance among schools such as the UW. Represented by brick and ivy-lined buildings, well-manicured lawns, professors in tweed jackets, BMWs in the parking garage underneath the university's Red Square, and what he would call "white people's food" served regularly in most cafeterias on the campus, prestige for Junior was something he understood as "white" and, therefore, elite and quite alien, and emphatically undesirable. This environment became almost suffocating for him, like being a fish out of water, both because he felt that this world was too different from what he was used to and because he genuinely believed this world did not like him. He was always afraid that people would think of him as out of place, that some-one made a mistake in admitting him (and that this mistake would be revealed soon), or that he could be easily and unfairly booted out for failing to succeed in something that he could otherwise do if he tried. He also feared that he could be eaten up or co-opted by this unusually exclusive and privileged white world.[43]

Junior, therefore, feared for his psychic safety, and, yes, he was constantly afraid that one day, he was going to be like the people he was not or did not want to be. But then, in many ways, in some contradictory way, this was the place where he also wanted to be. Inside of him, he was proud that he got in, and, for sure, he was glad he made it in. He and his parents had known it all along—that powerful attraction, that tempting prospect—that he would somehow get into college so that the lives of everyone in his family, and everyone who would follow in his wake, would be much better from then on, since he was, at last, in a big university like the UW. Junior was trying to grab a piece of the proverbial American dream, and he was going to make sure to relish his share of it by try-ing very hard not to give up because of and despite his alienation.

I am going to quickly jump ahead to another point before the students actu-ally say it, but this is where, on some level, the metaphor for school as an ocean can be brought up as a useful tool for understanding the simultaneity of fear and desire. The ocean. The university. One and the same, perhaps. It is that which we can admire for its beauty and majesty, and it is that which has the capacity as well to drown us in its very beauty and majesty. The ocean could eat you up. This sounds a bit like a made-up story, or a metaphor that is too easy to associate with Pacific Islanders, who themselves will say that this is worth saying and thinking about, but it sounds just too corny for them to mention it. "I think it's all understood," Tavita reassured me, "the ocean is our life. It is where we are. And it is us. But it has dark stuff too. If you don't know how to swim in it, you can and will die. And we just don't have to remind ourselves of that because it's like . . . oh well, everybody knows it." Needless to say, the university as an ocean had much more meaning than a representation of the simultaneity of fear and desire. Let us mine this further.

HISTORICAL (NON)MEMORY AND MISRECOGNITION

At the top of the list of self-descriptors articulated by students who understood themselves to be "underrepresented" at UW was "invisibility." This was what virtually all of my interviewees said in order to understand why they felt alienated, and it was the one item that was routinely invoked by students as the fundamental reason why they thought their school—their teachers, administrators, and classmates—oftentimes did not think about them, did not value their presence and demands, or, worse, did not even know about them.[44] Frequently, then, these students' invisibility—cast in the form of their small numbers and reckoned to be the product of and explanation for their alleged insignificant value—worked as both descriptor and reason, so much so that many of them could not figure out, at first, what to make of it. Did their school think of them as insignificant because they were not that many on campus? Or did their school not see them because it just did not know about them? Was it their fault that they were invisible? Or was their invisibility a result of something else that was historical and structural, and that is why they were not that many and they were not considered significant?

"I hate this feeling," Migetu said to me when we were talking about this. He continued:

> I'm always pissed that our numbers are so low. But you know what? I bring this up to them [the student recruitment officers and university administrators] . . . and then, they say, who? Who do we want to recruit? Chamorros? What's that? Man, I get so pissed. Absolutely fucking pissed! People are so ignorant. Some of them think we're a dog breed or something like that. Man, Guam is a territory of the United States. Guam is the United States! Why do people not know that? Don't they know their own United States country? Don't they know their own U.S. history?

Migetu expressed invisibility not merely as a result of his people's nonappearance on the UW campus, but as something that was the product of the nonappearance of his people's colonization in the memory of U.S. history. Guam was acquired by the United States through the Spanish-American War in 1898, but it was peculiar and unnerving to him that nobody seemed to know this. In our many conversations, he and I would make parallel references to the U.S. colonization of Sāmoa in 1899 through the Tripartite Convention (which also ceded Western Sāmoa to the Germans); the U.S. takeover of the Philippine Islands from their Spanish colonizers also in 1898, officialized similarly through the Spanish-American War's eventual culmination in the Treaty of Paris; the U.S. colonization and control of other places such as Hawaiʻi, Puerto Rico, Cuba, Mexico, the Northern Mariana Islands, and the Virgin Islands; the U.S. takeover of Native American land and property.[45] We were both aghast at the institutional invisibility or undervaluing of all these U.S. imperial conquests in U.S. society, and even on campus, with Migetu additionally expressing disdain for the damaging consequences of such a historical amnesia that now has found its way into the devaluing of previously and still colonized people from the Pacific and the Caribbean on campus, and both of us having to witness on the ground the personal realities of national forgetfulness of U.S. imperialism that scholars and I read and write about.[46] If institutions themselves have limited or no knowledge of these histories, how do we expect them to understand what these students have to go through? I wondered, as other scholars and students do, how deep the wounds are for those who are rendered invisible because of their forgotten historical status. And I winced at the thought of pain and trauma they must go through in daily moments when they are made to feel that people have lost their history, when they are unrecognized by their teachers, or when they are practically unknown to others.

"I've been thinking about this for a long time now," Daniela, a Filipina American student told me:

I've been in such . . . such misery since high school, when our history class had just one sentence about the Philippines. One sentence. And now, having set foot here [at UW], I thought, oh my God, it's even worse! To think that college teachers should or [are] expected to know better! I raised my hand, I talked to the history professors and, oh . . . my . . . God, they don't know anything! And then, I feel . . . shame. Like, I'm not worth it . . . that my people are not worth studying, or even knowing. What the hell? What's going on? It's not my fault. But I feel embarrassed . . . in front of everybody . . . and inside of me. I feel like I'm this worthless person. Like my history is not down . . . it's not important. Nobody cares! *Nakakahiya* [How shameful]!

"But Daniela," I interrupted, "why do you have shame?"
Daniela responded:

It's shameful because . . . because they make me feel like . . . I feel like our people are not worth knowing about. Like, we're not Americans.

We're not part of this country. We're from somewhere else, we're just visiting, and now, we were just rescued. And that we should be grateful for that. And that . . . I don't know . . . like our culture is not that great. Like, we were not civilized. And then, Americans came to rescue us and civilize us. So now, we should just shut up and be good Americans. But see . . . I'm not even seen as an American! Like, nobody in class thinks I'm from Seattle. Well, I'm from the Philippines too . . . or my folks are. But I'm an American like everybody else!

Here, the problem of shame as it arises out of a history of colonization and the continuing effects of imperialism was one that most of my students, like Daniela, constantly grappled with.[47] To them, it was indeed agonizing to be caught in a quagmire of despair that wove across their lives as UW students, underrepresented students, and colonized students, with each status engendering for them what seemed to be either an abyss of hopelessness or a cycle of doubt and misery brought about by trauma. It was immobilizing, to say the least. And, as their teacher and mentor, I, too, wrestled with finding the words to comfort them and looked for any way that could take them out of their despair and bring them into some kind of positive space. We held many discussions about these connections between historical invisibility, trauma, and shame one-on-one, as well as in small groups, and some of them found their way into our classrooms. Eduardo, a Chicano- and queer-identified and Pacific Islander–allied, student narrated:

I think that, looking back now, I see how things add up. Like building blocks! We do this in MEChA, you know? And we did in your class too, yeah? First, we have to understand that when we were colonized, our land was taken, and our minds were taken too. They killed many of us, they destroyed our culture, and then they told us that their culture is better. No. I mean, they believe their culture is better, so they destroyed our culture! Ha! And they taught us how to think the same. That's why we have shame. Like, our culture is not good. But I think that [that] shame is stupid. We had . . . we had big civilizations before they came. Better than theirs. It's just that we were colonized.

Daniela continued:

We were colonized, so now we have to un-colonize. Did I say that right? Huh? Yah? We have to stop blaming ourselves. [We have to] stop punishing ourselves. We should not be shameful like this. Maybe shame is not even the right response? I don't know . . . but it's hard. It's so hard to even just think about this. And it's not even good to just think about this. No? Because we grow up hating ourselves, our people, even our culture. Hey, didn't we talk about this in class? What was the term we used? Internal colonialism, ya?

As their teacher, I was a bit shocked to hear about the very same stuff that I myself had to struggle with when I was in college and graduate school. But deeper than that, I was not really all that surprised about the persistence of the kind of internalized colonization that Daniela named, particularly on a campus that was seeing more and more nontraditional students now being shepherded through conventional models of formal education. In school, itself an instrument of colonization from the point of view of many of those who are minoritized in it, issues regarding previous and continuing colonization manifested most starkly especially when one was introduced to the idea that knowledge is manufactured truth, and that many truths are constructed to benefit some and to control others. For "colonized" people, the potentially damaging, even numbing, experience of going to school got even more magnified beyond conditions of invisibility or nonrepresentation.[48] As we have seen, there was the alienation that Debbie expressed, the double sense of fear and desire elucidated by Junior, the indebtedness mused over by Kato, and the shame more recently identified by Daniela.

Students soon began collectively thinking about these conditions and feelings as stuff that was bigger than people's mere ignorance or personal prejudice, larger than their classmates' individual expressions of unawareness and seeming stupidity, and deeper than what appeared to be just happening only now. Contemporary colonization was something bigger than they were, something much more historically continuous, and, to them, much more powerful than what they had been and what they were able to be. And many times, that overwhelming feeling of being individually and institutionally invisible, of being fearful and shameful, for them became productive of inaction and isolation. Students just got tired, many times, of having to endure this kind of shaming both of others and of selves, and of having to live and go to school like this every day. Many of them retreated. They pushed back in silence. This was profoundly disturbing and sad for all of us.

To which Kapi, a mixed Native American, Hawaiian, Sāmoan, and Filipino American student quickly interjected, "And to top it all . . . even when people do get to know us, ah . . . all these stereotypes come out! Yuck! You know . . . we're exotic people dancing the hula all the time, we're all athletes and lazy and slow and stupid. Oh . . . my . . . freakin' . . . God! There's no winning here!" Yes,

Pacific Islander students were mostly the ones who were targeted by such stereotypes. If they were not invisible, they got assaulted by these typecast identities or got mistaken for who they were not. And when they participated in certain activities that potentially marked them as indigenous people from the Pacific, whether it was a cultural or a sports activity, many people assumed that this was who they all were. They were people who were always "displaying" their culture.[49] Huge crowds marveled at their dance moves, cheered at their agility in football, and were in awe of their long and flowing hair and elaborate tattoos. They became objects of desire and envy, but only because they were expressing their culture in what they thought were the right ways, the right times, and the right places. In these instances, Pacific Islander students bore most of the brunt of what many would call "racist love"—a kind of admiration and positive recognition of members of nondominant cultures because they exhibited stereotypes that were acceptable, nonthreatening, or harmless, and oftentimes desirable. Racist love has a tendency to prop up behavior and imagery that conform to white society's interests, as it is mostly referenced in relationship to the characterization and appreciation of "model" minorities.[50] That is, when minorities do better than expected, and then behave in ways that do not disrupt unequal power relationships, they are applauded. The Pacific Islander students here knew very well that this was what was happening to them, and they alerted themselves to not be deceived by such a dehumanizing and controlling tactic.

Kapi continued:

I think it's stupid when other people admire us only when we dance. Or only when we do well in football or soccer. I think that's racist. When they do that, we all know what they think in their heads. They think we're a bunch of exotic people who are not civilized, like we live in trees or something. Or we're only good at playing football, which is probably worse because that's like combining being exotic with being a dumb jock who does not know anything and is an alcoholic and most probably a mac daddy. That's very insulting. It's demeaning, I think. It's like we have value only as certain kinds of people. People don't think that we're also college students who are smart, maybe? Or who do other things besides football? But people don't see that! They only see the hula dancing and the tattoos and the long hair.

Racist love, for these students, had a definitive way of assigning value to their identities without their control, stereotyping them as particular beings who had fixed and simplistic characteristics, and thus misrecognizing them, or failing to see them, as people who may have had multiple and dynamic definitions of who they were. Worse, this kind of attitude and thinking also had a tendency to be internalized, flattering its recipients to the point where they were not able to see its damaging effects, breeding hatred to those in the group who did not conform, and also circumscribing whatever potentials or desires they had to be someone they were not expected to be. This partly explains why Tavita, earlier on in the beginning of this chapter, did not, or could not, imagine how a Filipino could be a person of color and a professor at the same time. Being a professor, to him, was not something that was even thought of as a career by members of his family and community. He and they thought that a young person like him was only expected to be a janitor or a construction worker, perhaps. Or a security guard. Or a gardener. Or an airport baggage handler. And someone who could also dance the hula or do the *haka* on the side.[51]

Undervalued, stereotyped, misrecognized, and, therefore, disadvantaged as nontraditional students of color, one could not imagine a quiet and easygoing life for these students. Oftentimes, they were made to feel unfit for a school like UW, as if a mismatch had occurred in which the school's values were simply unlike or in opposition to theirs and were therefore impossible for them to imbibe. They felt they could not even question these values, as if their school could only have a uniform template for all, whether it was a set of curricula that was supposed to be the same for everyone or one way of teaching that every student could just easily and satisfactorily benefit from. Or they would feel so much pressure to conform, to just be quiet, and simply ignore that which they felt they could not control most of the time. Frequently, self-blaming would happen, or targeting racist individuals was all they could do. As their teacher, I found it difficult to explain all of these to them as systematically, and systemically the result of, historical, institutional, and structural forms of racial violence, discrimination, and oppression. "It's not the people; it's the institutions," I would remind them over and over, conveying my preference for understanding oppression as a structural expression of hate and control, not always and only an individual one. But although these students were indeed experiencing degradation that had been brought about by historically entrenched and powerful forms of organizational arrangements, it was confusing and disappointing to them how such arrangements could also not be reducible to individuals who were racist.

These students saw themselves as individuals who were experiencing racism; they thought of themselves as individual targets of racist people. They were right. The questions for us, then, became, how are we to understand the workings of racism, sexism, xenophobia, even homophobia, beyond their statuses as "objects of study" and, simultaneously, in ways that do not devalue their operations and consequences on the ground? In specific, how do we explain that which causes fear and intimidation, invisibility and indebtedness, or shame and exotification as both a personal and a structural emanation? How are we able to consider the school—the *ocean*—as a place of difference and inequality, where collisions between cultures, histories, and values occur, and where power and control over one's life and destiny are played out, but without losing the sense that tides also change and that currents can be navigable in multiple ways?

RIDING THE WAVE

The vast majority of students I interviewed and interacted with had quite a mouthful to say about "diversity," which I put in quotation marks here to signify a strong inclination on their part to question its meanings and practices. I will highlight "diversity" here as one of the key and far-reaching contexts that constituted students' lives on their campus and one that was productive of the kinds of contradictions students faced, which, eventually, they contested in their own ways. We will cover some of those stories here. For now, I think it is worth examining how these students responded to the ways in which their school deployed the language of "diversity." We should keep in mind that my purpose in this exploration is not to indict university policies and practices related to "diversity." Neither our school nor our institution's prolific "diversity" programming effort was the primary and only target of students' critique here; instead, they were leveling their critique of "diversity" mostly as they experienced it in their capacity as members of U.S. society. Students' encounters (as well as my own) with "diversity," as I argued in the introductory chapter, cannot simply be understood as specific to the campus under study here. Profoundly, the "diversity" that students knew and experienced daily was part of a discursive and extensive chain of understandings that came from within and beyond their school, and exceeded their local boundaries, from large social and media events that highlighted, for example, debates regarding access to schooling, to books, articles, and court decisions that engaged with the meanings of difference in relationship to education.[52]

Three patterns arose out of this environment of "diversity"—the reduction of students' self-esteem, their quest to build small communities, and their particular insight on "culture" as a site of recovery and resistance—all demonstrating how students got caught in sites of incongruity and opposition that, in turn, imperiled, then later enhanced, their ability to experience meaningful schooling. The opportunity to provide meaningful education to all students, an imperative that was oftentimes lost in the shuffle of debates regarding defining and practicing "diversity," was one that my students managed to keep an eye on, despite the shortage of social space allotted to its discussion on-site and on top of having to continuously face the pressure to do very well in school—to be successful—just like many other students on campus.[53]

If the loudest message that students heard when their school talked about "diversity" was that students who are underrepresented were important primarily to the degree that they filled in good numbers for the university, the deepest cut that this rhetoric produced was the one that sliced at their self-esteem. It was ironic, then, that a vision or set of programs put out in the name of addressing issues of inequality turned out, in many cases, to be the one that exacerbated these students' undesired sense of difference and differential treatment. Many students felt that "diversity," as was practiced or understood by those around them, meant an unwanted focus on them as students who were merely brought in to populate the campus with color and were, therefore, beneficiaries of unearned and unfair advantage. Again, this was not utterly local; this contradiction also emanated from something larger than the university, something that was historical and structural. They thought that it actually happened everywhere—in government offices, in workplaces, in athletic organizations, for example—but they were oftentimes surprised and disappointed that their school was not immune from such practices. Not only did these conditions make students frequently doubt the reason why they were in a prestigious university; they likely made students feel that they were frauds masquerading as high achievers in school.[54] "I hate this feeling," Paul, a mixed Hawaiian and white student, told me in such an exasperated tone,

and I know so many of us feel this way. It is stupid and it destroys you, you know. It makes you feel so . . . not sure of yourself, that you're just here because you got in through some kind of handout . . . is that what they call it? Like it was a special pass that they give you, and that they gave you this special pass because you are not smart enough like the others who can get in with no special pass. I know that people who are like us were made to experience this before. And I know we, people like us, experience this in getting jobs, being politicians, you name it. So stupid.

A student from Palau, Charlie, extrapolated:

I don't get it. I thought that being a student of color in our school means that we are making the school a better place for us and for everybody. Isn't that what diversity is about? Why is it that we have this weird feeling that we are like question marks here? Like we are not supposed to be here if it was not for diversity? Like, now, the standards are suddenly lower? And that we came in because the school lowered its standards? That's bullshit, you know. But, you know, even when outside of campus, I hate it because people get shocked when I tell them I got into UW. Like I get questioned why I made it and not their daughter or their son who's . . . and they would say this really loud to make sure I hear it . . . SMARTER than ME (*said aloud with his eyes rolling*), or something like that. I hate it, you know. It really makes me question and doubt myself why I am here.

Charlie and Paul were not alone in feeling as if they doubted themselves most of the time, and their tremendous experience of uncertainty was indeed familiar to everyone else I talked to: Tavita, Migetu, Kato, Junior, Debbie, Kapi, and Daniela, to name a few. Virtually all of my informants had, in one way or another, expressed to me how their self-esteem, already low to begin with (experiencing minoritization even from their elementary, middle, and high school years), had been so ravaged by a campus and societal environment that had imagined them as students who seemed to be not worthy of admission or, worse, students who had cheated the system, even though they expected everyone to know that our state did away with practicing affirmative action many years ago. I recall countless hours when I had to counsel students out of this misery, by convincing them that they had a right to be here, that they deserved to be here, and that they had to find ways to keep an eye on their self-esteem so that it was not altogether destroyed.[55] "All of these doubts and blows on your self-esteem," I once told them, "may not go away completely. So, what can you do? . . . Well, you need to learn how to live through them, beyond them. You need to live with them."

"I know it's easy for me to say but . . ."

"You mean, like, ride the wave?" Tavita broached. I smiled. I saw his eyes light up, but his body looked awkwardly relaxed, like he was not that convinced about what he just said. So I wondered aloud if he was joking or serious. "I'm not kidding! This is like riding the wave, isn't it?"

Riding the wave, surfing in the ocean, or coasting along, so that one did not feel utterly hopeless and immobilized, was a set of coping strategies that helped many students manage their miseries regarding being in school or, otherwise, their daily struggles in life as a whole.[56] These problems were not going to go away, they were not going to be solved neatly and completely, and they seemed to students to be too complicated to deal with at great length and all the time. But "riding the wave" was regarded not as the only answer to their troubles;

rather, it was one among many, and it included within it a host of related strategies that students deployed in specific instances or circumstances that required exceptional responses. It was also a way to learn how to navigate properly their ocean, and how to acquire the facility and skill in understanding how their ocean navigated them, like the art and science of surfing. But it should be noted that all of these strategies and tactics were not altogether successful all the time. That was factually improbable. Nor did self-esteem issues disappear right after students deployed a "ride the wave" attitude. That would have come out as a fake statement, wishful thinking, or a joke. On the other hand, we also discouraged ourselves to think of "riding the wave" as merely a palliative strategy that was meant to temporarily alleviate pain, even if it appeared to do so. That would have sounded so instrumentally and unbelievably simplistic, anyway. And it would have also come out like a ruse. Riding the wave was a strategy utilized alongside or combined with a set of other strategies, and was always understood to be part of a process, a set of attitudes or stances out of many, and an element of an emergency tool kit that one reached into when the ocean currents were strong, seemingly unnavigable, or hopelessly unavoidable. And when it was invoked, and especially when it worked, many students felt both relief and contentment, at least momentarily.

"We gotta stay here, man," Grace, a Filipina American student who also identified as Pacific Islander, cried out:

I'm not gonna give up. Or, I don't know, I will try not to give up. So, sometimes, it's better to just go with the flow. I don't mean . . . to surrender. I mean, pick your battles. If you go against everyone all the time . . . and all together . . . like really all together . . . and with all your energy, man, you gonna break. And break to pieces, ha-ha. So, you gotta learn how to pick your battles and relax in the meantime. You know, just lean back, enjoy the moment if there's something there to enjoy, ha-ha. Be in cruise control, you know. Or, at least, for the time being. It cannot be fight, fight, fight every day. That will kill ya. It can be fight, fight, fight today. But just for today. Yeah? The next fight should be sometime next week, ha-ha. In the meantime, retreat a little bit, feed yourself some renewed energy, not think of it, then prepare for the next one. It sounds so easy, right? But we need to be like this. Or else, look at Migetu!

Grace's reference to Migetu, I thought, was a little bit harsh. She was talking about a student-friend who did a lot for the community, but who also suffered from burnout. So I thought he deserved more compassion. Migetu, as many students and I observed, had this propensity to tire out every now and then.

So we repeatedly told him to ride the wave. He preferred not to heed us most of the time. For as long as he was a student at UW, he commendably fought hard to seek representation and recognition for his people, he was intensely active in many student government entities (and made sure he was present even when he was not invited or required to be there), and he was always making a speech, participating in a teach-in, or holding some kind of a rally on campus. People jested that he was a campus celebrity; everybody else who was not as active as he was knew him at least by face! Even administrators—the president, the provost, and the vice president for minority affairs—knew him by his complete name, knew where he was coming from, and seemed to admire him. But they both loved and disliked, or were annoyed by, him. They were oftentimes upset with him, in the ways he bluntly challenged their authority, spoke too quickly, or aggressively demanded more than what they expected. I felt the same way sometimes. Migetu was a beloved student of mine who, I thought, cared genuinely about his community, understood the political significance of our advocacies, and had a deep investment and passion in transforming the way things were on campus. That is why I thought Grace's side blow to him was a bit insensitive.

But Migetu also had a tendency to overdo many of these activities, I agree, to the point of causing his academics to suffer, while also alienating other students and administrators who were standing in his way, and as he was frequently losing track of processes that required careful strategizing and patience for them to work. Worse, he developed battle fatigue and, occasionally, bouts of dispiritedness. On many incidents, I found Migetu craving for more things to do, except for studying or even attending to his family and personal life. We had many talks about this, because I thought he needed some intense guidance and compassion, or understanding.[57] And in our talks, he often reminded me, especially when I scolded him about neglecting his studies, how it was also possible for me to be out of it like him, and that I could also lose track of what was important to him, to his student communities, and to the school.

It was hard for me to hear this and, indeed, it was tricky for me to look at myself in the midst of such a deep, intense, and plentiful engagement with students. I paused for a while, talked with some other students, and wondered aloud with them on how we could collectively process this dilemma of being both a student and an activist, with teachers like me expecting them to do well in both, while also requiring them to take good or better care of their personal and public lives at the same time. I felt troubled about Migetu, even if I insisted on continuing my mentorship relationship with him because I thought he deserved and desired my care of him. Students were collectively shaking their heads:

"I don't wanna disrespect you, Professor Bonus," Tavita said, "but you're asking for the impossible!" Tavita reasoned: "You know why we do all of this, ya? We do all this because this is our school. And we have a right to be here. This is a public university. It is supposed to serve the people. Our people, ya? We have the right to learn and be better people just like everyone else. So we expect our university to help us do that. And when they don't, of course, we let them know. We want to make the university serve us. Because it is ours, ya?"

I was touched. Tavita's reasoning made me think about the powerful sense of integrity and dignity that advocacies in the name of ownership and self-determination can bring. These students wanted to take ownership of their school and feel legitimized as its members (or part owners), not just mere "bodies" for display in the name of "diversity." They wanted to convince themselves and others that they themselves had a stake in their education and that they were willing to sacrifice a lot even just to have some measure of acknowledgment of that aspiration for themselves. They desired legitimacy, worthiness, and humaneness. I then thought about the thousands of other students on the same campus who did not have to do this, this larger multitude of other students who came into campus already feeling a good sense of ownership of their school as something that was normal or regular to them and, therefore, unspoken and not even thought of, much less questioned.

"That is the first thing you want to tell yourselves," Tavita and I told high school students who attended a workshop we hosted for those who were applying to the UW.

> You have to tell your selves that once you get in, you become part owners of this school. Or, in fact, even when you're applying, you should not think that this school does not belong to you. You own this. You are the state's and the nation's kids, and this is a public school. So this is yours. And when you convince yourself that you are one of the UW's owners, then, of course, you want to take care of it, right? Same thing as when you own something precious. You want to guard it, protect it, make it better, be proud of it, love it! Keep that in mind! Write it down! You own the UW!

If society and their campus were imagining and practicing "diversity" as an answer to limited representation and, therefore, one that could be addressed principally by increasing the numbers of minority students on a campus such as the UW, my students were thinking and dealing with "diversity" as a call for greater recognition of who they were beyond their bodily and numerical presence. When they heard school administrators and professors talk about "diversity" as a necessity for greater understanding among students, for the enabling of additional perspectives in the classrooms, and for the attainment of harmonious relationships across groups, they shunned all of these in favor of pursuing diversity so that everyone gets to claim the right of ownership of a public good, so that everyone gets to experience what it means to be privileged and underprivileged (and feel a measure of discomfort about it), and so that each and every student in the classrooms, and their teachers, gets to address social inequalities. They wanted their school to say that our campus needed "diversity" not because we wanted certain people merely to be accounted for, but because we desired to address past and present injustices, or because no one group should have the monopoly of exercising the right to be educated.[58] My students felt as if they were being used to simply or narrowly populate the campus with color, and they were asking more than what was expected of them. Here is Heinzy, a Sāmoan American student, and other students after him:

> This diversity thing-y is kinda crappy. I feel like they're just using us for decoration. And then, they expect us to just shut up and listen. And then, when we get to talk, they shut us up again. I scratch my bald head all the time, ha-ha-ha, because they let us in, but they prevent us from saying anything. You see what I'm saying? Like we have no right or something. Like we are stupid or whatever. Look, we came here to study, and we could see through these things. It's our right to be here. And so . . . this diversity thing . . . needs to . . . we need to put some balls in it. I don't know. That's something we have to dig in for.

> PAUL: I was listening to the [university] president once, and he kept on saying that our school needs diversity because it's better for businesses to . . . I don't know . . . operate as better businesses? I was like . . . you gotta be kidding. Like, we want more diversity so that we can sell more things to different kinds of people? Like, what the heck? Are we doing these things so that corporations can benefit some more? From us? From people of color? That was not down, I thought. That was kinda . . . exploiting . . . for him to say that . . . to fight for diversity for businesses to have bigger profits or something like that. Why do we need to connect diversity with making money? That's kinda silly.

> GRACE: This diversity thing. We should not be fooled by it. . . . I don't represent diversity. I represent inequality! Ha!

Were these students representing the solution? Or were they representing the problem? It was a dilemma with no clear-cut answers for the students, and it did not help that issues of diversity constantly nagged them both internally and publicly, like an open wound that would not heal. As their teacher, I saw how distracting and disconcerting this situation was to them. These were conditions that made them susceptible to anxiety and despair, consequences that were so untypical for the vast majority of traditional students I knew. It became a running joke to my students and me that this experience—of being both a figure of "diversity" and an emanation of the anxieties that were its result—explained how underrepresented students got to be acquaintances and friends. We laughed about this frequently because we thought it was ironic. But we also thought it was so true on the ground. Our students first recognized one another, and sought commonalities with one another, through the color of their skin and their shared historical meanings associated with it. And then, they got to bond through and because of their similar miseries. Tavita and I, in the same workshop, said:

> You don't only own your school. You gotta own your community in it. Just like what our ancestors taught us, and what our families always teach us, you are not just you. You are not by yourself. Each of you carries your entire family and the communities you belong to, along with yourself. So, when you get to UW, always remember that you are a member of these communities, including the ones you will see here. Whatever you do, you do in the name of these communities. When you fall, all of us fall with you. But when you succeed, all of us succeed with you! So, make sure you find that community, or communities. Be [a] part of it, nurture it, shower it with your love. It will be your ocean—the one that will embrace you, protect you, and love you as well.

Invoking, owning, building, and sustaining collectives were tremendously significant parts of these students' vision for themselves as members of their families and communities, particularly on campus. It also became their mission to live by what they saw as the ocean's meanings and reasons—the full extent of the vasa. It was a practice that helped mitigate the consequences of alienation or, at least, circumscribe the effects of isolation. For when students began to light up as soon as they saw someone they could have "community" with—and I have also seen this captured on video, in several documentaries that my students have produced—it essentially became a lifesaving experience for them to be with each other.[59] Social science theorists have a trove of explanatory formulations that can rationalize causes of group or community formation, and these student collectives—especially those organized around Pacific Islander, Chicana/o, Latina/o, Native American, Southeast Asian American, or African diasporic identities—that I have observed for this study and helped guide through mentorship exhibited seemingly no particular exceptionality.[60] On many levels, they were just like all other groups founded and existing on campus: organizations created to bring people together under a common set of identities and interests, sustained through the active pursuits of such interests, and bound by dynamic definitions of sameness and difference. Almost all of those student organizations formed through minority racial or ethnic identities have had long histories of underrepresentation as the bases of their formation.[61] But what set these groups apart, at least those that I studied for this project, were the following: many of them were relatively newly formed, they had more porous or flexible racial/ethnic boundaries, and they seriously focused on "culture" (as expressions and processes produced through colonized histories and resistances to them) as a site of their political lives and advocacies.

Pacific Islander students' regard for their collectives, both Polynesian and Micronesian, and, to a certain degree, Filipino, was especially intense because their numbers were so low. The Micronesian students addressed this by teaming up with another Micronesian-focused student group outside of UW, at Seattle University. The UW Micronesian students were already quite established when I first arrived on campus, perhaps because of the strong alliances they were able to develop with communities outside of UW right from their organization's onset. As for the Polynesian Student Alliance (PSA), its initial formation was fueled by the concentrated recruitment efforts of its founding leaders that specifically targeted indigenous Pacific Islander students who were dissatisfied about their marginalization in the largely Asian-descent membership of the campus's Hawai'i Club, otherwise known as Hui Hoaloha 'Ulana. There was a big to-do with this issue of indigenous islanders' separation from Hui, especially when it was publicized, for it pitted Pacific Islander groups against one another and caused many of them to divide their collectives or otherwise decide strictly on their loyalty to just the one group they chose to be in, as in a zero-sum situation. Some students thought they were all being too "political" and decided to stay away from the fray. But many others picked up the cause for self-determination and joined the ranks of the curious, the interested, and the "let-me-see-what-this-one-will-amount-to" students during the alliance's inaugural meetings. High spirits were in place. Students were thrilled.[62] They were less than 1 percent of their university student population, and yet they found, at last, a collective voice—an ocean of voices that were proud and ready to be recognized.

"But what about the Filipinos? Where do they belong?" Daniela and Heinzy both asked loudly. I wondered about this as well, being a Filipino American myself, who was, through the years, getting more and more invested in the lives and politics of Pacific Islander students. Tavita replied: "Huh? I thought all this time [that] Filipinos were Pacific Islanders! Are they not?" And then Daniela said, "Well, technically, they're from the Pacific, right?" "But aren't the Japanese too?" Junior wondered. Tavita: "Why don't we just leave it up to them to decide? If they want to be with us, that's great. If not, well, that's okay too." I liked and agreed with this idea, but I also speculated whether students were being flexible because I was their teacher, to whom they owed some kind of recognition and respect. I myself knew several students who identified either as Filipino American or as Pacific Islander, and there were also those others who identified as Filipino American or Asian American, or mixed.[63] I similarly encouraged them to decide whatever they wanted, but even if they seemed to be open-minded about the suitability of Filipinos in their Pacific Islander–based politics, I would definitely not discount the possibility that this was disagreeable to other Filipinos and Pacific Islanders. This situation, nevertheless, exemplified to me a kind of openness, flexibility, and innovation in community building that I found among the students I interacted with the most.

If there was any other issue that stood out in Pacific Islander student organizing beyond their people's lack of representation in their school—their own version of a "diversity" issue that mattered for them—it was the preoccupation with their indigenous, even "diasporic," culture as some kind of a bonding agent for all of their constituents, what would be considered as everything that was contained in their ocean, including what they have yet to know. This ocean had vast treasures of knowledge and tradition, including histories of oppression and resistance, and it was also an open sea of possibilities. Culture, for the students in this case, then, marked the most significant ground from which all of their demands for recognition as students rested and arose. They imagined their culture primarily in their community's ways of thinking, attitudes, and values, of understanding their histories and place in the world, and as it was articulated in various expressive forms. It became their defining mode of representation, as it became the central feature of their mission in their fight for recognition, in their demands against social injustice, and as the most important tool in their quest for both recovering what they thought was lost or stolen from them and for expressing their soul and their meanings as people of the ocean. Kapi noted:

> I like it when we kinda almost require everybody to dance. I like it when we perform our culture. Everybody in our group needs to know how to perform any Pacific Islander dance or song, or poetry, what have you.

That's how we know ourselves and our traditions. We have a big ocean of all kinds of things we can be proud of. Let's know them and tell everyone we have all these things that are important, or sacred, or just plain Pacific Islander. It will force all of us to bring into the open what we are, instead of hiding. Dancing in public makes us proud. No more shame and . . . you know . . . embarrassment . . . because we wear these islander outfits and everybody can see our bodies and tattoos. No more of that! We are our culture, and we should show everybody else who we are . . . using our culture.

Similarly, Junior added:

I don't know. I just like to dance. Period. I grew up learning all of these from my village [in Sāmoa] and I am proud to show everybody that I know these things. They can be intense, you know? I do the fire dance and, yeah, people get scared and there's all this fire and I'm twirling these sticks around. A lot of people like that. And it's a good feeling to see that. They don't see that a lot. So when we perform, it's a good feeling. It's a way of showing who we are, proudly showing what we represent, what we hold as valued . . . important.

I've seen big audiences watch Junior do the fire dance during Poly Day, an annual set of cultural and recruitment events on the UW campus that are focused on Pacific Islanders. He truly was its star performer on many occasions. But it was also amazing for me to see the ways in which many Pacific Islander students took the lead in doing outreach to high school students. And they did so by couching their recruitment of these students on the likely probability that Pacific Islander students would be able to practice their culture on campus if or when they got admitted into the UW. This was their version of a practice of "diversity"—the version in which one was not encouraged to erase or set aside difference, but instead encouraged to celebrate how different they were from the rest, yet still feel that they could be accepted and valued.[64] Kato echoed: "It's nice that our recruitment of high school kids is not all about coming to UW so that they can be smarter students, or be successful as UW students. We recruit by telling them they can be who they are here, culturally. There are Pacific Islander students here. They can practice their culture here. They don't need to, you know, assimilate or be like others, and give up who they are, like leave it outside the campus, just practice their culture at home. They can practice their culture here. They can be who they are. Right here."

In the practice of community bonding, in which indigenous culture was at the center of students' energies, whether it was recruitment- or performance-driven, Poly Day was always the event to look forward to. It was something that students devoted so much time preparing for, from dancing and singing rehearsals carried out by professional and student instructors at least three months before the event, to participating in workshop development sessions undertaken by minority affairs staff members to instill proficiency among student "ambassadors" in university admissions policies and processes. I also conducted classroom- and community-sited preparations for the workshops on Pacific Islander histories and cultures. By the time Poly Day commenced, many of these students would have been thoroughly knowledgeable about all these cultural performances, histories, contemporary experiences, and school policies—their vast ocean—that they would have never learned in the usual classrooms on a regular basis. Yet, as Tavita alluded to in the beginning of this chapter, these were knowledges that mattered to the students, but were quite devalued, in the ways they were rendered as "extracurricular" by their teachers and co-students. Tavita explained to me that other people around him thought that his preoccupation with Pacific Islander matters was impractical, unnecessary, or even distracting. But he imagined it the opposite way: that stuff he learned in his regular classes, such as English and chemistry, was as impractical as it was disconnected from what he thought was his regular life as a person. So, when he told me that he did not know much about "practical knowledge," he meant he was not knowledgeable on those things that did not relate to his identity and culture as a Pacific Islander. He also did not care much about these "regular things," even though he forced himself to master them to be able to excel in his studies.[65] Profoundly, Tavita had an altogether different regard for his culture, for *Oceania*. They were the kinds of knowledge and practices that gave meaning to his life and the lives of his allies both as students and as people from and of the vasa.

Over several years, I observed how Poly Day worked. It started in the morning with a welcoming session for high school kids, who were bused into campus; a series of workshops then followed on college application and Pacific Islander cultures in school (Tavita, Migetu, and I jointly conducted workshops on the vasa several years in a row); and afterward, a sampling of islander food was provided for lunch. The highlight of the day was the stage performances of all the major groups of the Pacific, including, sometimes, even performances of the high school students themselves, who during a yearlong outreach and college-preparation program had also been taught how to dance. This performance happened at Red Square, an open-air venue strategically located on the UW campus, next to the central administration building, the undergraduate and main libraries, a building that housed large lecture halls, and a performance center. Most of the work was done by UW students, many of them volunteers and active members of existing organizations, in alliance with others, and in common ground with many members of the UW administrative officers and staff, to bring to the fore, for at least one moment in the campus calendar, everything the students thought was worth sharing about Pacific Islander culture. These students were transforming themselves, they were publicly showing it, and, by so doing, they were transforming their school.[66]

Of course, what got lost here, in the midst of all the celebration and excitement, but maybe just momentarily, were many of the students' daily struggles against what they usually thought of as a daunting and oppressive campus. It was not good to do any kind of emotional, negatively sounding accounting here, students told me. Furthermore, one could not expect a day's achievements to have a long mileage or one event to solve everyone's miseries permanently. Nor should one forget that different people obtained different reactions from events like this. Tavita, Migetu, and I thought many times of having a more substantive discussion of histories of imperialism and Pacific colonization in our workshops, but that would have entailed setting aside time for rumination and processing of what might be painful or challenging (or unfamiliar) matters for many high school kids. We needed an entire week just to barely scratch the surface! In addition, Kapi and others wondered if performing in public amounted to more exotification of islanders by the diverse audiences who watched them, or if such performances resulted in the further reinforcement of islander stereotypes—that they were only good at hula or that they all performed only sexy or exotic dances in body-revealing outfits. Kapi expressed concern:

> I always worry that when we dance, people don't get the point. In the Hawai'i Club, dancers dance to entertain and to show off their moves. But with us, we dance because this is our culture. There's meaning to every move; and the body is just the . . . the vessel, you know? There are messages in each dance. Many of them are sacred too. Like, you don't just play and dance. You almost, like, pray. And in each song, there's history, there's culture, there's crying sometimes because of colonization, or things that have been lost or devalued. You know? I don't think people get that. They just see us as exotic sensual dancers. It's kinda sad.

Culture was, indeed, an unstable site for performing a politics of recognition. Performed in the ocean that was their school, students turned to it to find their community's expression of who they were from their own perspectives and to search for meaning in their lives both as members of that community and as students who also wished to belong to a larger community. They used culture as a space for knowing themselves, for defining themselves, and, occasionally, for crafting a version of themselves that varied from the ways their parents taught them or from how their teachers treated them. This ocean behaved smoothly when it was positively generative of new things, but it was also sometimes rough when these new things got shown to the public. In all of the performance planning processes, there were no strict scripts that were followed, for different leaders and more vocal members changed every year and had their ways of influencing others to be conservative or, sometimes, daring in their performances. Some of them were approvingly met with big applause from their audiences, and some earned the derision of a few community elders for going against the grain of tradition, for example, doing a dance move differently or having a woman do a man's dance. Yet, for all the many years I conducted this study, Poly Day never had a no-show. So many students and staff members always worked behind the stage curtains to make it a reality time after time. And so much of their labor always remained unnoticed, their names not even mentioned in any public or permanent way. This was how the students' campus community was. Everybody took care of the ocean, no matter the outcome and with no expectation to achieve praise or fame after the work was done.

COMMUNITY DESPAIR AND COLLECTIVE FORTITUDE

The university was and has been a place of assault for many of the students I interacted with. Students who were the first in their family to set foot on a large college campus, and those others who were seen differently, faced very little doubt right from day one of school that the probability of hardship they would face for the coming years was going to be high. They knew they would encounter difficult times, and they knew that giving up on school always loomed as a firm and probable option on their horizon. At some point, they anticipated this to be a dreadful fork in their road, and this was probably the biggest reason why school appeared to be so forbidding and perilous to them. These students held on to what seemed to them as the luck of the draw, represented by their providential entry into college. And they knew all too well that this fortunate circumstance was fragile and could be taken away from them anytime without advance notice. No wonder they felt so insecure; their tenuous sense of stability was frequently bombarded with such blatant and persistent assaults on their senses of worth and self-esteem, resulting in numbing thoughts of failure and doubt each and every day they were in school.

In conditions such as these, some students tended to be quiet, remained on the sidelines, or unobtrusively opted out of school. Others reacted with an intrepid attitude, seeking out comrades initially to break their isolation by meeting others who were like them, then turning their acquaintance-based relationships into social and political circles, and eventually transforming themselves into communities of support, activism, and advocacy. They had to empower themselves in the process, and they did so by convincing themselves that they were the true owners of their identities and that they were also legitimate part owners of the school they went to. They were not always sure-footed about their moves, but in naming themselves in relationship to the conditions they commonly faced, they found that power of community whenever they were with one another.

This power of community, of turning to one another for sustenance, of building dignity through collective self-respect, and taking pride in the immeasurable wealth of their cultures, fundamentally rested on bringing the ocean into the students' school lives. In a place where everything seemed to be unfamiliar, scary, mechanistic, and uniform, the ocean—even when it was only imagined, or *because* it was meaningfully imagined—held out the potentials of discovery, solace, and transformation. Instead of being pinned down constantly by their school's relentless domination of their sense of personhood, students invoked the profoundly palpable command of the vasa to bring themselves together into the tight embrace of their own traditions, values, and respectability, securing for them, even in fragile ways, the right to determine their worthiness as people and their capacity to transform the very place that undermined their potentials. This imagined oceanic community often acted as a viable response to conditions that were overwhelming to students. It was a staging ground for seeding coalitions as much as it was a set of attitudes and practices that were enabled in reaction to uncertainty, invisibility, and misrecognition. But, as we shall see in the next chapter, the ocean in the school was also, and in some ways unexpectedly and in others intentionally, a productive site for generating a host of other alternative ways of finding meaningfulness in school by transforming what it means to be students in it.

2

PIPE

Collective Mentorship as a Politics of Partnership

Spring quarter. It's already close to four o'clock. I've been waiting for the mentors because we have to pick up the food! It's gonna come from Hawaii BBQ [a restaurant] and, hopefully, there's parking there. I hope. At this time, maybe not. Grrrrrr, grumble. I always get annoyed when we don't have parking over there [on University Way, or "the Ave," a busy commercial area by the campus]. That means I have to park farther away, making it such a hassle for the mentors to carry the food trays. Or else I have to drive around in circles until the food is ready to be loaded into my car. And then. . . . And then we have to drive all the way to the ECC [the Ethnic Cultural Center, about eight blocks south of the restaurant], park in the faculty parking lot, unload the freakin' food [trays], bring them into the study room, study, then feed the students at five, then study again 'til six or seven. Are we even ready? Don't forget your backpack! Don't forget our bag of school supplies! Don't forget the bag of plates and utensils and napkins! By the time all of us get settled down, study tables will be over, I'm sure. Who will lead the grace this time? Will students be there? Or will it just be me? Did they forget to announce this? Or did I see something on email? Were students informed? Oh my God, it's already six? We don't have enough time!

. . .

Chill, Professor Bonus, we have all the time in the world!

. . .

The long passage above is an excerpt from a collection of field journals that I have been writing in for more than a handful of years now, ever since several students and I ventured to test out a pilot peer mentorship program on the UW Seattle campus, way back during the spring quarter of 2001. The remark that followed it came from Tanielu, a Sāmoan-Filipino student who became the program's director many years after that pilot program. Tanielu came from a long line of successive student mentors and directors that originated with Tavita, a student we have met already in the introduction and chapter 1, who, along with Migetu, was part of the founding group that conceived and implemented this specific program, called the Pacific Islander Partnerships in Education mentorship program (PIPE). These excerpts come from May 2010, and Tanielu is quoted here from that same source as well, because I invite most of my students to write in my own field journals. In this chapter, I trace the history of PIPE as a particular mentorship idea that students and I thought of, and discuss a collection of mentorship practices that we collectively worked on and that eventually led to what is now a set of several mentorship programs targeting different underrepresented student groups on campus. As I do so, I will provide an analytical narrative using journal entries like the quotes above—many of them mine and some of them the students'—and excerpts from individual and group interviews that I conducted over more than an eight-year period for this book. Several insights will come out of this narrative, bookended, on one hand, by a strong conviction on the part of the core group of students involved in conceiving these programs that schooling cannot be meaningful until the conditions for it are such that the importance of "culture" to education is respected and, on the other hand, by a principled belief in all of its participants that mentorship is a "partnership," not a one-way relationship between a counselor and an advisee, but something that ought to be practiced through and within a collective multistranded and multidirectional formation.

In this chapter, as in the entire book, I mean to speak of "culture" not merely as a static set of beliefs, traditions, values, symbolisms, and practices that belong to a specific group of people who are bound by such a collection, but as a dynamic process of meaning making undertaken by people within a field of social, political, and economic relationships of power.[1] That is, in this work, I am much more concerned about culture not as a fixed compendium of objects and behaviors of a group of people but as a contested site of individual and collective identification—the endless social construction of meaning as defined by selves in relationship to others—as well as an activity that performs conversations and negotiations about the past, the present, and the future.[2] Hence, when students and I say that "culture" is important in education, we mean that such processes of negotiating one's identity (mostly expressed in plural and collective forms, and within historical contexts), from the points of view of those who are minoritized or underrepresented, are key to understanding how meaning making is connected with successful schooling. In effect, then, it was when the students were able to engage with their collective identities in relationship to their experiences of historical and current domination by others that they understood better what schooling was for, how to do better in it, how to critique it, and then how to attempt to change it.[3]

This did not mean that those who were in the majority, specifically represented by middle- and upper-class white students, did not have "culture." They did and they do. However, white "culture" in this study was regarded as the dominant culture, especially by the nonwhite students, and it was understood to operate within and through processes and institutional patterns of domination and control. As several scholars additionally suggest, dominant culture, precisely as an indicator of its dominance, appears as a *nonappearance*, something that unrecognizably stands as the norm or the center in everyday life and, therefore, something that is assumed as the unquestioned way of doing and living, so that movements away from or outside of the "center" are perceived to be out of the norm.[4] Students grappled with this kind of normalized "culture" when they thought about theirs. Thus, one of the central points that students will be making here is that such "cultures" of domination have to be exposed and engaged with, as well as contested, vis-à-vis the "cultures" of those who are nondominant, in order to come up with a transformed environment of schooling.[5]

The other end of the set of arguments regarding mentorship that is written about here was constituted out of the very practice of meaning making through culture that I have just outlined above. Students and I, right from the very start, contended with the palpable structures of hierarchy, especially in terms of status, ethnicity, sex, religion, and age, that were present on our campus and within our communities when we were thinking about a mentorship program that would best serve our needs and desires. Many students expressed some anxiety in imagining how particular communities of students and study sessions might end up replicating hierarchical arrangements of power that they already experienced in their classrooms (in relationship to their teachers and classmates)—structural conditions and arrangements that made them uneasy, concerned, and distracted in their quest to become good students. What was the point of duplicating the same environment in our cultural communities and study groups? Our tentative answer was to form a mentoring *partnership*, a kind of relationship between mentors and mentees that was not absolutely nonhierarchical, but less hierarchical in form and practice than what they were used to. This was also envisioned to hopefully help in mitigating the anxieties and limitations brought about by inequality or, at the least, in circumscribing to a certain extent the effects of unequal relationships of power among mentors, students, peers, and professors like me.[6] The success of this practice rested on the notion that it was going to be tested out in the beginning as a kind of experiment, making it a site of *process* rather than thinking of it as a finished product with a surefire set of procedures that was expected to work in any and all contexts and instances. That would have been a wasteful fantasy, we all thought. Instead, our mentorship partnerships then were, and are to this day, works in progress, with ebbs and flows in an ocean of dominant and nondominant cultures vying unequally for prominence, acceptance, and legitimacy.

The kind of mentorship that students advocated for was surely not thought about in one day; it arose out of a set of conversations we had with one another regarding what to do with the low retention and very low graduation rates of those who were underrepresented in their school, particularly Pacific Islander students.[7] There was a good deal of trial-and-error investigation during the initial years of this program (as mentioned already, it is still being tweaked as it continues to exist today), and it should be noted that the idea of "mentorship partnerships" as the descriptor for the very first incarnation of the program that we institutionalized was provided to us only later on by our inaugural benefactor, Myron Apilado, at that time the university's vice president for minority affairs.[8] Apilado, himself a scholar and practitioner of various student development models that he applied to his own pet programs in his capacity as chief student services administrator in the university, proved to be pivotal in the successful launch of this first mentorship program we advocated for. Without much deliberation and fanfare, and with such generosity, it was he who quickly trusted our instincts and offered us monetary and institutional support right away.[9]

Students, in the beginning, did not have a clue that what they were campaigning for had an academic or formally prescribed name, and I myself was not familiar at that time with the proper scholarship on peer or partner mentorship in school settings, except for my experience of having been mentored when I was a college and graduate student and later having similar mentorship relationships with senior and similarly ranked colleagues when I became a professor. In covering the histories of these mentorship programs, then, I focus on a process of learning that took place among our experiences, or a kind of evolution of a set of ideas and practices that organically arose out of everyday conversations about education and various situations of schooling we found ourselves in, as well as through my and, sometimes, students' forays into the more conventional academic literature on multicultural education, including conversations with scholars and colleagues invested in this field.[10] We were also implicated in conditions that saw the rise of "diversity" as a prominent agenda in our university campus, one that appeared to be positively engaging on the surface, yet was revealing in the ways that it promoted "respect for others" while silencing criticisms of differential power across diverse groups. We suspected that this was a consequence of the increasing stress upon schools like ours to treat its students as consumers who needed to be managed, pleased, and efficiently graduated. This was a neoliberal university formation that was being felt across the nation at the time of this study. This coverage, then, will be guided principally by a recounting of the particular conditions that students experienced of what education scholars call subtractive and consumerist schooling, a retelling of their respective insights about collective work in their school as an answer to their cultural and economic subtraction, and an analysis of the benefits that accrued to them and their communities as a result of their schooling interventions and in correspondence with their thoughts regarding school transformation. I also include in this analysis the critical questions that were raised (and continue to be raised) concerning the challenges and limitations of the practice of "mentorship among equals" within an environment of historical marginalization, as a way of raising our consciousness regarding the fragility of alternative "cultures," the realities of continuing structural domination, but, more significantly, the boldness of persistent advocacy that these students exemplified.

This chapter was also written with a fair measure of consciousness and self-reflection regarding my role as an advocate, cofounder, faculty director, mentor, teacher, and adviser of and for the programs described and analyzed here. Because of these positions of power that I held over all of the students who were part of such programs, I tried to be very careful in protecting them from potential punishment in case their responses to my questions or comments about the programs were disagreeable to me. This I did by conducting most of the detailed interviews after their participation with the programs expired or when they graduated. Moreover, only very few students gained access to my notes and ethnographic drafts. And when they did, they were shown just small portions of them, usually for my clarification. The program portraits that I paint here, including my selection of students' voices, are, thus, the products of my interested, yet unequal, relationships of power with students.

MYRON: So, what is it, Rick?

RICK: I think students are here to tell you something, and to ask for something.

MYRON: What is it?

MIGETU: We've been thinking of our very bad rates of graduation, and our very bad rates of retention. We're not only the lowest in [student] population here, we're also the lowest in graduation. And we're the highest in dropping out! We're just concerned about all of these.

MYRON: I know.

MIGETU: And yeah, we think this is not the students' fault. They can succeed. They just need help [to do so].

MYRON: I know. We should do something, then. Why not encourage them to do to the IC [the Instructional Center]?

MIGETU: No, we want our own, really. Something special for us. Because we're different. And we have different needs.

MYRON: Okay. How about some scholarships? Financial help? Grants, maybe?

RICK: I think we have some of that already. Or we can apply for some later. But we also think that money's not the only solution, ya?

MIGETU: Yeah. I was thinking we need help in studying. Our kids don't feel good here, and it doesn't help their studying.

RICK: . . . like a studying or mentorship program specifically for Pacific Islander students, perhaps?

MYRON: That's sounds good. Give me a blueprint and we'll fire up one.

MIGETU: But we . . . or our school? . . . should provide some kind of funding for it, you know? We should not make it free and voluntary, like how we [usually] do things. That's not good enough. We . . . those of us who will work on this . . . we should get paid. Like, this can be our scholarship. Enough of students giving things for free. We should have some kind of scholarship here. But it shouldn't be some kind of money for doing office work. It should be money for helping ourselves and others.

RICK: We can call it stipends if you're having trouble with paying or receiving compensation, so that it's like scholarship money for the mentors, not like salary for their services.

MYRON: All right, you got it. Stipends. That's good. Good idea.

MIGETU: But these monies are meant to be shared, not just for the mentors.

MYRON: I agree.

RICK: And we should feed them too. It's not good to study on an empty stomach. We could use some money for food, like refreshments, while studying.

MYRON: Food, yeah. You got it!

This was how I remembered our beginnings with the Pacific Islander Partnerships in Education project, or what we have since referred to as PIPE. It was quite quick and straightforward. When Migetu wrote the first draft of our proposal, he called it the Myron Apilado Mentorship Alliance, to honor our primary benefactor. The acronym would have been poignantly MAMA! But then, we decided on thinking of another name for it, for Apilado was not too keen on having his name up there. The joke was that, among Migetu, Tavita, and me, we later thought of calling the project the Pacific Islander Mentorship Program, but the acronym for that one would not have been as desirable and acceptable to others as PIPE. P-I-M-P. We laughed about this frequently. The word "partnerships," as suggested eventually by Apilado, and after I performed some research on mentorship programs elsewhere, was highlighted not just to cue ourselves to start thinking of the program we were aiming for as a non-hierarchical collective of mentors and mentees, but also to signal degrees of inclusion right from the very start—that this collective would entail and be open to the participation of college students of all kinds, administrators, faculty, staff, even nonuniversity folks such as high school students and teachers. We desired to serve Pacific Islander student communities first and foremost, but at the same time, we did not want that preference to exclude others. It was illegal and not right to do so, anyway. We were then instructed to begin as a pilot program.

Apilado directed us to plan and outline some major elements of the program's principles and goals, its elements and mechanisms of operation, as well as its proposed budget. As PIPE's first and founding faculty adviser, I worked with a small group of students in the fall and winter quarters of 2000–2001 to quickly draw up some cornerstone ideas, basic plans, and a simple budget. In the winter quarter, we held some meetings, before eventually launching PIPE in the next quarter.

Winter quarter. I want to think of ways to introduce and workshop these ideas we have about PIPE to our beginning set of mentors. I want them to have a set of solid ideas about what PIPE is all about. I need to tell them to think about this as a collective. It is a partnership, as our name says it so. But it is also work. It is work. So I want to talk about the work they have to do, how many hours they need to put in, and what expectations we have, and how they're going to be evaluated. But this stipend that they're getting, like how Migetu and I put it, I want to explain it to them that they're not supposed to see this as payment for services. This is not about money they will earn. It is a stipend. So, it is like scholarship money that's given to them, so that they can support themselves and their mentees. They should use this money for their studies, not for anything else. They can use it to buy books and school materials, or food to eat for themselves and their mentees. That's why they have to regard this as something else besides salary. Not like capital for labor exchange. Or something besides payment for services rendered. It should be something they deserve to get . . . because they've been good students, and good enough to mentor and help others. They deserve to be helped. And supported. As they support other students like themselves. I like this idea.

The mood was upbeat when I initially met our first set of mentors. I remember telling myself to restrain my own excitement and let the students run our inaugural meeting and workshop with the rest of the group, so that I didn't rob them of their well-deserved place on our small stage. They deserved their own airtime. Here's Migetu, in quite a compelling and straightforward fashion:

We've been trying hard, and we've been trying desperately, to think about solving this crisis that we have among our people. We're not doing good, you know. We have the lowest rates of graduating, the lowest in retention, and we just have too many of our people who are dropping out of school. This cannot be our own fault, right? Our school cannot keep on blaming us. So, we've been meeting with Dr. Apilado and Professor Bonus here. And we were thinking that we need to do something about this. Something for our people. Something also for those who will come after us. So now, we're here. And guess what? We're gonna study together. This is part of our culture, anyway, you know. We help each other out, even though our teachers don't like that. They don't like it when we do our own cultural things. Like when we do family things or community gatherings. So, we have this now. Why can't we practice our culture here? We deal with our issues together. So, yeah, why not study together? Since studying is always a lonely and sad thing to do. . . . That's not who we are! That's how our teachers want us to be. To be doing things on our own. But that's not how we're gonna do things here. From now on, we're gonna study together. That will be our culture thing to do. We pray together, we eat together. Why not study together too?

TAVITA, *nodding his head*: Yup! Study in the vasa! Study and eat! That's what we need to do! Paddle our boats together, let's do it!

The rest of us looked at one another and giggled a bit, teasing Tavita for that unexpected remark, even though I thought it was indeed a noteworthy and appropriate thing to say. And he snickered back at us too, which indicated to me, through some ironic way, that he was serious in what he said; it's just that it came out humorously. But seriously, I thought that what was said here warranted some attention. When we initially started to think about the foundations for this mentorship program, two things stuck out in our conversations. The big one was the poverty of the campus environment or—not even that—the lack of anything substantial in the school environment that was meaningful enough for these students to be successful in such an environment. Many believe that it is enough for students to integrate into their university environment by themselves as if every student comes into the campus equipped with the same resources. Or that students just need to conform, to follow rules, and expect to be treated like everybody else in order to succeed, thinking perhaps unfairly that these are the only ways to achieve fairness in treatment among all students. But what if students have contrasting ideas of school behavior and performance? What if certain students have a critique of school that practices domination over them? What do we do with students who are devalued and disregarded by their school? How do we deal with ethnocentric curricula and teaching? The mantra I heard over and over again was, "How does one survive in a place that's set up so that one is not able to survive in it?"[11] And many students thought how incongruous it was to think that many of them survive in school despite such controlling and impoverished conditions. "So, why can't we set up conditions so that students like us are able to have a fairer chance at success?" That was how the study group component of this mentorship program was conceived. It struck me at that time, as it still strikes me now, as something that was quite bold for the students to say and believe in with such passion, even though these were students who were themselves "successful." These students were very good students, with outstanding grades. But they were thinking of others whom I myself had not seen or even considered. They were thinking about those others who were not succeeding, or, in their forward-looking attitude, they were thinking about students who would potentially be unsuccessful when it was their turn to go to and be in college. These were students who would likely feel isolation, alienation, or invisibility because they did not see themselves as belonging to their school. These student mentors insisted on pointing the fingers somewhere else besides the usual blaming that was inflicted on them for their failures or inability to be successful on campus. They were brushing against the grain, or the dominant way of thinking, about student success and failure. And they were resorting to something that would not distance them from their formal schooling. They wanted to be better students by improving their academic space, not abandoning it.

To wit, numerous scholarly studies and many personal experiences of faculty and students I have known demonstrate that the inability or failure of certain students to succeed in school cannot be appropriately and justifiably explained solely by students' lack of intelligence or drive to do well. Rather, it could be because the schools or the schools' ethnocentric environment have continued to devalue, set aside, or even ignore the needs and interests of these students, who would have succeeded in the first place had their necessities been met.[12] Many, then, unfairly expect students to do well in an environment that is structured to make them not do well.[13] The PIPE mentors were recognizing this unwarranted finger-pointing at students and were now proactively taking steps to directly provide a set of tools to assist in the fulfillment of their project to retain and eventually graduate Pacific Islander students. What set them apart from many other mentorship programs, I thought, was in the ways they deployed their retention tools as stuff that sprang from the practice or, at least, observation of a traditional cultural value of collective work—the vasa, as Tavita interjected earlier, comically and earnestly—that they directly applied to mentorship and effectively integrated with their schooling.

Christian, a Filipino American from the first cohort of mentors, commented:

I like this idea . . . this idea of this [program] being our ocean. It's gonna be a place for us. We can practice our own culture here and . . . also . . . of course . . . not forget that we are also students that need to succeed. And it goes two ways too, you know? We can't really succeed if we lose our culture, but we also can't succeed if we do not study. Yeah? You think? So, why not do it together?

Annie, a Tongan, also from the first cohort of mentors, responded:

I like it too. But . . . this will be a challenge, you know. I want to try it. People usually don't imagine PIs [Pacific Islanders] studying. They always see us as dancing this and dancing that. Or playing football, what have you. But studying together . . . yup . . . that's something that we do in our culture too! Well . . . we do a lot of things together . . . like we're all family. So why not study together as a family? And if others see us, well, then, woo-hoo, that's a PI student studying, what do you know? Who would've thought?

I did think, at first, that having a "family" to study with was not a uniquely Pacific Islander "cultural" practice. I thought that many others practiced this as well. But these students had a strong sense that thinking about this group as a "family," treating others as if they were family members (and, therefore, as bonded with one another in a deeper and more permanent sense), and doing this within a "family-like" setting were all profoundly islander inspired.[14] As Steve, a Chamorro-Filipino student later said when this question about the uniqueness of PIPE came up during the next year and the years that followed: "Definitely, PIPE is different because it's more family oriented in a way, and I can relax and be myself around them, unlike [in] classrooms where you're kind of nervous and listening to the professor. And it's not as intimate and [it's] a lot more professional than PIPE. It's a different feeling in PIPE. It makes me feel at home. No pressure. Just do what you need to do."

Indeed, during the earlier years of PIPE, queries regarding its viability and exceptionality came up both from students who were part of it and from those who were not. Many PIPE-affiliated students felt as if they did not have to defend themselves, other than saying that PIPE was like home for them, and I sympathized with them. Having study group sessions, what was to become the signature activity of PIPE, was not that unusual in most educational institutions or any school setting, for that matter. And building these sessions around notions of "family" belongingness and cohesiveness also appeared to be not as uniquely islander-ish to some, especially as it appeared to outsiders. Yet PIPE had a particular draw to many of its students who saw a set of commonalities of attitude and practice that was being acknowledged within the program, itself conceived in the first place as a dialogue between dominant values that were opposed to theirs and alternative values that they had, which showed respect for where they came from and who they were. For one, it was in PIPE where they thought they did not need to give up their values in order to integrate into a larger culture that did not appreciate or recognize them, like being forced to assimilate into dominant society without gaining acceptance into it. They would constantly hear from their professors and classmates that they should just learn to blend in, set aside what made them different, and just act like "normal" students. But they resisted, thinking it was so strange and unfair to make them give up something they valued just to make the rest happy. They thought it was a kind of "diversity" practice that was insulting to them, or something that reminded them of their ancestors' colonization histories now finding their way into their school's version of fostering assimilative campus environments so that all its "consumers" remained happy but unreflexively compliant. They felt that their campus had an expectation that "diversity" was meant to flatten out or ignore differences at the expense of working toward addressing and acting upon social injustice. At the same time, PIPE leaders were also conscious and critical of internal family practices that were considered just as oppressive, such as devaluing the worth of women, including nonheterosexuals and those who were nonreligious and nonconforming. Later on, in writing up a grant proposal and nomination for a diversity award on campus, I asked several students what made PIPE unique in its practice of "culture," and here is some of what they said:

PIPE is all about family and community; isn't that islander enough?

Community service! That's what we do all the time. And we do that in PIPE too! We study with our community and we serve our community!

Respect! We do a lot of respect! We respect our elders who put us through school. We respect our culture, our traditions. We respect each other! That's why we end up respecting ourselves, all of us, in the long run! That's hella islander! What else can you ask for?

We give back! We give back to our ocean—our community, our family, our students, the ones who will come after us. We don't forget to repay and re-... I don't know, replenish? We know how to show our appreciation.

We call on our ancestors all the time to guide us. We pray to our ... creator! Our ancestors and creators are not dead. They are alive in us! They are all here with us now. This is why we're something islander special, you know?

We are a community in PIPE! No one sits here as individuals. We're all together.

Well, the thing is, we're unique because this is our space. This is ours. We carve out our own space here. And we decide what goes on in our space. That makes us who we are, yeah! We're different from others; that's why we have our own space here. So it can be our own. Our own space in the school. Finally!

And in our own space, we can have our own rules. Like, this whole thing about getting paid, but not really getting paid, yeah? And these things about looking down on women and gay people, and those who are not Mormon or Catholic or Christian. So many others we don't pay attention to. Or put down. To heck with those! We want a really good and fair and honest family in our own space here!

This ownership of space was definitely a critical component of students' assertions of uniqueness and an instance of cultural deployment of values they wanted to express together, and critique together, and for outsiders to notice. They were also articulating such an ownership within the contexts of their experiences of invisibility, isolation, and domination.[15] And connected to this was their quest to be in a space that was not completely immersed in consumerism. Note the earlier discussions regarding what to do with the funds that were going to be granted to PIPE for its first incarnation. Student leaders were quite hesitant to be seen as mentors who were getting paid for their services; they were anxious that their persistent insertion into capitalism, as I thought more about it later, appeared to be inconsistent with or even in opposition to the values they held as islanders—that working for one's family and one's community could not be compensated for in terms of cash or conceived of as redeemable through any form of monetary exchange value. I have seen Pacific Islanders dance in public and receive money for doing so. So I asked some students how this situation was different. Student leaders told me, "There are some aspects of our culture where money as payment or gift don't apply, and this is one of them." I smiled, and thought, what an interesting way to deal with capitalism within what seemed to be still an ostensibly capitalist space![16]

Offensive to them as community/family workers, getting paid for services rendered as mentors did not jibe well with the actions they performed in the name of their devotion to their community. And along these lines, cultivating mentorship relationships that merely replicated hierarchies between seniors and younger students, including among mentors, mentees, and me, their professor and program adviser, was also a practice of a dominant culture that students thought needed to be reformulated, for even just a bit. Our program included the word "partnerships" in it, and students contemplated how it might be operationalized without compromising the program's integrity. How might a "mentorship among equals" be executed without disrespecting or not recognizing a senior student's deeper and broader experiences in college? Or a professor's authority within and outside of the classroom? Or someone else's stature or advantage that might be useful to others? Here was Christian's suggestion:

> Well, we can start with requiring mentees to mentor their own mentors too. Like, making their mentors accountable to them, you know? If a mentor asks a mentee, how are your classes doing?, then a mentee should also ask their mentor, how are your classes doing? Right? You get it? Then, if a mentor asks their mentee to tell them the grades they got for their exams or term papers, like how we require mentees to actually show us the term paper with the grade in it, then mentors should do it too, like show their papers and grades to their mentees. That means both are accountable to each other, you know. It's not just a one-way thing-y. It's a way for both to check on each other, and to call out each other when things are not going well. Ya? It's also so that they show that they care for each other. And younger people can be trained to do that early. Ya?

> TAVITA: Well, what about Professor Bonus?

> CHRISTIAN: Ha-ha. We should all ask him how he's doing too, and to show us what he's been up to. Ask him for his reports about us. And all his student evals. And the things he writes about. He says he writes about stuff. He should show them to us. He should make us read what he writes! We should teach him to be like us, to be answerable to us too! Ha-ha-ha!

Students joked that doing this was not tantamount to revolutionizing a hierarchical system in total, but that, in a serious way, it was an attempt, at least, to make the conventional mentorship practice less rigid and mentors less domineering. They encouraged each other to be true to the practice of partnerships, and I, as their teacher and faculty mentor, felt inspired to do the same with them. I began requiring all of the mentors, who saw me at least once a week for group and individual meetings, to make me accountable to them as well in terms of everything I did, from preparing for my lectures to submitting an essay for journal publication, and from grading students' exams and being evaluated for my teaching performance, to taking care of PIPE's budget and annual reports. These practices didn't happen regularly or smoothly at all times, nor did they improve exponentially over time. Oftentimes, I did not want to show my student evaluations (when they were not great), I couldn't find the time to share what I was writing (because I'd rather have spent time continuing to write), or I considered some of my field notes confidential (especially when I wrote about sensitive stuff regarding students). But it was enough for me and all of our founders and eventual leaders that we kept on trying, so that at the beginning of every quarter, we reminded ourselves to be accountable to one another, and at the end of the quarter, there was at least a short report that we produced that outlined how both our mentors and mentees, and we ourselves as well, held our individual and social selves together. Our reports were not all glowing, either, for there were good as well as challenging times. We were implicitly expected to write reports by those who funded us. Occasionally, we were anxious about revealing everything, lest we lose support if there were negative items exposed. But we all decided to report both the good and the not-so-good. Some of us resented this, but at the end of the day, and as a collective of partners, we nevertheless felt convinced that being answerable to one another, including our benefactors, was a good thing. This system kept us truthful to ourselves as it encouraged us to be honest with one another and the institution we were a part of, despite being critical of it.

COLLECTIVE WORK

Autumn quarter. I've been reading Subtractive Schooling *by Angela Valenzuela, and I can't help but see my students in this book.[17] And I'm gonna use it for my class too. This book is an ethnography of two high schools in Texas and, among other things, yes, she makes the claim that our schools or our school[s'] teachers have a tendency to devalue the wealth of knowledge and culture that students bring to class if they don't conform to the dominant or the standard practice and definition of what is valuable knowledge or what is legitimate culture. This is so what PIPE has been saying. She calls this the practice of subtractive schooling. And then she says that if teachers only ADD instead of SUBTRACT what students bring to their classrooms, they would all potentially and positively flourish.*

. . .

"Subtractive schooling" was a term that stuck in my head permanently after I read it and connected it with what PIPE students were advocating for. Not only were students campaigning for school spaces that were less consumerist and less repressive particularly in handling students' communal work; they were also asking that the values and practices they observed as nontraditional communities on campus be respected. They desired to be allowed to nurture themselves and others.[18] These students took the initiative to start transforming their campus environment even though, at that point, they were provided the opportunity to do so only outside of their classrooms and strictly within the aegis of the "student services" arm of the university, not through its academic units or actual classrooms, where curricula mostly promoted the interests of dominant cultures. Nonetheless, everyone thought that collective work needed to be attended to right away, whether in the classrooms or outside of them. This proceeded with the notion of "study tables."

Study tables simply meant having a room where a group of students study together. Our original plan was as basic as having a study session once a week. And our plan has remained so to this day. We usually commenced at 4:00 PM, in one of the rooms of the Ethnic Cultural Center, to study quietly. Then, at around 5:00 PM, after saying grace, we ate together, usually slices of pizza and a cup of soda or water. We studied during or after dinner, and then we ended at around 6:00 PM. That was it. Some mentors would designate the first hour as the "quiet" hour and then the next hour as the "discussion" hour, in which noise was to be somewhat tolerated. Other times, the first hour was set aside for a guest speaker to talk about topics such as graduate school opportunities and application procedures, or some other relevant subject such as effective studying skills, healthy sexual practices, the teaching profession as a career, or becoming a health professional. Then, during the second hour, we would occasionally have a social gathering, whether it was celebrating someone's birthday (it was usually mine, I'm embarrassed to report) or planning an upcoming social event. It was as simple as this. Sporadically, a professor or university staff member or a high school kid would visit, just to study with us, or mostly observe us. When PIPE won a campus diversity award, and a reporter asked me to explain when the "magical" moments, as he referred to them, happened during our study tables (where he got that assumption that we had such moments, I wasn't able to ask), I was stunned to realize that I had very little to say about what happens when students and I study together. Our "study table" sessions were usually uneventful, and I would always kid around with students, especially the new recruits into our mentorship programs, that we didn't have "Oscar Award"–winning moments when we studied together. We didn't have memorable dramatic blasts, other than my infrequent bursts of song when I got overwhelmed by something I was poring over or I just wanted to break the silence. When I asked students later on what they remembered most about our study tables other than studying, they pointed to my random eruptions of song or to a cough I would make that sounded like "ahem-hungry-ahem" or "huh-thirsty-huh," which would signal to everyone that it was time to eat and that somebody better announce it. These made students laugh. And I laughed with them as well!

While, on the surface, study tables gave an impression that nothing eventful was happening, I confess that it was also the premier site where I thought most deeply about what mentorship was to me and to others. Here was where I ruminated on mentorship—as an idea, as a partnership in practice, or as a site of collective work—as it was partly happening. The more I participated in study tables week after week, the more my relationship with students grew and became deeper, tighter, and held together in more complicated, sometimes difficult, but productive ways. In PIPE, I would always think about those students such as Christian and Annie who helped start it, those who came after them, such as Steve and Paul (a Pacific Islander student many remember as having been gregarious and loud right from day one), and Matthew (a Tongan student, who just happened to check us out one day, from out of the blue), and those who had been there before but had left already. Every time study tables was scheduled, I was drawn into it because it also became my family on campus, my bonding site with the students I cared about the most, and my refuge from the chaos of research, teaching, and service that my job primarily entailed. Here are two entries from my journal, one from 2004, and another from 2010:

> I'm tired, I'm beat, I'm ready to go home, but there's study tables today. And I'd hate to disappoint the kids. I want to be with them when they study. I want to show them that I study too. That I'm also in the same struggle. Well, maybe a more advanced struggle, but a struggle to flourish in school kind of struggle. To survive and flourish in a space that was not meant to be for us. [A struggle] similar to theirs. I want to model to them that studying is good. It is what scholars do. And if they want to be scholars like me, they better be studying.

> I like seeing students study, actually. When I see Rene, Andres, Joyce, Horky, Trixie, and the rest study, I get proud of them. I don't tell them this because I don't want to flatter them. But I'm happy to see them and [I] am very proud of them. All these stereotypes of people of color that

describe them as lazy, stupid, nonintellectuals, bad students, good for nothing, [and so on], they all fly out the door when I see them. And I know they're observing me too. They see that I'm studying with them, and I'm so pleased when this happens. Because the feeling gets stronger— or the motivation—that we're in this together. We don't need to feel bad about our situation; we can do something about it. We can be together in our struggles.

This practice of collective studying—for the most part, *quiet* collective studying—also unexpectedly made the students bond with one another in ways that were different from how they did so in more action-driven events, but generative of a kind of emotional web—quite indescribable to me here—that was solid and meaningful. Here is what some of them said in a survey that I once took:

I love study tables! It brings us all together and it's a relaxing thing. No need to worry about someone watching you, or that you're required to finish something or get done with homework here. It's just two hours. But two hours as opposed to nothing is . . . something worth more.

Bonus is here, so I just go when he's studying here too. He doesn't pressure us to be good students all the time. He's okay. He's just here mostly for moral support.

Other people get freaked out when I invite them to study tables. Like it's something strange for them to hear me say. Study? With me? With you? They don't expect me to invite them to something like serious studying, so I break the stereotype to them, you know. I tell them Pacific Islanders study too, you know. We are serious students. We don't just party like they do. Or do sports all the time. Or sing and dance. I think it's good for us and good for others to see us studying, so they have a different and positive view about us.

Study tables is our 'ohana [or "family," in Hawaiian]. It is our 'ohana in session. In serious and fun session!

Our vasa, study tables, yeah!

This is our culture, you know. Our school doesn't value much who we are and what we do. But they should value this! They should see us do this. Because we ain't lyin', this is another side of us that many people don't see.

I get distracted many times during study tables. But I try to do better next time. It's good to study together, and others and me gossip too, so it's bad. But yeah, next time, we should study more. Bonus gets mad. But he gossips too ha-ha! We should all take this more seriously from now on. It's our ocean we need to take care of!

Against a kind of subtractive schooling environment that many Pacific Islander students were thrust into, study tables became a welcome relief as it provided not only a space for being together in the context of isolation but also a site for building and sustaining relationships in the name of a common oceanic cultural sensibility. It became a place of networking—one that brought together a community or communities of peers who, beyond a more social and nonacademic gathering within and outside of campus, would not have met one another, where new students were introduced to more senior ones, and where all the students who were involved in it got to experience a more scholarly, yet less uncomfortable, moment of academic work with a college professor. To me, PIPE study tables became the place where I myself got introduced to many new students, if I had not met them yet through the recruitment programs I participated in. Older students made it a point to bring unfamiliar newly recruited and recently admitted students to my attention during study tables, for they knew that this was a positive space where they could do so. This was a good space to show new students another side of us. And without fail, these new students would always be pleasantly surprised to meet a professor in the flesh, standing or sitting next to them, in an undergraduate academic setting, eating pizza with them, and maybe even sharing a joke or two with them. Whenever there were other professors or staff around to be introduced as well, it was the same effect. These study tables became a welcoming space for those who were beginning to navigate our ocean, as it was to those who were already seasoned paddlers.

It was during study tables for the PIPE mentorship program that I was reintroduced to four students. Their names were Justice, Zackary, Lusse, and Kody, all Pacific Islanders. I say reintroduced because I already knew them from when they were high school sophomores, juniors, and seniors (Lusse was Junior's sister), during those few times when college students and I visited them at their campus in Tukwila, a suburban neighborhood about eleven miles south of Seattle, to conduct our recruitment workshops. These visits were usually undertaken through a separate but allied UW outreach and recruitment program called Pacific Islander Opportunity Network for Educational Equality and Representation (PIONEER), created and staffed by students themselves, and it was quite understood among all of us who were involved in the visits that not only were we recruiting these high school kids—basically, encouraging them to fill out the UW application forms, and to fill them out well—we were also receiving them into our college community. We were welcoming them into our community. Our informal slogan was "The earlier, the better," and our corresponding thought or vision was that we wanted to have them become familiar with us and treat us like "family" at the time of recruitment and long before they would potentially step into college, our ocean. We wanted them to be in "community" with us right now so that if they indeed ended up at UW, they would already know a community of people like them on campus. They would not feel as isolated as those who came before them. So now that all four of these Tukwila high school students had been accepted into our university, I was so delighted to see them come to their first college PIPE study tables. And I was even more pleased that they looked as if they were so at home in this environment, which they had already visited as high school students several times by then.[19]

Ever since PIPE study tables started, networking within a family-like milieu was a front-and-center activity, and it was even more enhanced by the requisite serving and consumption of food and the invitation to join the study sessions that were always extended to students from other racial or ethnic groups. As someone from the original cluster that started PIPE and who agreed with the rest that serving food was vital during study tables—whether it was as simple as starchy pizza pies from Domino's or as complicated as mouthwatering chicken katsu with rice from the Hawaii BBQ Restaurant—I also always wanted to convince myself that many students were drawn to our study group sessions for reasons other than the free food available. That was often not the case, though, but in some positive sense it was apparent. Both Pacific Islander and non–Pacific Islander students, we jested, would be able to "smell our food from a mile away," and it wasn't all that easy to turn your back on a freebie lunch or dinner if, like many struggling students, you were constantly hungry or had little money to spare for food. Mentors and I thought, however, that if this was an effective way to draw distressed students into our ocean, then we should just go ahead and do it all the time! Better than nothing. And the more, the merrier. Besides, we also understood that no student could study properly on an empty stomach. And if we could provide the pertinent resources to make such hungry students succeed, then feed them we should!

I have met countless students this way—they were merely checking us out because somebody told them there was free food in the room where we were hosting study tables—and I have also encountered even many more who would have perilously spent the entire afternoon and evening studying without any kind of nutrition, had it not been for study tables at PIPE. Study tables provided collective nourishment; grace was said before each meal, with all of our hands held together in a circle; and the social interaction that went with every spread, no matter how spartan (when we were running out of funds) or extravagant (especially during holidays or birthdays), brought us imperceptibly but qualitatively closer to one another physically and emotionally. No loud fanfare. No big production numbers. Although some student directors and I complained that preparing for study tables could be time-consuming, enervating, or complicated, as I wrote in the passage cited at the beginning of this chapter, the decision to provide refreshments in PIPE paid off in the long run. These were always appreciated, and they humbly but effectively facilitated studying and interaction. And more basic than having food as something that brought us together in our family, and indeed it did, food was what vitally enabled all of our students' survival.

Food was the reason I met Tutru. Or, at least, that was my recollection. Tutru told me later that he first visited PIPE because he wanted to review for an exam with his friends Zackary, Kody, and Justice, who, along with Lusse, graduated with him from the same Tukwila high school. They were all friends, and they counted Tutru, even though he was a Mexican American, unlike them (they were all Pacific Islanders), as part of their "family." So it was just natural, and completely acceptable to me and to us, for him to be present in one of PIPE's study tables. I remember him eating a lot during that time I first saw him, hence my first indelible impression of him. This annoyed me a bit because I had this hunch that he was just eating and not studying, contrary to what was the idealized norm for everyone in study tables. And then I got even more annoyed when I heard his loud voice overpower all of ours during "quiet time." Although he appeared to be studying as well, these things, to me, were very unacceptable! I became more and more irritated.

So I motioned to Justice and Zackary to come tell me about this guy. They told me who he was, and then someone else reminded me that this was the same guy Palolo was talking about. Palolo, a Sāmoan-Filipina alumna, was a former mentee of mine who had been guiding several students from the Tukwila high school and other schools for recruitment, and I remembered her suggesting to me at some point that I should meet (and mentor) this kid, as a way of passing along the reins from Tutru's high school environment to his new college setting. It was one of those instances in which our networking operated—students got recommended and passed down, from one mentor to the next, were given opportunities to experience our kind of mentorship, until they eventually became mentors themselves (which happened later to Tutru). "Wassup, Bonus?" Tutru softly said, as he approached me, with his head bowed down politely. I secretly smiled, for I knew that this student had most probably been briefed on how best to approach me, which was to call me by my last name, as was standard practice already for many years among all the students who were closest to me. I asked, "Are you here to study?" "Of course," Tutru quickly responded.

Then why were you so loud? Don't you know this is a quiet study session?

Oh, this is how I study. Ha-ha. In loud ways.

Huh?

Yeah, my voice is naturally loud. So I naturally study loudly.

I rolled my eyes at him.

Sorry, Bonus. I'll . . . I'll try to be quiet. I didn't mean to . . .

It's all good. Good to see you here.

Thank you.

Tutru was not going to be the first non–Pacific Islander student I would most closely mentor and include into the inner circles of PIPE and our study tables; he became only the latest, at that time, in a long list of what Pacific Islander students and I have appropriately described as those who may not be "technically" in our racial or ethnic category but are, however, equally precious allied occupants of our ocean in the school. Before him, there was Kabru, an Ethiopian American. After him were Horky, a Khmer American, and Turtle, a Vietnamese American. With all of them, I felt quite happy and appreciative. They chose to ally with people who were not ethnically or racially like them, and they humbly devoted time and energy to Pacific Islander advocacies in very genuine ways, not expecting anything in return. That was why Pacific Islander students and I cared deeply about them.

Early on in PIPE's history, or upon its first year of operations, many non–Pacific Islander students were invited to join our study sessions. I met Eduardo and Angelica, Chicano and Chicana students and classmates of some of PIPE's founders, through Ronaldo, another Chicano student, who was actually a PIPE mentor himself. He was a PIPE mentor not because he was also a Pacific Islander student, but because he was intrigued by what PIPE was doing in study tables, and he asked if he could participate in it. Of course, the PIPE mentors welcomed Ronaldo without ado. And when during his stint as a participant in PIPE he voiced his desire to start a similar program for his group, we gave Ronaldo his own mentor slot, complete with a stipend and a requirement for him to mentor at least three mentees. This act converted his status from observer/participant to "official" mentor. He recruited his own students, many of whom he was able to pull in from another organization in which he, Eduardo, and Angelica all participated, Movimiento Estudiantil Chican@s de Aztlan, or MEChA. In 2004, these very students started their own "sister" version of PIPE, the Adelante mentorship program.

Adelante, whose name translated as "Forward" in English, stood in alliance with everything that PIPE was all about, its participants practicing what they also held dear to their hearts and, in doing so, trying to make their schooling meaningful to themselves so that they could succeed in it. They had their own version of study tables; I had separate meetings with them; and they conducted their own socials according to what they desired and decided as evocative and significant to them. Since two study tables were in session every week, now that Adelante had started its own in addition to PIPE's, students began to enjoy the benefit of attending one or the other, or both. Now, if you were a struggling student, you wouldn't mind having two free dinners every week, right? We were so happy that another administrator from the Office of Minority Affairs and Diversity interceded for us, resulting in a separate budget for Adelante that undoubtedly enhanced the viability of twin mentorship programs on campus. If collective work was the students' answer to cultural and economic subtraction, it was clearly imperative that university administrative support, no matter how small, was to be solicited successfully for this work to achieve its goals and flourish. Students tried hard to make sure the ocean's resources were utilized broadly, but properly and cohesively.

STUDENT AND SCHOOL TRANSFORMATIONS

Winter quarter. I'm kinda happy that the mentor directors are doing their job. Yehey! They've been meeting with me regularly. They're taking care of their mentees. And their mentees, as far as I've heard and known, are also taking care of them. This is way cool. Great job, everyone! I need to tell these [things] to them—make it verbal and out loud so everyone can hear them, so that everyone can be validated and feel good. This is important. Like having a public outing of congratulations and achievement. It should be good. When we do our banquet at the end of spring, these things should be repeated. But before that, oh my God, we should be looking for the next year's mentors. It's good to start early. Remind the mentors that they need to pick who the next mentors will be. Have them shadow the mentors, or have the mentors secretly ask them to shadow so they can watch what happens, so we don't need to reinvent the wheel the next time they get to be the leaders. We need to think all the time about the future, about who's next, and what's next. I need to discuss these [concerns] with students. Soon. Note to self: remind students to plan for the banquet and pick the next mentors. Oy!

. . .

Every year in PIPE and, later, in Adelante, I always reminded the students involved in them that these study tables and mentorship moments were all going to be temporary for them. At some point, I told them, all of them would graduate and leave the UW, and that this should be reason enough for all of them to plan for what they wanted to leave behind. I'd then noticed many students' eyes welling up, as if they were about to cry. And some of them did. I don't know for sure why. I was just reminding everybody about our mortality, perhaps, and dispensability, and, of course, the reality of their eventual graduation. But when I talked to them about these things, I was also convinced that these moments gave us enough reason to reflect upon ourselves, our collective work, and our place in the school. The organizational missions of PIPE and Adelante required that all of us turn in evaluation sheets every month, on average, depending on who was in charge and how effective that student in charge was in making us fulfill this obligation. These one-to-two-page forms, later handed in online, asked about issues that were dealt with during mentor/mentee meetings, items to be addressed with mentees or mentors, and appraisals of one's own performance, the faculty director's (an evaluation of me, basically), and the program's performance as a whole. Whenever we had the wherewithal or initiative, all of the mentors and I read and discussed these evaluations during our group meetings or even at social get-togethers. We used them to keep an eye on one another, to reflect and improve on ourselves and our program, and in their collected form, we considered them as evidence of our work for our eventual year-end report and budget request for our succeeding year's operations. We were, however, not all that successful in collecting these assessments from everyone, because students and I were inclined to treat this additional requirement as something that was burdensome to do and quite repetitive. Some mentors also half joked that Pacific Islander tradition (as with many other indigenous cultures too, they said) preferred oral narratives, not written assessments in the "Western" way. I brushed this half joke aside quickly, not wanting to create an impression for students that we could conveniently use "culture" to explain what we preferred not to do, or that we could rationalize our differences with others by referring to essentialized practices or notions about ourselves. But with myself and later with others, I began thinking more and more about differences in practices and preferences that set these students apart from dominant cultures and that put them at a disadvantage. Many students concurred, and some of them even said they had no qualms thinking about cultural differences this way. Here are the rest of the significant evaluation items raised by the mentors and mentees. On leadership skills enhancement issues, one student wrote:

> I think [that] as a person color, I've learned the importance of mentoring fellow minority students like me who are undergrad. Because talking to them, you kind of realize the same kind of problems that they also go through. We're not like all the rest of the students. Aside from academics, they are also going through other situational heavy stuff, which is very interesting, and so they also need that help. And they might be leaders in their own community as well, but they also need their own form of mentoring. I've mentored a lot of students who are leaders in their own little or big organizations, and they, too, need some assistance in some way. People need some kind of mentoring, so that's what I learned. You can be a leader, a very good leader. But even very good leaders need their own kind of mentoring as well. Or, at least, have someone to turn to, or someone to look up to at the same time. Like a guide. They need to own up to this. They cannot be good and great leaders if they deny the help they need. We need to work on this some more.

Some commented on time management:

> Personally, as a mentor, I want to start requesting my mentees' schedules and from now on, I'll manage my time accordingly to theirs. I'll ask them about their classes, and based on my experience, I'll give advice based on what I've done and what other people do. In terms of managing your time studying and working, a lot of my mentees work and are active in clubs, and so managing their time and doing well academically is a challenge. Oh well. It's something that we need to have to face being active. So I want to improve more on time and discipline. And I want to be a good example for my mentees when it comes to those.

> I've been slacking on PIPE actually, and focusing more on PISC [the Pacific Islander Student Commission, the umbrella student organization for all official and registered Pacific Islander–themed student organizations on campus], and trying to acclimate myself to this environment to see how my personal relationships and my schooling all fit in. I'm just

juggling everything, in addition to FASA [the Filipino American Student Association] and Project FAMILY [Filipino Americans Mentoring and Instilling Leadership in Youth, mostly a high school outreach program led by FASA students] too. I've been trying to get in contact with my mentees almost daily now, and I've been trying to see what their availability is, and see if I can meet up with all of them at one time for one hour. I know it's kind of preferred if it's individual, but one reason why I'm getting them together is for them to get to know each other and have them ask me academic questions, which benefits everyone else. It's good to see [them] as a group. We can bounce off ideas and support each other and collaborate. I kinda like this idea. I'll try this and see [if] it works. But no matter, I want to keep them close. You have to be in constant contact with your mentees all the time and let them know that you're available, and saying hi when you see them.

We are always late [in submitting our mentor reports]! What's the matter? Islander time? Islander habit? Ha-ha.

Several mentors suggested academic strategies:

I always tell my mentees that if they need to get a class to let me know, since I'm older and I have priority [in class registration]. I could get them the class, register for it myself, and then give it to them later by dropping it and making them register for it quickly. This is a trick that's really helpful to them. An unwritten strategy. Something good to do to work the system. We should tell the other mentors to do the same thing. This is good especially for the really in-demand classes like bio or math. We can do this to help them.

I gave a suggestion to my mentees today, to take the foreign language classes early so that they don't forget them. It's a requirement you know. I forgot mine, so now I suffer because it's an everyday class, and my Spanish class really distracts me from my senior-level classes. I hope my mentees don't do this, what I did. Oh, and the writing classes too. People forget them. They're required. But people think about them very late.

Mentees need to understand that [a] college like ours is designed for others, so we need to first acknowledge that. After that, then it makes sense to figure out ways to work the system. Either have strategies that will satisfy the system or dare to do something different. There's always risks though. The system can eat you up. So I tell my mentees to be careful!

Other basic mentorship issues were raised:

One of my mentees cried today. Okay, so heads up. If this happens to you, don't make it even more awkward. Just let them be. Make yourself approachable and at the same time, give them space. I've helped my mentees out when they feel kind of stranded and that they need someone. They feel a lot of pressure, especially from family. Even if it's not that obvious, there are hints, so be alert. I try to go out of my way to help them sometimes. We should all do [that].

I don't really like my mentor. I'm sorry. She just drives me crazy. Please help me.

I don't like writing these reports. Can we please just talk? Pretty please?

My mentor is hella lazy! And that makes two of us! That's all.

I think it should be okay to say that you're not doing well. I just said this to one of my mentees. And she was so understanding. I figured, I can't just hold it in. Since I've learned how to trust her too, like I taught her to trust me, I thought it would be nice to be honest with her. I cried. We both cried.

Nothing to report for now. Just regular school stuff. My mentee doesn't like studying, so I force him to go to study tables with me. I really drag him! Or, I give him a reward, like I take him out to dinner or buy him something. It's okay. I know, been here, done that. He also has a lot of family obligations stuff, and work, but I understand that. I told him that family and culture have to come first, but he needs to balance that with school. He needs to take care of school too! Like taking care of his family. He doesn't have to give up one for the other.

There is a long litany of issues that both PIPE and Adelante mentors and mentees have brought up over the years. Because mentors and mentees devoted a lot of time and energy in sustaining partnerships of nurturance and care among themselves, they excitedly found a fresher sense of themselves and each other as important students in a large campus ocean of mostly strangers and people who were not like them. Somebody else cared for them; someone else cared for their welfare and understood their family and community obligations. These obligations did not need to be given up, they began to realize, in order to survive in school. And school, just the same, did not always have to be treated as a lower priority, coming after duties to one's parents, (usually younger) siblings, and other relations. In fact, it was well worth convincing the students, as they did so with each other, that succeeding in school was to be seen as a fulfillment of a set of family and community obligations.[20] And the moment they realized this—that they had value as members of both their families and their campus—students began finding ways to transform their familial educational experience as coexistent with finding meaning in their schooling.

More than merely enabling its participants to develop better skills in negotiating and accessing the university system, these mentorship partnership programs also helped in facilitating better judgment in pursuing a career, balancing schoolwork with social and political activities, and taking advantage of what the university had to offer as well as what they could offer to it and to their communities. Regular interaction with mentors who showed care in keeping close watch over their mentees, and vice versa, also taught everybody the values of leadership, respect for each other, responsibility, and accountability. They called each other "fams," short for family, and, indeed, they treated each other as if they were family members, something that many of them thought was *the* glaring omission in their school lives.

So, beyond these evaluation narratives and observations, how are we to measure the "success" of these programs? This was the question that confronted my students and me every time we submitted our annual program funding proposals. It is the same question that teachers and administrators, and parents or guardians, would ask their kids every time a school term was coming to an end: How did you do? And, of course, the real matters lurking behind these queries were the letter or number grades that were assumed and supposed to represent student performance or, in this case, program performance. I was asked many times to collect grades and grade point averages for every student who participated in our mentorship programs, and I was told to collect them during their pre- and post-participation stages, in the testing mode and model of the social sciences. But in all these times, I refused to collect grades, not because I wanted to hide some version of truth that needed to be known, but because students and I wanted to champion our right to be evaluated on the ways we have been "successful" in a form other than number and letter grades. We thought that, for once, we did not want to be beholden to a system of evaluation whose basis of worthiness could only be systematically measured, if it ever was, by classroom performance or course coverage.[21] And we have insisted on this defiance against grades to this day.

This was not to say that grades did not matter at all. They did. But only in a limited way when it came to our mentorship partnerships. We would ask one another how students were doing grade-wise, but no one required the participants to record them. In doing this, no one really rewarded or punished a student for doing great or performing not so well in his or her classes, as far as grades were concerned. Perhaps grades mattered only to the degree that they were merely one part of a whole array of performance indicators that determined and constituted each student profile. For example, we started a list of students who were able to get into graduate school—in which grade point averages were used as but one of the many indicators to base admissions decisions on—or who won fellowships and grants or were selected for competitive student exchange programs. Grades were indeed required to be submitted to be properly considered for these programs, and grades did matter when it came to applying for graduation. But we thought these were things that were somewhat beyond our control. And since, to a good extent, we were in control of PIPE and Adelante, we thought we could take both of them out of a rigid and conventional regime of assessment that we did not find effective and meaningful for our own purposes. We just did not find grades to be meaningful on so many levels.

What instead we found effective and meaningful in our mentorship partnerships were the qualitative improvements in the lives of our students both as individuals and as members of collectives.[22] When students interacted with mentors who had similar backgrounds and experiences, or at least understood the meanings and consequences of difference and diversity, then points of identification and empathy got to be more intense, and pride was instilled in deeper ways, as mentors and mentees themselves acted as role models for each other. Students' experiences in mentorship relationships enabled them to become more thoughtful and effective leaders. Many of them had already been active students socially and politically by the time they participated in PIPE and Adelante. But in working with their peers and faculty, they gained a more perceptive outlook on human development and socialization, a more sensitive recognition of their potentials and the potentials of others, and a more grounded as well as balanced approach to student activism. They learned how to build and sustain a community of scholars and activists, which, we observed, carried farther into long-term processes of social consciousness development, especially for those who were first-time college students. They showed respect for one another, but they were also open to criticizing one another, so different from the ways their teachers wanted them to respect everybody else by discouraging critique. Over time, many students grew more and more reflexive about how societal transformation was to be done, how partnerships could be nurtured, and how students could build on the work that had already been done by student activists in the past. Many more learned how to be patient, diligent, and resourceful. And in learning how to help others, they learned how to help themselves. I can mention so many mentors and mentees here—such as Paul, a mixed-race Pacific Islander; Waffles, a Chicano; Debbie, a Sāmoan; and Tony, a Native American—who all grew quite exponentially, from being isolated and unconcerned or indifferent individuals to proactive leaders of campus organizations, student government, committees, and advisory boards, as well as off-campus community groups, by the time they had been involved with our mentorship programs for just about two years. These advances were all personal, social, and academic improvements that we thought could not have been expressed through mere grades and letters: we have enabled students to do well, and we have inspired them to do better.

If we needed to collect other physical evidence to express our accomplishments, there were the photographs that students turned in, the videos they made, and the attendance/activity or survey sheets they filled out during the weekly study tables. These were organized into binders and albums, and most of them have been archived. They also submitted term papers, PowerPoint presentations, group projects (such as scripts of mini plays, lyrics of songs, poetry, and oral narratives), posters, and short videos of projects that thematized their research into their undertaught histories and cultures, focused on their criticisms of their school or the U.S. educational system in general, or outlined the advocacies that they have created, nurtured, or fantasized about. They found innovative, creative, and resourceful ways of dealing with the ethnocentrisms and devaluings they experienced in their studies by proactively integrating their critiques and activisms into the classes they were attending. They made sure to circulate these among one another and to pass them on to the next cohort of mentorship partners within and outside of the campus. As students, they wanted to belong, participate actively, and engage, not so much as consumers of knowledge, but as producers of it. And they were willing to share and spread their good work.

It was not as if students found taking pictures awkward during studying, and nor did they feel immodest that they were partly determining their own schooling agendas and activities as a result of the things they learned during mentorship sessions. In fact, they were glad that the program was taking them seriously; they wanted their school and school funders and supporters to notice them; and they wanted to show one another how serious they were in nurturing the programs they themselves established and take pride in what they had learned and done. They wanted to stay true and accountable to the vision that had been set by those before them. And even if they thought they were imperfect, they desired to keep on improving, to not be content with what they had, and to make better the things they cared about. A good example of this attitude was the serious but evenhanded leadership displayed by Kabru, a black student from Ethiopia (by way of England) who made it a point to regularly visit PIPE during study tables. Kabru was a friend of Junior's, the Sāmoan-Filipino student we met in chapter 1; Kabru and Junior went to the same high school together and got accepted to UW as well, and Kabru joined us in PIPE right in his first year in school. Later on, he inherited a mentorship program for African and African American students that had been established a few years earlier through the leadership of Angel, who, in following the footsteps of what Adelante did as an offshoot of PIPE, wanted to build a similar program for another group of students with our help. Angel came up with a rather cumbersome name, the Black/African Students in Coalition, Peer Leadership, and Mentoring Program, or BASIC PLAN. In a visionary way, she intended it to be inclusive of African diasporic students on campus, who, like PIPE and Adelante students, were similarly looking for ways for their campus to be much more welcoming of their growing population of minority underrepresented students from recently immigrated African families and their offspring. In its first year of operations, in 2008, it was quite successful; it received funding similar to PIPE and Adelante. But by the next year, interest in it had waned. So when Kabru took its helm, he wanted to reenergize the program's positive record and think of ways to make it better. He offered a new name that was more fitting of African culture—Ubuntu, a Nguni Bantu term that was popularized during the presidency of South Africa's Nelson Mandela and refers to a philosophy of human kindness, within the historical context of Africanization—and he infused the revitalized program with a new sense of forward-looking leadership and accountability.[23] He was inspired and motivated to do something better for his communities. He, thus, collaborated in constructing a "contract" for mentors and mentees that was eventually used by the other mentorship programs (see figure 2.1).

While all the mentorship partnership programs professed the belief that all students deserve to be provided opportunities to succeed in school, they also, in many ways, staunchly argued that many underrepresented students would not avail of any opportunity given to them if school was not made meaningful to them. It was as if asking students to make sense of school, while not making an effort to have school make sense to students.[24] This was the same spirit behind yet another outgrowth of PIPE: the establishment of a mentorship program for Native American students, called Yǝhaw̓ali. Written more properly in this way, the name is a Lushootseed word that means "the place where a kind of beginning or something currently going on happens."[25] Lushootseed is the lan-

Ubuntu Mentorship Program
Mentor Contract: 2010–2011

I, _____, understand and agree that Ubuntu is a program designed to empower and decrease the attrition rate for all students at the University of Washington. As a mentor, it is my responsibility to do all that I can to make this possible without abusing my authority.

As a mentor, I understand there are responsibilities requested of me in order to make Ubuntu an effective program. Therefore, I acknowledge and will commit to the following:

- Attend all study tables and meetings and
- Help set up and clean room before and after study tables
- Regulate study table hours
- Meet with my mentee(s) once a week, outside of study tables
- Regularly update and meet with student director
- Regularly update and meet with faculty director
- Ask and provide help for mentee in any area
- Provide biweekly reports on mentees
- Help with the ordering of food, planning of events, and recruiting of mentees
- Participate in the activities of the program
- Fulfill other relevant duties that may arise in the mentorship program

_____   _____
Signature   Date

_____
Student Director

_____
Faculty Director

FIGURE 2.1

guage spoken by the Duwamish people who are native to the Seattle area, and Yəhaẃali's founder, a Native American student named Solomon, thought that such an opportunity for collective student support through mentorship might positively work in ways that were similar to what other students in the existing mentorship programs had already experienced. And so, befitting the no-frills and no-fanfare tradition of the other programs, and with the help of the college's American Indian studies department and faculty, Yəhaẁali was quietly born.

To save some monies, Solomon asked the Adelante students if his group could temporarily join their study tables and share in their concomitant food expenses, as well as solve an impending problem of (lack of) space in the Ethnic Cultural Center. Adelante mentors practically shrugged their shoulders, almost as if to say that this was clearly the most "natural" and expected thing to do. Of course! They overwhelmingly said yes. This temporary situation of a partnership across groups—traditionally treated as separate and discrete singular categories—has now lasted for more than eight years. Honestly, I myself have found this kind of endurance surprising, but the work of collective support and the work of student and school transformation that all of our students had a hand in, in all of these mentorship programs, have likewise truly changed my own perceptions and practices of partnerships as transformative processes. Here is an excerpt from my journal regarding this situation; it was written after the Adelante/Yəhaẁali study tables, during their third successful year of collaboration:

> Today, I am so embarrassed that I cried in front of the students. I'm embarrassed, but I'm not ashamed about it though, if that makes sense. I walked into study tables of A/Y [Adelante/Yəhaẁali] and there they were, all seriously studying, next to each other. I know for a fact that Luis is from . . . [name of a fraternity] and George is from [name of another fraternity], and these are rivals! Shit! How could they be studying next to each other! And then, all these Native students, wow, sitting there next to the Chicanos and Chicanas. I was kinda touched by the sight. All the stereotypes and bad stupid assumptions lashed out to us out there, even by our own people who believe we don't have the capacity to be serious students—all of these came rushing to my head. Wow, this is amazing. So, why am I crying? Paul looked at me and was so puzzled by what he saw. What happened? he asked as he came up to me, so I forced a smile on my face, just to quickly show him that I was not in trouble or being dramatic. Nothing, I said, nothing. I said that I was just happy to see him. Now I have to explain to him all of this when I see him tomorrow, ugh!

THE UNPREDICTABLE OCEAN

Spring quarter. It is already 5:00 PM, and the students and I are anxious. I. Am. Anxious. LOL [laugh out loud]. We've been waiting for those other students since 4:00 [PM], when we were supposed to start our study tables. They were rumored to be on their way. 5:10.

5:20. 5:30. No show. Nobody came. Except the usual five mentors. No mentees. No other student. What's going on? Can someone explain this to me? We're just on our fourth week of study tables. And no one seems to be paying attention. What's going on? I'm ready to walk out. So ready to give up. So annoyed. Frustrated.

. . .

In our mentoring partnerships, students were collectively encouraged to take ownership of and responsibility in their schooling. This allowed them to feel that they were not just a number, and they obtained the sense that the university was figuratively a smaller place that they could potentially navigate if they were just patient enough to learn from a few others, strive to do well in the midst of various kinds of pressure, and try to remain in focus in the middle of numerous kinds of distraction. But of course, no true account of these programs would be complete and realistic if we were all made to believe, even among ourselves (that is, me and the students), that everyone did well all the time and that all these programs flowed smoothly on all counts. As was expected, conflicts of all kinds arose at every moment, and at every step:

> This mentorship is not going well for me, God damn it! My mentor's crazy, crazy! I don't like her. Please help me, Bonus. Please change my mentor. Please save me. Can't stand her no more! Eeeeek!!

> This week, we didn't do too well. That's why Bonus got pissed. I was pissed too! Mentees didn't come to study tables. I think they were not informed, if you ask me. Or we didn't inform them as much. Or on time. But it's just a fluke. No big deal. We'll do better next time, don't worry, Bonus. It's all gonna work out. I'm pissed, but we're gonna make this work, trust me.

> This week . . . well . . . this week has not been good. Too little time and too many things to do. My uncle passed away and everyone [in my family] had to help out. I was so required at home to drive this, do this, do that. So I skipped class many days and now I'm trying to make up. My teacher don't understand though; she said I'm getting a zero in the quiz I missed. Man, that was the day my uncle got buried. That was the saddest day for me. How does she expect me to be absent for that? It's okay, I'll take the zero. Don't care.

> Sorry I have nothing to say. Same as last week. I always run out of time to do things. It's just too much. I wanna give up on other things, but you

says I don't have to; just balance them out. I'm gonna try this. Easy for you to say. Try and understand me please!

This week, shit, my mentees ditched me. The three of them. All three of them! One after the other, OMG [oh my God]. I don't know why. I think they don't like me. I don't know. I don't know. Can somebody please help me? I'm thinking maybe this thing is not working for them. Or for me, ha-ha. What's goin' on?

Whenever disagreements or any kind of friction occurred between the mentors and the mentees, or between them and me, and within each of these groups and other students outside of them, I did not usually intervene until the issue got to be bigger than what students could handle, or critical enough in the ways I sensed so, or was brought up to me directly by the students. We were all convinced, although uncomfortably so, that conflicts were part and parcel of any kind of association, and that we were not unique in this regard. Well, our numbers were not really that big, so certain issues got magnified more than usual, and the consequences of any incidence of attrition—whether temporary or permanent—were always damaging. Whenever we lost any one student in our study tables or, worse, lost a student from the school entirely, all mentors felt the blow. It was scary and oftentimes debilitating. And even though we learned from these crises, cruising through them was easier said than done. Struggling through these emergencies was oftentimes an ordeal, as one would imagine, specifically in relation to time management matters, family versus school conflicts, and mentor-mentee compatibility. Our strategies involved a set of alternatives to a zero-sum situation of having to force students to give up one valuable thing for another. They did not have to do this, we thought. We tried not to ask students to give up their political and social activities on campus, or to forget about their families, nor did we ask them to focus only on schoolwork. Rather, we cultivated in them how to balance these different components so that they ended up as better-rounded students, even happier students who were not forced to give up on any important dimension of their lives as students and social beings. We encouraged them to integrate their values, traditions, and cultural practices, even their on- and off-campus activism—conventionally seen as stuff that was outside the boundaries of formal schooling—into their classroom work, such as their term papers and their academic projects. In doing so, students and I were convinced that when the connections between what was learned in the classrooms and what was lived outside of the classrooms were strengthened, their understanding and experience of formal education became more relevant to them, enriching, and diverse.[26] We therefore believed that schooling and community (and family) priorities did not have to be arranged vertically all the time, as if one was always and only more important than the others. Instead, we advocated for a more horizontal and intersecting arrangement of interests, experiences, and expectations whose importance was interrelated with others, nuanced, and contextual.

Still, crises of different versions and degrees of difficulty would inevitably happen. Tavita referred to this condition as living in "an unpredictable ocean," where all of us got to learn strategies to address problems and tensions as they would come to us unexpectedly, and where it was critical to take these things in stride by refusing to be always beaten down by them, as we were a few times. Still, as their faculty mentor, I felt I did not need to be in the students' faces every time something unexpectedly bad would occur. I wanted to make the student mentors and directors more responsible in managing their members, and, most of the time, they did their job fairly well. It was during those times when I, their own mentor, had friction with any of them that things did get dicey. When it came to my own position within the scheme of things in all of these mentorship programs, the vision of "mentorship among equals" was challenging to me as well as to all the students involved. We could not possibly think of a way to make this work without my having to lose some critical measure of power over students: power that was meant to guide them especially when they were offtrack, or power that was there to make sure that students were protected from any kind of harm while they were at school. Many times, I felt that students were looking to me to lead the way. I was not hesitant about pulling back when I sensed that my intervention was not necessary. But I was also not willing to let the students be by themselves if I thought they were in jeopardy. Still, this issue about my power over the students sometimes lingered and strongly exerted a presence, particularly when I had students brushing me the wrong way.

For example, I once scolded Justice, Tutru, Zackary, and Kody for being late for our weekly meeting (an activity integrated into our study tables), by abruptly canceling that meeting once they arrived in my office, about fifteen minutes after our appointed time. I wanted to teach them about the consequences of disrespectful behavior and to impress upon them that time, at least for their mentor, was precious, especially if their reason for being late was that they were not mindful of our scheduled appointment when they were playing pool in the student center, a building across the street from my office. I yelled at them somewhat, told them to leave my office, and shut my door on their faces. But I did not think this would be anything more complicated than a symbolic slap on their wrists. However, a few days passed after this incident, and not one of them reached out to me. From what I heard someone close to them report, it seemed they were hurt by my treatment of them. So, I thought, how could they be hurt? They were the ones in error! But their distancing behavior spoke louder to me. When I saw them in class (they were taking a course with me, at that time) after a few days of virtually no communication, nobody attempted to say anything to me (unlike what they would have regularly done before), and their smug looks while I was teaching annoyed the hell out of me, as if they didn't care. I was furious! We were approaching our final exams, but they completely ignored a study session that they knew I was conducting. Against my better judgment (as I learned later) and simply because someone close to me, another student named Ili, who was more senior to them, advised me, I initiated contact. I texted Tutru to ask if they were studying for exams and if they needed my help. All I got was a curt "yes, no, thank you."

Almost a year and a half into mentoring these young men, it felt odd that something as simple as tardiness and the mild punishment that came after it would immediately result in the seeming conclusion of our relationship. I was annoyed, disappointed, and sad that I had invested so much time and energy and resources nurturing our relationship, only for it to be ended like this. This was not to say that I was looking for some kind of return on my investment; it was just that I could have devoted my resources to others who might have turned out to be more appreciative of our work. Some people say that conflict is a necessary part of any relationship, for it is through conflict that those who are in the relationship learn how to navigate, resolve, and strengthen their bonds. I believed so as well, and part of the conflict that I was dealing with here involved my recalcitrance to approach them, believing that these young men needed to learn how to show respect and humility and demonstrate the capability to admit a mistake and apologize, especially to someone who had shown great care and devotion to their well-being. I thought this incident would deepen and tighten our mentorship, and it did, as I looked back and thought about it months after this incident. But the critical step of resolving it, I thought, should have come from them, not me. I learned later that they were indeed thinking of making the first move, but I beat them to it. I tried to learn a valuable lesson from this, and I was quite happy that my relationship with these students withstood this test and made us more wary of losing one another. But recalling the earlier moments of this conflict, and ruminating on the fact that they were showing me that they were not willing to do anything about what happened to us, even when I was reaching out to them, caused me to be a bit infuriated. Such a bold display of immature audacity for nineteen-year-old men, I thought. I admonished all of them later on, during calmer moments, that they should never do that with me again. I told them that I felt as if I were ganged up on, that it was unfair to leave me alone, and that it was not right to always rely on their mentor to fix things during times of trouble. After all, I was just one, and they were four. They nodded their heads, expressing their tacit agreement and apology. It was the first big "fight" we had. And it wasn't the last.

Yes, there is no such thing as a perfect mentorship relationship; everybody knew this. And I do think that most every student I mentored tried, at least, in different ways and however they could, to be collaborative and nurturing in our mentorship programs. My students and I crossed uneven paths together, treaded oftentimes murky and, sometimes, hard-to-define waters of interaction, but we did try hard to make things work in our unruly ocean, given that the contexts and spaces within which we nurtured these relationships were not exactly free from conflict or completely supportive of what we were attempting to achieve. I reminded myself many times to keep positive, and I trained myself to have a disposition that expected good things to come out of mentorship, not bad, even when bad things occurred. Still, I felt surprised, dazed; I even found myself in a self-blaming recourse whenever things did not actually work out, shaking my head in the process, while so thankful to the universe that these things happened only rarely. Incidents like these made me pause for a while just to painfully confront the realities of an imperfect ocean in the imperfect school we inhabited, but, more positively, to think of ways by which these could be lessons for me as much as for the students on how to conduct ourselves despite and in spite of our imperfect worlds and imperfect selves. And in all these struggles, we could hopefully and mercifully move on. In this light, I also thought about the students I cared so much about, and my seemingly too-present presence in their school lives. Here is my journal entry on that thought:

> I feel for the students, good and bad. I am so visible and present in their lives at school [and beyond], and so when they get into trouble with me, or when they choose not to deal with me for a host of reasons, I imagine that there is not much out there for them to replace me with. They do not have a lot of choices. Or, if I were to stop being immodest about this, I imagine that it would be tough for such students to simply avoid someone like me. We are a small and tight community, I know almost all these students by nickname and background, and I am usually present in many of their functions and activities. I know their families too! They

must feel terrible about how life in school can be so unfair to them, and how I may bitingly contribute to that unfairness. That's why I let them be. I should do it more. Indeed, they shouldn't be forced to deal with me if it is against their will. Nevertheless, I could also imagine these young men [Justice, Tutru, Zackary, and Kody] as probably already carrying on with their lives, not realizing for now what I think they have lost or what they have gained. They probably have other more important things to do with their lives. With or without me. I, on the other hand, feel compelled to reflect on my loss in order to save myself from misery and dejection. I tell myself, there are so many more students to mentor out there besides them. There are still so many opportunities out there to nurture, to care, to enable meaning and connection, while building respect, humility, and love within our families and communities. The ocean currents do not stop, I convince myself, at least while we are resolved to stay in them.

The study tables and other spaces that students inhabited as underrepresented collectives in school were fragile, but only to the degree that the institutional structures and the people in power who supported them affected them so. This did not mean that such students were monolithically and totalizingly beholden to everything and everyone who was more powerful than them. They were not, as these gestures of proactive transformation, in the spirit of collaboration, have already shown. Materially, they have also managed to run their programs despite dwindling resources and mentorship budgets that have been diverted elsewhere. But their programs' robust existence, and potential to continue running, depended and still depend so much on convincing their institutional benefactors that they are worthwhile to run regardless of their "small" size, and even though PIPE has been successfully running nonstop for more than ten years now, and the rest, for at least more than eight. To date, these mentorship programs do not have offices, dedicated staff and faculty (other than me), and a permanent budget. Every end of the year, I have routinely sought the help of students to assist me in writing our next year's program funding renewal application, but since most of the students are already too tired by this time to do anything, I have ended up doing this by myself most of the time. It helped that we had a few administrators who persisted in believing in our work and a community organization that supported our efforts whenever we were short of financial resources. But it has been the students' show, first and foremost. The PIPE program won an on-campus diversity award, was featured in a national resource catalog of top college student programs, and, along with its allied programs, produced many students who eventually succeeded in their classes, graduated, found decent jobs, or entered selective graduate programs and professional schools. These were accomplishments that we listed in our reports so that we could get noticed and be recognized, and obtain funding and other kinds of support. But I also thought that the most commendable work—what was rarely mentioned out loud—was the simple yet significant work of a collective of students who just wanted to keep sustaining one another while at school.

On this collective effort, Andres commented:

> I can't really complain a lot about our struggle to find and keep support, because programs like these are not common around the university, and this program is new. It's [in] its fourth year. I think as time goes on, we could probably pick out more things because we'll probably encounter more problems that we'll learn from. The largest things I'd have to say about the program are pretty good; we have community, people to network and work with for support, to keep us working. We have a steady meeting spot for study tables here at the ECC [Ethnic Cultural Center], and this is the first year that we've had that. Previous years, we'd always move locations around campus. This year is the first year we're a registered student organization, so congratulations to all the mentors for helping us achieve that status. We also formed a large group of mentees and wannabe mentees, and this is thanks to all the hard work of the mentors of the program; our fruits are showing. We have a lot of potential to be gained from this program in terms of getting to know others, learning cultures, and gaining knowledge from each other. So, the benefits are overwhelming; I think as the program goes on, we find out just how strong communal programs like this are beneficial; this is because of the many crosscutting ties that we are building with other people and with many, many communities here and outside. We all come together here.

On the whole, PIPE, Adelante, Yəhaẁali, and Ubuntu were all political projects invested in engaging with and intervening into students' desires to transform their school. In these projects, students attempted to conjure a set of opportunities and spaces that were not in existence before or, at least, were not available specifically for the students to avail themselves of. Faced with what seemed to them to be a congeries of alienating, impersonal, and imposing institutional structures of schooling—stuff that many of them had not seen before, in such magnitude and majesty that they felt their university expressed—they advocated for a chance to build and sustain an alternative set of communities that were meaningfully designed to honor their extraordinary desire to become successful students. In acting upon such a desire, these students wanted to make sure that the terms by which they could accomplish their goal should not disrespect their dignity and humanity as underrepresented students of color who were coming from communities that were not steeped in the prevailing cultures of conventional college attendance and performance.[27] These were explicit in the original blueprint of the mentorship programs very early on, and they have endured for a while now, despite being under the specter of an unwelcoming and fear-provoking institution, and in the midst of neoliberal moves to reduce support for programs that do not appear to be worthwhile investments either because their beneficiaries are too small in number or their "outputs" cannot be adequately measured.

These students simply wanted to make their school respond to their desire to be successful in it, and their first impulse was to ask for a space of their own. This impulse, however, had an impetus that was propelling it from the background, something that was challenging them to understand deeply the paradox that they were in: of how to succeed in a place that was designed for them to not succeed. In order to address this paradox, they first had to perform a critique of what success in college meant for them and what they did not want to give up. Clearly, to me, these students were not willing to do certain things: they did not want to leave or give up on their school, nor did they desire to be completely integrated into it at the cost of giving up parts of who they were as students from minoritized or nondominant cultures. The solutions they offered patently refused a capitulation to what their school mainly demanded of all its students, that they behave like everybody else, and that their faculty and staff treat them the same way as the rest, a kind of domestication of unruly subjects whose unruliness needed to be contained, so that everyone uniformly ended up as efficient citizen-workers upon graduation. I have no doubt that this kind of critique of assimilation—all too familiar especially for Pacific Islander students who first took the helm in summoning their special advocacy for collective mentorship—was borne out of a long history of continuing colonization and imperialism that these students of color had already been dealing with on so many levels and aspects of their lives upon arrival in their school. Faced with the liberal formation of a market-driven and consumer-centered institution that was their school, such students needed to then reckon with the ways in which the campus policies and actions they saw seemed to be anchored in the imperialist agendas of domination they were familiar with. And in terms of dealing with difference, they felt that their school also subscribed too much to the pluralist project of enabling harmony for all through the flattening out of such differences.[28] Hence, the frequent calls for respecting other cultures without critiquing uneven relationships of power within and between them, or the emphasis on adding "diversity-themed" classes into the curriculum without changing the overall ethnocentrism and core of the curriculum, did not fare well for these students as advocacies they wanted to support.[29] To them, progressive change did not happen this way. And they thought it was time for them to do something about it.

Seeming to appear peripherally, although so apparent in their daily lives as students, and even without the invocation of its formal name, imperialism in schooling—as students have pointed out to me time and time again—cannot be seriously engaged through compensatory practices of integration, temporary repair, or decorative and nominal alteration of educational institutions. They have seen these happen before, and they were tired of seeing these happen without changing the situations they were in. What they wanted was for their school to undergo transformation, and for it to do that—for it was expected that it would not do it on its own—they had to be proactive about it. They had to start with themselves, not as individual advocators, but as collectives that were set on negotiating with and through the prevailing structures of power in their lives as students. Collective work undergirded their political actions, at the same time as collective trust in the values they held in their indigenous and local cultures underwrote their insistence to be self-determined in their efforts. They started well, they had fitful episodes, and the processes by which they persisted entailed messy pathways that were simultaneously infused with nurturing collaborations and an enduring hope that things would somehow work out. Now looking back in self-reflection, I see how such hard-earned investments have led to qualitative expressions of empowerment for these students, ultimately advancing the value they now accord to themselves, their communities, their school, and their society as people and places that are open to possibilities and, therefore, transformable. So even though I do sound immodest and self-interested here, I am proud to say how honorable it was to have been part of the lives of such students who dared to transform themselves and their school in ways that brought to their ocean the values of their collective work when they were ignored, the courage to act when opportunities for change arose, and the compulsion to remain hopeful whenever they experienced despair.

3

THOSE WHO LEFT

December 11

Dear Professor Bonus: I'm so very embarrassed and I'm sorry to tell you that I have finally decided to quit school. No more school for me. Yes sir. No more. There is no turning back now. :-(And I'm very sorry. BUT, *but, but I also want to tell you I am happier because I can have freedom now to do what I want, and that is to work with my step dad and help my mom and my sister with my little brother and also my nephew too. Work, work, work! That's a lot, huh? So, you see, school has been that one thing and that one and only thing that was preventing me from doing all this. Working is the one that makes me wanna be living. For the longest time, I was asking myself if school is what really is the one for me. And we know that my grades where [sic] not that good anyway, but they show you why I'm not interested in even going to any classes. Honestly, only when I met you did I find something good about school. You cared for me very much. You taught me good things, like how to be a good person for my family, for our community. Even until now. You're the only one who did that in school for me. And thank you for that, Bonus. But honestly, that's not enough. It's not your fault, but I just cannot be in school anymore. It does not mean good things for me anymore. Better for me to be useful in life by not having bad grades, but in helping my mom and dad and sister. I'm so sorry . . . you having to take care of me is now all a waste. I hope I'll make it up to you someday, you'll see.*

With all love to you,
Sonny

. . .

January 29

I had a long talk with Teeny today. She was distraught as ever, like meeting me was something that was physically breaking her body down in pain. I was unsure what to tell her, but from what I can detect, she is in no position to continue with school, even though I can see that she's been trying very hard. I told her to take a leave [of absence] next quarter, or maybe, even better, during this one, and then she could just catch up later. She can do that. She's been getting really low grades and not even attending class, even though she's always there during meetings [of student organizations] and in all of our performances and events. She even goes to study tables! I don't know what she's studying though. Is she? It's amazing to see her "working" during our meetings. She's such a dynamic speaker, a motivator, and a role model for so many students, especially for young Pacific Islander women. And she has a great, thoughtful, and wonderful grasp of all the issues we're facing, from deep academic and intellectual points that she can articulate with no difficulty, to mentoring others to find meaning and to develop their communities of care in school. She's on top of things. And then, now that I've asked her to meet with me, she gives me this [sassy] attitude first, which I ignore. Until she later somehow communicates to me that we may not see her anymore, starting next quarter. In some ways, I'm glad to hear this. But I'm so worried for her, for us. We're going to lose Teeny soon.

. . .

Sonny and Teeny, both Sāmoan American and local within the state of Washington, were two students I mentored under PIPE (the Pacific Islander Partnerships in Education mentorship program on campus, detailed in the previous chapter). The first entry that I started this chapter with is a short letter given to me by Sonny, something that I had requested from him right during the time when he decided to not return to the UW, not even to finish the term he was in. At that time, he was in his junior year, and he knew from PIPE that journal writing, and writing to me in particular, a mentor in the program, was something students and I did regularly. From then on, I invited him to continue being in touch with me, asking him if I could keep our mentorship relationship going, and if I could possibly include him in my study. He agreed.

The second passage is an excerpt from a journal entry that I myself wrote a few years after I met Sonny, a small part of a large set of entries that served both as field notes for me and as personal ruminations on just about everything and anything connected with my experiences with students both on and off campus. It is a slice out of the same habit of journal writing that I tried to teach my mentees to acquire. This excerpt—and we will see many more like them later—narrates a part of Teeny's struggles in school. Clearly, it includes many observations and some quick analyses, but it does not say much about or explain at length Teeny's specific circumstances and deeper challenges. In fact, these struggles appear in this excerpt as vague and somewhat contradictory. So, as entry points, I just employ them to pry open an initial set of doors and windows regarding student departures from school, an ethnographic analysis of which I offer here.

Both Sonny and Teeny had also been students in my own classes; they earned average and above-average grades and were quite active in on-campus organizing, especially in matters concerning their community's history, culture, and educational interests. Like all of the students mentioned in this book, these two regarded me as their teacher, mentor, confidante, and, to a certain extent, friend. But they were a different set of students who struggled persistently at the onset of their second year. As Pacific Islanders, they mainly felt marginal and isolated on their campus particularly because their numbers were low, and they could not keep up with the mostly academic, social, and financial demands of their school, their families, and their communities.[1] And, out of all the students I kept a close eye on, I won't hesitate to say that Teeny and Sonny were the kind of students I looked after the most, especially after I first quietly suspected that they were about to leave. I was careful not to say this out loud to anyone else because that would have been quite inappropriate. Students like them get to be labeled so quickly as "at risk." But I was also afraid that, even if I had good intentions to help them, talking about them would have drawn unnecessary attention to them and their plight, and thereby would have jeopardized their relationship with me, their co-mentees, and the rest of the people who knew them. They are two students among the nine who left school whom I will write about in this chapter.

STUDENTS WHO "FAILED" AND THE SCHOOL THAT "FAILED" THEM

In looking at the lives of certain students who encountered their school as alienating, forbidding, or disconnected from their communities, I found among them a good number of those who chose and were able to change their school, transforming it instead into a place of nourishment and meaning by taking ownership of it and making it adjust to their desires and advocacies. These students looked for potential spaces of opportunity, seized untested or unfamiliar ideas, took risks, and worked persistently to improve on unusual group-devised strategies. They tapped combined energies to ensure cooperation and *collective* success. However, for a number of reasons, they did not succeed all the time. Nor did all of their advocacy projects consistently run well and for a long time. These, we have observed in previous chapters and will now know in even deeper instances. A big part of their so-called unsuccessfulness constituted the experiences of those I consider as members of this other set of student communities who have physically removed themselves temporarily or permanently out of the university. But, were these students really unsuccessful? According to whom? Why and how is their departure from school an expression of their failure in it?[2] This chapter explores alternative answers.[3]

I will paint a somewhat different picture of school departure here. Or actually, I will use a different set of brushstrokes—different, that is, from the usual student-centered blaming that is likely to come out of many teachers' and parents' mouths and to which many of my students referred in instances of potential or actual dropping out among them—to paint a picture of school departure that tells us more about what students thought was wrong (and good) about their college experience, the different expectations they had about it (that were mostly unmet), and the various estimations they had of what could have worked better in their formal educational processes that would have allowed them to stay and flourish in college.[4] These students were all voluntary dropouts whose parents, teachers, and acquaintances would have likely considered them "failures." But, in an overwhelming and deeply felt sense, the students did think instead that it was their school that failed them. The action that they chose to take was to leave the place that they considered was unsuccessful in meeting their expectations. They were dissatisfied with what they thought was their inability to change their school (after they tried many times), brought about by what they perceived to be their school's resistance to change or improve, or do something different and unexpected. So, in many ways, their utmost dissatisfaction with the very place they thought would work for them ultimately determined their decision to give up on it.[5]

The students' disappointment with their school, however, did not mean that they thought there was nothing wrong with themselves in particular. They did. At various points, some of them thought they just had too many responsibilities alongside their studies, while others opined that they could not focus enough. But they also pondered a great deal about the limitations of their self-culpability, especially after they had already left school. From a distance in terms of space and time, such limitations became more pronounced for them as they compared the differences of the experiences they had between their on-campus and off-campus lives, and as they were able to assess the effects of living in "the belly of the beast" from places outside of school that ironically appeared to be safer or less scary for them. Such "structures of domination" in college, as these students would allude to later, and argue centrally, to refer to things such as insensitive pedagogy, dominant culture–centered curricula, expensive tuition, and campus climates of racism, sexism, and homophobia, were oftentimes invisible to many other students, especially those thought of as belonging to dominant and majority groups. But it is through these students' experiences of being subjected to these conditions in school that we get a glimpse of usually hidden campus agendas and unnoticed or unrecognized operations.[6] These invisible conditions and practices turned out to putatively impose limitations and unjust exclusions upon these students, who, in many ways, received messages from their school that they were unfit (or not ready) for a certain kind of mainstream formal college education.

In large measure, I seek to present these students' comments and critiques, all expressed through my contextual ethnographic formulation and analyses, not so much to say that they must not be understood only as an airing of gripes and complaints about a school that appeared to be underperforming, at least from the perspective of those who left it. Perhaps, some of them will sound like that. But more significantly, and in the spirit of respecting the school and the students who left their school and were so willing to talk about it, I offer them as testimonies of a struggle to understand why contemporary colleges in general oftentimes continue to have a restricted capacity to enable the success of all those who enter them; why schools can remain blind and uncaring to those who are not able to fit their narrow and unchanging model of an achieving student body; and why a critique of the presumed and oftentimes unquestioned universality, or *unimodality*, of educating college students is necessary to begin to grasp the reasons why certain students who attend the university unnecessarily and unjustifiably leave it in the middle of their formal educational experience. These students' narratives will testify that the cumulative effects of our blindness to school underperformance can be realized most emphatically by considering the accounts of those students who left the very school that initially admitted them.

In the field of education, there have been many competing accounts and criticisms of philosophies of schooling that range from reflections on the meanings of university education for a contemporary Western first-world society, to debates regarding curricular change that emphasize immersion in liberal humanistic values versus skills building for an increasingly technology-based workplace.[7] For this specific account, I will pay the highest attention to how students who have left their school engaged in these debates, and I will do so not in the strict sense of my asking them where their views fell in these debate positions, because I did not ask them that. Instead, I will take notice of, and recount here, why students left their school and how they thought differently about their school in three aspects—all connected to their ideas regarding the roles of schooling in the lives of people like themselves.

First, as opposed to the predominant way of thinking about going to college as a place to learn and produce knowledge, imbibe a skill, or hone a craft, these students thought about their school as, and expected it to be, a place, foremost of all, to *discover* themselves. It was a place to search for meaning, to uncover interesting and unexpected phenomena about life, and to freely navigate through an ocean of educational possibilities. Second, and more intensely, these students came to the university to search for, nurture, and sustain a *community* to belong to. They imagined themselves less as individuals in pursuit of individual growth and enlightenment and personal success and more as members of collectives composed of students, faculty, and staff aggregated in or through collaborative visions and formations.[8] And instead of conceiving the school as a stepping-stone to something else, as a temporary place to be in, with the eventual goal of leaving it once academic training was over, these students had an attitude that seriously considered school/community/family (almost always understood or anticipated to be joined together) as something more evolving, intersecting, and boundless. Third, these students thought that they were different from the majority of students who went to school to access resources just for themselves. Access to resources for such underserved and disadvantaged students had a different meaning. It meant *securing resources for their collective selves, including their families and their communities.* And, just as how school was understood to be constituted by and constitutive of their communities, they regarded school and its components as public goods that had to be shared, valued, and, therefore, protected and cultivated. School resources to them, then, were community resources. No one was usually thought to individually own them. All of these college permutations, expressed in physical, social, and intellectual, as well as idealized or imagined, terms, from campus buildings, departmental offices, and laboratories, to library study sessions, classroom discussions, computer-based exchanges, socials, and, most especially, the bodies of teachers, the staff, and the students, were linked together into a holistic understanding of school as an oceanic entity whose values were considered as coextensive and coexistent with islander communities within and outside of it. School/ocean was a set of social communal relations.[9] Therefore, when any one or a combination of these elements was insufficient, unmet, or misunderstood by their school, these students found their campus community deficient enough to make them decide eventually to leave it.

I started writing this chapter at a point when all nine students—six men and three women, all from working-class backgrounds—voluntarily left the

UW during their second, third, or fourth year of attending it. They represent the approximate 32 percent of Pacific Islander students who are not able to graduate within six years of attending the UW (the highest number of non-graduates among all racial groups), or, on average, part of the 51 percent of the national population's cohort of Pacific Islander students who are not able to graduate within six years after entering a four-year university.[10] When I was close to finishing the first draft of this work, two of them went back to campus and eventually graduated. But I remained in contact with every one of them throughout this study, and I still am in contact with many of them to this day. Here, my interactions with them are excerpted as glimpses of what students go through before, during, and after exiting or momentarily stopping school. Departure may appear to be a long or drawn-out process. But usually, in these cases, it was not. Students would rather leave unnoticed if they can help it, and, of course, nobody would want to announce to everyone their intent to not return. Even when they visited campus, very few chose to talk about the circumstances of their departure from school. Or give any updates regarding it. It is because student departures to them were primarily painfully productive of stigma. They were definitely not easy things to talk about. And when many students and I attempted to convince those who we knew were about to depart to stay, we oftentimes inadvertently reinforced the assumption that there was something not right about the departing students themselves. We almost always thought there was something wrong with them that needed fixing.

"WE'RE IN SCHOOL TO DISCOVER!"

April 7

Had my second meeting with Marie today. Ugh! It's hard to meet with her these days. And also weird, given the fact that she has secretly decided not to go back to school. I feel like it's just too uncomfortable for her. Next time, we should meet in a place much farther from school, like away from it. Over here, we're too exposed! Or she's just too vulnerable. Anyhow, today at least, she seemed much more relaxed, although she also seemed to be troubled, or a bit anxious about me being here. Or scared? I tried to make her feel okay by doing small talk with her. But I told her that if this were too uncomfortable for her, I will not continue on. She said it was okay to go on. So I asked her why she's not coming back [to school]. Especially now that she's close to graduating. Very close! And she shrugged her shoulders. Just stayed quiet. With head bowed down. Was she crying? After a while, she started to speak. Just softly. She said she left because she thought school was not interesting anymore. She had a sad look on her face. She said that everything she did outside of class, like going to events and parties, and attending meetings for PIPE or participating in kava, were all interesting and good for her.[11] She liked doing them. But everything else she did in her own classes [was] just boring and didn't make sense to her. She wondered why she was studying these things they were dealing with in class. The word she used was "unrealistic." She said that these classes were unrealistic; they were not grounded in her real world, they did not matter, or, that she didn't find anything useful about them. Useful to her life. She said that these courses did not refer to her own interests or needs, or the lives of her people and everyone she cared about. These "school things," she said, mattered only to white people. So, she basically found school to be disconnected from who she is, and the communities where she came from and live[s] with. What's the point of spending time and energy in school? she asked.

. . .

April 11

Dear Proffe. Bonus (still misspelling Prof.!), This quarter has been quite eventful for life more than our school. There's a significant other who makes me better manage my time. :=) So, it's kind of good, ha-ha. We like each other. Other than that, I was working too much again like I do all the time. Because I need to! And teachers, well, of course, do not understand that. Besides, the classes are not that important to me now. They're all about white culture I don't need to know more about anymore. Imagine, I have to be forced to learn about white people's history, and whites don't have to learn mine? My history? Fall quarter, I need to make up an incomplete for one of Prof. ——'s classes. Adelante! [mentorship program] planning has been more so heavy than last quarter. I've set up a meeting with Arnaldo although I'm dodging your office for fear of your scolding, ha-ha. Hey, this IS the part of school that I like the most. Or, actually, the only one I like, ha-ha. Because this is where I feel my community. I'm steadily setting myself on a better path now, but I gotta run and meet Jennifer in MGH [Mary Gates Hall] now. :=) I will e-mail you a visual schedule during ——'s class @ 2 PM. 'Til then, I'm running errands for Adelante! And the frat! Oh yeah, good news, the frat is back so you can catch me on campus mean mugging the rival fraternity, as I do all the time. :=)

Daniel

. . .

From the purview of many students such as Marie, a Tongan American, and Daniel, a Chicano—people I talked to and wrote letters with—and many of those others who left school without graduating from it at the time of this ethnography, the university was not completely an impossible place to be in. School was not such a bad place for them. At the same time, it was also not exactly welcoming either. They considered major elements in their school—

the restrictive curriculum and sets of expectations, the faculty and students who did not understand them, and the overbearing self-entitled culture of whiteness—as viable reasons to seek alternatives to spending time in it. All of these, of course, were discovered later. Before life on their college campus, they were students who did well in elementary and high school, who got themselves successfully into a competitive university, and they were ready to continue with what they were productively doing. But something changed when they were in college. Their minds opened up and, as if all of a sudden, they felt a sense of liberation from the tight constraints of the high school they knew before. So, they felt the impulse to roam widely on their college campus, with an avid sense of potential discovery and a newfound feeling of excitement in unearthing a set of possibilities they never thought existed, especially in taking college courses, deciding on their own curricula and schedules, making new acquaintances, working on new friendships, planning social activities, and joining communities that mattered a great deal to them. They were quite enthusiastic about being grown-up students. "I remember stepping into college for the first time," Sonny recalled:

And I just got so so excited. High school was a bummer! It had all these rules and things to restrict you. Not good. Not good at all. Like, you were in chains, man! And then, now, in college, it was . . . like . . . it's like you get to be a free man! Amazing, huh? Like, you are suddenly in charge of your own! No one really looking after you, telling you what to do. Like, you can pick and see what's good for you. And you make your own life . . . like, work for you, man. That was fun, at that time. I really, really liked it!

"But did you get scared too?" I asked. Sonny responded:

Hell yeah! I was super scared uh-huh! Remember when I talked to you about this? I was so excited. But I was also scared shit. I was shaking! Literally! Like, I had to be grown up about all this new stuff at the same time. Like, I needed to make decisions for myself all of a sudden. And I had no one looking over my shoulders, yes. Like, I could decide if I wanted to go to class today or not, ha-ha. Or just go to the gym, ha-ha-ha. Just kidding. But I'm serious. I really liked that part of growing up in school. I miss that. Learning new things here and there. It was scary but it was nice!

Until, that is, the "official" requirements of college attendance caught up with him. Reading my notes made me remember how Sonny started college with such a fresh and enthusiastic demeanor. It was right when I met him for the first time, when he was introduced to me during one of our PIPE study tables. I immediately observed and felt how happy he was to be in college, and, soon after, I saw him regularly in serious studying mode. He was well motivated then. He wanted to be a good student. I also noticed how excited he was about meeting other Pacific Islander students, so he started joining clubs and became active in student organizing. He enjoyed doing these activities so much more than studying, and then he soon carved up more time for the clubs, more than actually going to his classes. So right during the beginning of his second year, he started to come to class late or just decided to ditch them, one by one. Many times, he didn't show up for weeks. He came only when there was a scheduled exam. This coincided with new demands that his mother, who was mostly a single parent, brought upon him. Sonny explained further:

> You know, when I got into UW, my mom was super proud and super excited for me. I just turned eighteen and I was ready for something bigger and better, man. But see, my mom thought of college in a different way. You know, she had this idea that college was gonna make us all rich. I mean rich with a capital R right here and right now! Ha-ha-ha. Not later, I thought, when I graduate, just in case, ha-ha. But right now! She started expecting me to bring back the dough, like I suddenly have this pot of gold that I just found in college. What's going on? That was scholarship money! Or money I got out of my loan! And more than that, she started assuming that I have all this time now in the world to help out with her stuff and my sister and my brother. Whoa! I don't have the money, and I don't have the time to help them! I have to go to school! Now, I'm so stressed!

Sonny began to get overwhelmed. He was caught between two situations and cultures that wielded different demands upon him. On one end was a set of expectations to do well in anticipation of material benefits, such as working for a ticket that would eventually amount to a big fortune. On the other was a penetrating sense of excitement and wonder at what was unfolding before his eyes, something that he could not exactly pin down yet, but that caused him to be very enthusiastic about the choices before him, which seemed to have no limits. "I feel like an open book that is not written yet!" he told me one day. And when I asked him, not too long afterward, what he wanted to pursue, career-wise, he surprised me with, "Whoa, I'm just barely discovering things! How come we're already expected to have a career [path]?" I felt bad rushing him this way. But Sonny's defensive reaction to my question made me think twice about the pressure that many other similar students take on to work toward a so-called career early on and quite quickly.[12] Many parents would even prefer having students decide on a career before college. To be sure, Sonny's imagination of college was something that was perhaps connected with pursuing a career. But he instead wanted to spend more time exploring and discovering what he wanted to do, without being distracted by having to make a career choice right away. He was bent on taking his time exploring opportunities. He was on a quest to find out more about himself and what he wanted to be. And he desired to be more relaxed, not rushed, about being a student, by watching the realities of college life unfold before him, in a pace that was unhurried. Something slower. Something more measured. Sonny wanted to enjoy and live life without the pressure to always be on top of things right away and all the time or to have a far-reaching vision of who he was going to be, already determined straightaway. And then, he also did not want to be labeled as lazy or clueless, or as a shifty and unambitious college student, despite his insistence on deferred decision-making. Of course, being his mentor, I was a bit unnerved by this, just as many of Sonny's teachers were, I imagined. Or his own mom. And it was not only because he refused to be focused. It was because he appeared to be delighted in his defiant laid-back attitude and out-of-focusness. "Don't get mad at me, Bonus," he once said to me, "I just want to enjoy my college life, you know. I just want to take it easy and find out things slowly. I want to enjoy college, get to know more of it, you know? This is a good place, and I don't want to be rushed. I feel like I'll never ever, ever have this time and place anymore after my stay here, so I'd rather enjoy it. And make the most of it, you know?"

I was not quickly convinced. Many educators like me have this mind-set about what the best ways are for making the most use out of the college experience. And many parents think this way as well. We tend to imagine college as, yes, a place of discovery, but discover quickly, one must![13]

The very same predicament haunted Daniel's college life. He was an on-the-go college student, running here and there, busy with so many things and with no time to waste, yet, at some point, he appeared to not really advance toward a firm goal. In fact, I asked him many times verbally and online what his goal was. He just ignored me. Or distracted me by changing the subject. And whenever I ran into him, he either gave me confusing answers or simply shrugged his shoulders, accompanied by a wry smile. At one point, Daniel was way into his senior year already when he showed me his class schedule, and I was aghast to see a plethora of courses that did not cohere with his major (which was political science, at that time). "You're taking calculus, marine sciences, archaeology, and a women's studies class? Shouldn't you be done with your electives by now and trying to work on your classes within your major? Shouldn't you be on track already by now?" He replied, "Well yeah, but these classes caught my eye. They sound very interesting, Bonus. Why can't I take them? What's wrong with taking them? Don't you think they're good classes to register for?"

"Next quarter," he continued, "I will take Chicano history, don't worry. That's to make up for the Scandinavian lit class I dropped last quarter. I've taken so many classes about whites, now's the time to take classes about my own people!" Still, I thought, taking a Chicano history class wouldn't be credited toward his major. Not when he was already done with electives. This was something I had seen over and over: students earning credit for so many electives—in their quest to discover new and interesting courses—beyond what could be counted toward their declared major. They were usually so hungry for anything that caught their attention and curiosity that they eventually lost track of that one thing they were expected to focus on, which was to graduate with a degree in a field of sorts.

It was also Marie, who said to me over and over: "I don't get it. I thought college was a place where all these things you learn in high school and stuff get all exploded. I thought it was going to be exciting and refreshing, and all that."

"In what way?" I asked. Marie replied:

Well, that's what my parents told me, that college was going to be like you learn deep and wide and lots, and everything in between, and that you can question everything, take on whoever and whatever. And take courses in different areas and different topics, like in whatever you like. Well, that's what I did! That's what [I] was told I should do in college. I did it! But I got punished for it!

"What do you mean?" I asked. She responded:

Well, I think parents, teachers and advisers . . . also many students . . . don't realize that not all students operate on the same track of going through college. I thought . . . this way like you too, in the beginning. But later, I realized I thought . . . differently. But many other folks, they're kinda insensitive to how different some of us are. We're here to learn, to learn things that interest us, yeah? Not to be tied down to one thing. Like, I see many students who already know right from the start what they want to be. Like, they want to be a doctor or a nurse right from day one. So, they take all these biology, chemistry, science classes, all the same things. They think they'll make lots of money getting these degrees. Hmm. They're so focused on what they want and what they need. And they want to make money soon after. That's great! I'm happy for them! But, you see, there are those like me who take their time, who are still searching and trying to find out what they want . . . people who only realize now how narrow high school was, and how open and wide college is . . . students who discover that there's so much more beyond white history and white culture, and white languages and white readings, you know? Imagine? Now, for us, it takes time to take in all of this! Four years are not enough! I'm a super senior, you see, and now that I'm forced to take classes only in my major, I'm actually so bored and uninterested, and I'm so upset too because I couldn't take what I really, really want. It's not good, this system. It sucks for those who like variety and fun! Those who want to take things at a slower pace. Or a different pace altogether! Nothing bad with that, ya?

Indeed, college students whose mind-set is oriented toward discovery and a wide embrace of variety in their coursework have a tendency to take their time and postpone funneling into a specific major much later than usual. True, there are other options for students like these: they could design their own program of study under the rubric of individualized studies, or they could major in interdisciplinary studies offered by other campuses. Still, these options required thematic coherence and curricular direction. By their junior year, many of these students would have been still exploring options and changing their minds about career choices, causing parents and advisers to scratch their bewildered heads for what is oftentimes seen as wasteful indecisiveness.

"I roll my eyes all the time," said one adviser to me, without a hint of discreetness, and with a lot of exasperation continued:

They're seniors and they haven't declared their major. Or they've declared it, but not following through, not taking any of their major requirements. I don't know what they're waiting for. They're wasting their time and money, I think. They need to move on.

Maybe they need more time to decide? Or they need more help with deciding, perhaps?

No, they're being shifty and indecisive and unfocused. And wasteful. Wasteful of our time, our professors' time, of everybody else's time, and wasteful of the school's resources too. They need to be better students. They need to get good grades, get into the best majors, graduate with the best degrees so they can make money soon. They need to graduate. They need to move on, because there are other students after them who are moving in. And moving in fast! They need to make way for them!

"Yeah," Marie said, as her eyes rolled, with both sadness and disgust. She continued:

I've heard that said to me many, many times. Not only advisers. Also teachers! Like, all of my teachers say this! Yeah? More than I care to remember. It's so sad because I think we emphasize too much on learning about something, learning about this and that fact, instead of learning how to do something and learning how to not focus on just finishing that something. This is a skill, you know? We learn how to identify what's interesting around us, how to navigate through choices, how to have a good and open attitude about things. [That is] really important stuff. Not just the facts and the statistics and the date. But, here, we focus on learning these things, like learning all kinds of information, instead of learning how to learn. Like, learning the hows and the whys. Instead of the whats. You know what I mean?

"Wow, that's deep," I said, just to say something at that moment, I'm afraid to say.

Stop mocking me, Bonus.

No, sorry. Sorry, Marie. I see what you mean. But. Wait. Let me process it too. I want to think more about what you just said. Hmm.

"Many times," I continued, "I do think that some students take too much time to decide. It's expensive to go to college, you know? And the more you stay undecided, the more you spend time and money, right?"

Well, so who's at fault here? You're the one who taught us how to look at the system, its workings and limitations, yeah? Don't good teachers like you teach us that the important thing is to analyze or process the information, not just memorize and give it back to the teacher during the test?

Hmm, of course, Marie! Of course!

Marie's thoughtful opinions about what she and other students like her go through did make me think more than twice about the struggles of fitting into a particular mold of a proper student, or a student required to fulfill a suitable college attendance and completion process. Surely, is it the students' fault if they do not proceed on this path? Or is it the system's? One is given at least a year or two in the beginning of college to explore "what's out there" in terms of courses of study and other activities while on campus. And then, there is this expectation—indeed, a requirement—that one has to make a decision to focus on something or some things by the time one reaches the third year, so that all throughout the senior year, one is housed in a discipline or field of study, from which one eventually graduates. This is most definitely a mold that fits a multitude of students, at the same time as it weeds out those others who are not able to do the "right" thing. College is a cattle call, of some sort. This is hardly a new opinion, but it is one that devalues, for sure, the experiences of those who are weeded out. And, especially at a time when so many are also already concerned about rising tuition costs, little room is left for those who "take their time" discovering the process of college learning in ways that are more protractedly measured, gradually introspective, and time-consuming in some misunderstood way.[14]

No way did these students who "consume" their college education in this manner deliberately plan to attend college to be different from the rest. They simply learned how to do college differently on the spot, or as they were going through the process. They knew that college was going to be different, they were expecting it to be so, but they did not know how that difference was going to unfold. For many of them, it was a refreshing revelation to discover forks in the road. "The choices were fantastic," Daniel recalled:

I was definitely floored! I was thinking like, this was like going to a buffet restaurant, you know? Ha-ha-ha. You see what I mean? Lots of choices and variety. Like a buffet! Choices here and there, you know, like, to take advantage of all these new and exciting courses that are being offered by the school. I don't know. But I thought, try them, of course! Whatever appeals to you! Most of them, you never even heard of before! Like, tongue twisters, even. Or sounding hip and crazy. Most of them, you just wanna take because they sound interesting. Most of them, too, you want to take with your friends, maybe? Until . . .

Until what?

Until your adviser tells you, you cannot choose anymore. Uh-oh.

"You cannot choose the courses you want to take?" I asked, a bit surprised when he began to echo Marie's plight. Daniel answered:

You don't have a choice anymore. Like, you're old and you're overdoing it, and you're overstaying. And you're wasting time and money. And your adviser announces that to you. And it's followed up by an e-mail message. Like, the computer says that to you point-blank. It's like a final judgment, see. Like a prison sentence. Choose a career now, or else. . . . This sucks, you know. This, and this alone, made me quit school, I think. I wish there were other options. But this time, it was the computer that shut me down. Like, I couldn't register anymore. It was not even my adviser who told me this. Not a person. It was the fucking computer! What the freak! The stupid machine won't let me register anymore! So stupid (*shaking his head*).

All I could do at that time was shrug my shoulders. This was getting to be a pattern among my students. After a few seconds of thinking, I ventured that there had to be some other option, like having them talk to their adviser to ask for a reprieve or permission to have just one more quarter of freedom before finally deciding on a major. I realized later that this had been done before, but only in exceptional cases, and only very rarely. But I did not want to belabor the point any longer. The point to be made was that these students were behaving like regular students, or how I thought regular students were supposed to behave. They wanted to remain as students. They were sincerely interested in studying, even committed to it. And the breadth of their interests exceeded the scope of what the university structure typically allowed, both in terms of time brackets and disciplinary training, as well as in navigating knowledge sites. It seemed to me that these overextending students could not imagine, or refused to imagine, that there were limits to the breadth of educational opportunities that were before them. They were interested in stuff happening within the classrooms, and they were equally, if not exceedingly, interested in stuff happening outside of their classes as well. All the activities they participated in, mostly labeled as "extracurricular," both those occurring in student organizations and those sited in nearby communities, were activities that they wanted to seamlessly connect with their formal education. They wanted to learn from multiple sites.

Indeed, many of these students—Teeny, Marie, Daniel, and even Sonny, just to name a few—spent a great deal of time discovering, learning, and enriching themselves and those around them in places outside of classrooms, doing work that was mostly described (by their teachers and advisers) as not only noncurricular or extracurricular in their devalued senses but also wasteful, excessive, and unnecessary. Or beside the point. I am not the only one who was able to sense the irony here. "It's funny we learn more about the curricular . . . in places called extracurricular," Teeny once commented to me around a group of students who, like her, preferred the joys of learning outside of traditional classrooms. She went on:

I definitely believe there's more learning that takes place in our orgs. Right in school. But not in the classrooms. This is one classroom we have going good, I truly believe [referring to the office of a student organization she was active in]. We learn a lot here in PSA [the Polynesian Student Alliance], FASA [the Filipino American Student Association] even PIPE! And our school doesn't think this is worthy [of] the money, you know? Like, the things we learn here are not courses we have to take so that we can rake in money later, ya? Here, we don't charge tuition, ha-ha. We learn, we discover, we teach here, yeah?

"Huh? Like, what? Like, how?" That was me, teasing her.

Teeny rolled her eyes, adamant about communicating her seriousness to me:

Well, we learn together, that's for sure. We learn together with people who learn like us and want to learn things that we want to learn. You see that? We learn to have the right attitude, you know. Like, how to be in our big ocean of things. Like, how to be one with your people, to talk with them respectfully and to discuss common things with them, like history and society. To discover and learn about your people. Like, how to be with your own community! And that's on top of learning your own culture with people FROM your own culture. That's not even done AT ALL in our classrooms here! Not at all! Why should we be punished for being students who want to study? Why is doing this all wrong? We're just being good students, right? What's so wrong about discovering, and learning, knowing, and getting meaning, and being good people? Being good students? Isn't this the right attitude to being a good student? Isn't that what we're supposed to be? Shouldn't we be in school to learn and to discover and to engage in the process of learning? I would think so, right?

By the next school quarter after this conversation, Teeny did not return to campus. She visited us several times to show support for certain events, and, within a couple of months, she told me she found a job that she decided should be a better way to occupy her time. Sonny and Marie left school completely, but they stayed in touch with me, while Daniel returned after taking a break for two school quarters.

What does it mean to be with your community in school? What does it mean to study with your community? Being around a very tiny population of Pacific Islander students at UW, one learned the value of community as a lifesaver, to put it very plainly, though in many significant ways. To explain this logic, here is an excerpt from a workshop I conducted on campus with a dozen UW Pacific Islander students (and their allies), mostly directed at eager high school kids, also mostly Pacific Islander students, who were about to enter our school or who were hoping to get into it as college students later. We held this workshop session in one of the meeting rooms at UW's Ethnic Cultural Center. There were about thirty of us in all, gathered together on a rainy and dreary Saturday afternoon. I was the only teacher, the one who primarily led the workshop; the rest were students. They were typically rowdy at times, but they paid attention when it was called for. We started by asking all the high school students to sit on the floor in a circle facing one another, with me and one UW student standing up in the middle of the circle to lead the exercise, while the rest of the college students stood or sat outside, but close to, the circle. I made sure to move around the circle as we proceeded with our activity, so that everyone had a good chance to interact with me and with one another.

November 20

> All right, let's do a guessing game here. (*Clap, clap.*) Learn something new, some kind of logic. You get it? Yup! Let's pay attention! Come on! (*Clap, clap.*) Let's hold it together! Okay. First, let's see. Let's guess . . . how many Pacific Islander students are there in UW? How many do you think there are? Students who are Pacific Islanders. Anybody guess? Anybody!
>
> Five thousand! (*From a shy volunteer.*)
>
> No! Too high! (*Cheering, laughing, and clapping in the background.*)
>
> Ten?
>
> No, too low! That's too low! (*Some jeers.*)
>
> Twenty?
>
> No! Okay. Guess what. It's about . . . It's about two hundred students!
>
> Huh? That's tiny. Wow. (*Cheering and laughing first, then cheering subsides.*)

Now, let's see. This time, guess how many students there are in total, at UW. How many total number of students at UW? Anybody guess?

Five thousand? (*Cheering rises again.*)

No! Too low! (*More cheering.*)

Uh-hmm. Nobody can guess?

Ten thousand? (*Cheering subsides once again, with high school students looking perplexed.*)

Well, guess what? Guess what it is. It's about thirty-five thousand. Yeah? So, students, what is two hundred out of thirty-five thousand students? Calculate the percentage. Do your math. Let's see how smart you are. How many percent is two hundred out of thirty-five thousand?

Wow, that's not even 10 percent? (*One student said loudly, but rather anxiously.*)

Yup, it's not even 1 percent! It's slightly more than about one-half of 1 percent! Do you know what that means? That's like 0.0 percent small, ya?

I don't do math. . . . (*Laughter.*)

Yeah, me too. (*More laughter.*)

So, what do you think happens to students—Pacific Islander students— who come to the UW? What do you think is their experience like?

Wow, that's hard. I can imagine that they'd be very lonely. Just by not seeing people who look like them. (*Said one student sheepishly.*)

It's a sea of so many other people right from the very first day of class! So many, many people who do not look like you. So many people everywhere, and you can't spot one who remotely looks like you! Yup, that's hard, as you can correctly imagine. When this happened to me, back when I started college somewhere else, I literally cried. It was so overwhelming!

Uh-uh. I can see that. (*Laughing, but getting more serious afterward.*)

That's why COMMUNITY is important. (*I sat down and motioned the students to move closer to me.*) Come closer! Let's huddle! We want to build community with you right now. (*Turning my head around frequently.*) Even when you're not in college yet. Especially NOW that you're not here yet. You know why? So that just in case you end up at UW, then you do not need to invent a new community all by yourself. There's already community here. There are communities of Pacific Islanders here, you know? Even though we're small, we already have them! Right here! And there are other communities you can identify with also. They've already started and built these communities long before you even thought of coming to UW. Look around you! Look! (*Me pointing at UW students.*) These are UW college students who are together as families and communities here. If or when you come on board, you will see them. And you won't need to feel sad that you don't know anyone like you. You won't need to feel as lonely or isolated. This is why we reach out to you. We don't want to know you for the first time when you come here. We want to know you now, and build bonds with you now, BEFORE you come here. Way before you come here. So that, when you arrive, you already know some people, you know some students, some staff, and you know at least one professor. That's me!

This speech was usually followed with instructions on how to contact me and how to continue interacting with the year's student leaders. We asked all of them to write down our names on sheets of paper already provided to them, including our e-mail addresses and offices. Next, we played a little bonding game, or did an exercise to help us get to know one another better. At the end of the workshop, we sat down again in a circle and drew up some sort of a "promise" statement. We promised one another, "We will try our best to come to UW." And that when they indeed come to campus later in their lives, I told them, they were required to look for us. Or to look for me, at least. I told these middle and high school kids to write these things down as part of their promise that they would have to keep right now, sealed with their and my signatures, for use later. I made them promise to go to my office (the address of which they wrote down earlier already), show me the promise statement that we just wrote together, and then use it as their ticket to lunch on campus with me, on me!

I devised this workshop as a result of many years being with very small groups of Pacific Islander students. Two students stood out in this regard, Teo and Senior, themselves students who left school during their senior year (pun unintended!). But at some point, they also expressed a strong desire to come back, and my suspicion was that the only reason why they could not and would not was that they had racked up so much debt that they owed to the UW from way back when they were still students. Their debt had accumulated through the years they had been away from campus because of nonpayment. Teo was Tongan, Senior a Sāmoan. These two represent to me a most dedicated commitment to community work while being UW students, something they managed to continue to do even after they left, even as they both worked part-time as staff members of a local high school and a community organization, respectively. They continued to participate as volunteer workshop leaders in our high school outreach programs, such as the one I described above.

It's a bit tricky to connect the dots here. If they had a high regard for community work when they got to campus, and we built community with them even before they came in, why did they leave? I knew Teo and Senior even before they set foot at UW, when we were outreaching to their high schools. In significant ways, they did represent the value and advantage of building community early on in the pipeline, not later on when students initially get admitted into our school. For, the moment they got into UW, both of them were already familiar with the campus (they had visited us so many times previously as high school students), they knew what pertinent organizations were in place and were eager to take them in, and they already knew me, an authority figure in their new school. I don't remember the exact date I treated them to lunch right when they came in to the UW as college students for the first time; but for sure, I did take them out for a meal, even many times later on, as regular college students. But I got to be tight with them right away. And other UW students did too. They remembered Teo mostly for dancing during the audience participation section of their annual Poly Day at UW's Red Square.[15] And they remembered Senior as well; he was someone whose presence even before he got admitted was quite strong. He sang with a booming voice, he knew several islander languages, and he was an expert on indigenous cultural practice. On campus, he was like a young person who was thought of as an elder. We turned to him for advice on traditional music, he taught us old and new chants, and we trusted him with devising innovative ways of performing and presenting Pacific Islander culture onstage. So, what happened to him that made him leave school? Here is Senior, explaining:

> I think my thinking of community was just so strong that I paid attention to it more than paying attention to my studies, no? In the student organizations, I was learning a lot. I was also teaching a lot. I was so engaged. Imagine, I was doing all my teaching and learning in school, but not in the classrooms! I found lots of fun and excitement in PSA [Polynesian Student Alliance] but I found schoolwork to be so boring. So uninteresting. It's hard to explain. But the more I'm away from the belly of the beast [outside of school, that is], the more it comes to me that I had expectations from the school that didn't pan out. I was kinda disappointed. And I

was, I don't know, angry, I guess? I wanted school to be more like what is connected to me, to who I am, deep inside. So, when it was not connecting anymore, I slowly, slowly drifted away. I lost energy for courses, no? I don't know. I didn't pay attention anymore. Until I felt I was not ready to go back.

What do you mean by "belly of the beast?"

Yeah, the belly of the PIG, I should say, hah (*laughing*)! It's like being at the center, the top of the mountain, and inside the oppressor, ha-ha. It's like, you know, being in the place that's like the headquarters of the people who don't like you, or want to control you. Like, being with people who don't like you, or don't care about you. Everywhere, there you see them (*pointing at a random group of people*), racists and all. Also homophobic and sexist people, too many haters! Yeah, it was not a good feeling being in there, you know. The thing that made me stay, at least for a while, was the orgs, our activities, our after-school stuff, our community, our dancing and singing together, you know? That is my definition of school. That's what was important to me. I thought our school could do better. But yeah, I drifted away. I took out loans—this is another story—and then I just did not return the next quarter. And the next one after that. And the next, and so on. Now, I'm busted, busted deep, ha-ha. Now, you know.

I felt sad about what had happened to Senior. It seemed to me that a student who was heavily involved in the life and culture of his school, at least in those aspects of school that mattered to him, would be the one who would potentially stay and flourish in it.[16] I thought more about this, having had a similar conversation with Teo during a time when students were asking me if Teo was still a student at UW or not. He was conducting a high school recruitment workshop on campus, similar to what I had been doing, and I, too, wondered at that time why he had not been around:

No, Bonus, I'm not enrolled, not registered. Sorry!

Hmm. But why? You wanna talk about this? I don't mean to pry though.

No, ha-ha.

Okay.

(*Pause.*) But I'm here because I'm a community member. Isn't that enough? Huh? Isn't that okay?

Of course, it is, Teo. It's okay. You're welcome to be here. Anytime! You're good! No one's checking. (*I felt a little awkward here.*)

I wish people would be more understanding. See them? (*Pointing at other attendees.*) They're not students like me! They're alumni! They wanna keep in touch, you know. Even if they graduated already. I'm just like them, right? I miss everybody!

I know! It's so nice to see them and to see you visit every now and then, even when they're already done. (*Still feeling awkward.*)

I mean, I wish there was this thing called community and school that's one and the same, like there's no difference. You know? (*Long pause.*) Like, I wanna be here, in school, just like I wanna be with my family or community, you know? (*Looking down for a while, then looking at the students.*) Like, look at all these students rehearsing for Poly Day! They're here, doing all sorts of things, getting busy. (*Pause.*) And yet, they don't get grades or any kind of school credit for what they do. Can you believe that? No? I wish it was something different. I wish school would do things differently. Or treat these students differently, so that students think of their school in good ways. Like, students go to school to learn about their culture. And they learn about this and that in Poly Day. That should be school for them, you know?

Yup, I see what you mean, Teo. Some of us try to think that way.

Like you! You're here. You're a professor. And you support what we do. But you're not paid to do this, huh?

Well, not really. But I don't mind.

That sucks, huh? See, I wish we change all this at some point. This is our community. This is our school. This is how we do things. We should honor all of this.

It was both easy and hard to agree with Teo. One could say that it is, indeed, time for schools to appreciate what different students bring to school— their diverse cultural backgrounds, their different and differing traditions and epistemologies, their alternative perspectives on learning and being educated. Teachers call these "funds of knowledge" that not only should be valued and appreciated in the multicultural and multidimensional classroom; they are actually what enable students to succeed.[17] On the other hand, there is also the argument that in basic or fundamental learning, there are universal standards that all students need to comply with, and even course materials that all teachers need to cover no matter what culture they come from or what backgrounds and perspectives their students have. It is the teacher's responsibility to teach students the requisite knowledge in the field, the appropriate skills in learning, and the right ways to help students grow their capacities. All of these are not culture-bound; they're simply universal and universally applicable tenets of schooling.[18] Why should we do schooling differently?

Because not all students learn, succeed, or make meaning in school only this way, as demonstrated by the likes of Teo and Senior. I want to extend Teo's points here. But there is a student who is able to explain it better than me. It is Tavita, from the previous chapters, who had now graduated, who had turned into an informal part-time informant for this ethnography, and who, during the time he talked to me about this, was attending graduate school in another state. We met for coffee and some pastries in a coffee shop not too far from UW:

It's the structures of domination, Bonus. I learn that from my social studies course in ethnic studies, ha-ha.

Huh?

Well, it's this idea . . . or practice too . . . that . . . let me see . . . the ways people do things are kinda set in stone, you know . . . that they are supposed to be universal, and, so, people think of them as THE truth. Yeah? Or, like, they appear to be so. And they . . . these truths are supposed to be disinterested, like, you know, neutral, or without culture. But actually, they are! They come from the main white culture, you know . . . or, don't we call them structures? Yeah, structures that are in place . . . like rules and procedures, yada yada . . . and they make it seem like everyone should just follow. Or [is] required to follow. Obey and just do things like it's the regular things to do. So, everyone is dominated or controlled by them. And those who do not follow them are labeled as, you know, mistaken . . . or wrong, or not civilized enough. . . .

Wow, good thinking, Tavita!

Shut up! I know you know this already. And our students know that too. Structures of domination, no?

I do! It's just that it's so easy for us to say all of these things when the real challenge is to see what's happening in the trenches, you know. Students get inundated by all sorts of pressure, especially those disadvantaged ones like Pacific Islanders. They have this, you know, enormous pressure to succeed, to have a career, to support their families, et cetera, et cetera. But they also have this . . . I don't know . . . extraordinary struggle to keep holding on to a culture of their own, in this world that's asking them to assimilate into a dominant one.

They know they cannot push back on their culture and their practices and traditions just because they're in this big school. They know there are punishments for not following the rules. So they have to deal with that. Not all students experience that. Only those like us. It's such a struggle. You know what I'm saying?

Well, in fact, the pressure is GREATER upon them to succeed as students AND as Pacific Islanders, an equation that many people assume is not at all possible, or even something that's not worthwhile doing because it doesn't make sense to them to be so exposed to what looks like a losing game for them.

That's why so many are inclined to give up. Makes the system win a lot too, you know. Too many students lose out.

Yup. That's why we have Teo, Senior, Teeny, and Sonny, and so many others.

And some more like them coming too. Hmm, so sad!

Later on, in another get-together session, I continued this conversation about conditions of college attrition with Senior, during a time when he had just come back to Washington after being away for at least a year on a teaching stint in one of the Pacific islands. He told me he was thinking of going back to school to finish it up. We also met in a coffee shop, but this time in one that was farther away from campus. He exuded much more positive energy this time, as if he was refreshed by his trip. Everybody assumed he had graduated already, since he did accept an actual teaching job, for a high school there, I thought. But he surprised me:

No, I haven't graduated yet, Bonus! I walked, yeah, but nothing official yet, ha-ha.

But why? What happened? Is there anything the matter?

I left with some classes still incomplete. I got some money to pay, and I think I still have one or two more courses.

Wow, that's it?

I know. That's it!

So what do you think happened? What's the matter?

(*Long pause.*) Well, I think things just caught up with me. I was so busy doing all these extracurriculars and all the outreach programs and all these things that I dragged behind school stuff. I left it hanging. I put school at the end of my list. I was having so much fun! And then, I think . . . I think, I forgot . . . no . . . I think I combined the two things, you know. I thought being a community person and a student were the same. Well, I wished they were, you know. Because I wanted to do both. I tried to make it work. I thought that being a student meant serving your community and doing good for your community meant being a good student. Does this make sense to you? You believe me? You get it?

I can see what you're saying, Senior. Well . . .

I just wish that people would understand that in our culture, this is all one thing . . . one ocean, you know . . . that our lives are wrapped around each other, whether we as students or as community folks, parents, teachers, family members. Doesn't matter. Or should not matter, you know? We're all one whole.

Like, not differentiating between school and community?

And between family too, Bonus. You know that, yeah?

I can sense that. (*Nodding my head.*)

I think we islanders have a way of thinking that all things are all con-nected. This one, for me, I thought about not right away though. We get to know this more when we get older, when we get to be college students. That's what happened too. Things slowly unfolded. We see the connec-tions soon enough. Like, waves have no end. Or beginning, ha-ha. That's why . . . that's why we get . . . I don't know . . . misunderstood many, many times. Like, you know, we're very close to each other like family, even though we're not related by blood, you know. Like, you know, school is something you go to and leave afterward, you know. Well, me, I never left school, ha-ha. I didn't want to leave school. In a way. When I found community in school, I always thought it was going to be forever. Like, I was not going to leave it, like, forever, you know?

Like, it's not just a temporary place to be in, yeah?

Like, it's not just merely a stepping-stone for something else, like, a temporary place that you go to and then leave afterward. No! This is what most students think about when it comes to school. But for us islanders, no, you know? We think of this differently. Ask these PI students around us. School is community, not just a place you visit and then leave. It's community and it's family forever and ever, ha-ha.

It was Senior's logic that helped me make sense of what was happening as well with other students. In a contradictory way, those of us positioned in a school setting find ways for students to discover and nurture communities—the more intimate and the more accessible to a wide variety, the better—and yet, when they do find community, we remind them that it is not as important as doing well in the classrooms. We do understand that students tend to do better in school when they are more engaged with what happens within their school grounds. This engagement makes them feel integrated into their university environment. But we also want to make them connected with off-campus environments. We try to make them connected with what happens in communities that are not simply confined to the classrooms.[19] Simultaneously, we send frequent messages to our students that community work is something they should do on the side, something that they can just add on to what they are studying, and something that cannot substitute for "real" academic work. Senior understood this; it is just that he believed that if we did not do away with the dichotomy between community and classroom, we would not understand why some Pacific Islanders like him gave up on school, or, more skeptically, why we would not be as successful in helping Pacific Islanders, and others like them, do better in school.

In some ironic way, then, it was "community" that caused Senior to stop going to school, and it was the same that made him keep in touch with it regardless of the loss of his college status. I was awed at the ways in which he showed devotion and care toward a place—his school—that seemed, in contrast, not to value him as well. "I'm just a statistic," he would remind me then, and again when I saw him more frequently later. He did find lifelong friends at UW, but even after his friends had long graduated, he would show up in some event or another either as a spectator or as a participant, whether as a guest lecturer or a workshop leader, or simply just a member of the audience who applauded and cheered the loudest. He was our biggest fan and supporter. I don't think he felt bad about doing this; I didn't think he felt too sentimental or that he was lonely about the passing of time, for example, being old and being with new kids he didn't know yet. He and Teo would have these mini reunions and just fondly hug each other, joking at some point that they would always be like this, forever returnees, but also forever members of the community. Teo always repeated to me, time and time again, "UW is family, Bonus, and family never goes away, ha-ha."

"So just come back for good and graduate, Senior," I said one time. "Just finish up from where you left off and . . . get this thing out the door, ya? Don't you want to do that?"

To which he retorted, "I like school, Bonus, don't get me wrong. I miss school very much. I miss everyone. I miss our community. So much better to be in school than where I work now. In retail. I like school. I think it is school that doesn't like me."

"WHAT'S MINE BELONGS TO, I DON'T KNOW, US?"

I have introduced you to Sonny, the student who, earlier in this chapter, talked to me about giving up on school to work full-time to help his family. Sonny and I go a long way back, and our relationship, for sure, has had its ups and downs. When he was still in college, I scolded him many times for showing up late in our mentorship meetings, or, oftentimes, not showing up at all, and for forgetting or ignoring our little "promises" to each other, as in promising to bring his journal or promising to show me his graded essays (which, I eventually found out he habitually threw away). These were things we did in PIPE in the context of our mentorship partnership. Simple stuff. We also "celebrated" small and big successes, for example, slapping each other high-fives for earning a decent grade in math or for showing up to all of his classes on time for two weeks straight. That was a rare feat for him! But there was one time I scolded Sonny for something that he and I grappled with for a while. And that was about money.

"My money is none of your business, you know," Sonny said to me, his voice soft but also confident in a rather angry way, it seemed to me. It was a surprising moment for me to hear him with an adamant voice.

"I know that," I snapped back, though reminding myself to stay calm. "But you can't be using ALL of your loans and scholarship money to feed your family. That's for your school stuff!"

Don't be trippin', Bonus. I got it.

Don't be mad at me too!

Oh, I'm not mad at you. I'm just saying that this money I get is not just mine. It's not just mine, you know?

(*Long pause.*)

Well, it's not just ALL mine, you know? There's people around me that need it. And . . . look . . . it's not just family. Heck, I buy Leo and Sione [his school friends] and . . . whoever . . . lunch or dinner when they're hungry and don't have money! And they pop me a nickel and dime or two, too, every now and then. So don't be trippin'!

Sonny was not alone in thinking this way. Many of his peers in the Pacific Islander community seldom used their scholarship money strictly for their own needs in school. They used it to help with household expenses, or to pay for a sibling's tuition or a parent's plane trip to the islands, or to contribute to a relative's funeral or wedding or to some other special occasions, which were frequent. I suspected that other students of color on scholarship did the same, and, discreetly, my reservations were confirmed in a conversation with several of them. Leo, mentioned above, a black student whose parents were Afro-Caribbean and who later graduated, explained to me:

I think it's kind of like a secret, you know, but also an open secret, ha-ha. Like, everybody knows this and everybody does this. Is it an islander thing, you think? Heck, when you're poor, you just do the best you can, you know? And in our culture, you know, you cannot just keep your money to yourself, right? You cannot be selfish. That's like a bad thing, you know. Not good. Me? I help out my family [in] any which way I can. I buy groceries for my family every now and then. And I buy the school supplies for my little brother who is in school too. I also give to my grandma because she has these medicines that nobody could afford! I helped out some homeless dude. And then, I bought dinner for, you know . . .

And then, I found out the same thing from Mork, a Khmer American student:

Wow, you don't know this? You didn't know? Why are you so surprised? (*Laughing for a while, then getting more serious.*) When you're poor, you cannot just, you know, turn your back on your family, huh? And if you've got the money, why would you not use it to feed your family? Hey, I'm a good kid. I don't turn my back on family, you know. And it's not just me, it's everybody else!

I know that. I . . . I just didn't realize it was that extensive and . . . deep . . . and frequent. And, like, a lot of kids do this? Really? I didn't know. I didn't know it's used to pay for so much more than I realized. Yeah?

Yup, it's common. You know this guy who spent it all to pay for his dad's gambling debts, ya?

Okay, don't tell me anymore! Stop!

I do understand why poor, working-class, or even middle-class students would do these things or, at least, have this attitude. If there is a need, how else could they help in addressing that need, especially if they have access to resources that will fill that need? How can anybody tell students that this scholarship money is just for a particular purpose and not for another? Here is Junior, our Sāmoan-Filipino student, concisely explaining this matter during a group conversation:

Well, it's their money once it's given to them, right? Nobody should tell them what to do with their money, yeah?

Well, it's not what Anne [the financial aid person] told you, ya?

I know. She said I can't use it for anything else other than school stuff. Like, it's illegal if I did so. But . . .

But?

But, heck, I can use it for whatever I want. It's my money. I earned it! And I don't need to tell them!

"I think it's islander culture, you know," Tavita, again, chimed in.
"So you think there's a cultural explanation for this?" I asked, being semi-sarcastic here.

Ha-ha. Well, there is and there is not. I don't know. Is it wrong to say that in islander culture, a lot of things are collectively owned? It's not like we're stealing or doing anything wrong technically. Or whatever. It's just, like, saying that individual ownership is not as highly thought of as collective ownership. So, it's like, it's sharing. Like, scholarship money; it is seen as not really owned by one. It is owned by the family, by the community, yeah? That's how we think, I think.

Well, we can say that that is cultural. But we don't want to say that that is all a function of culture, yeah?

I know. I don't want to stereotype. Or think that culture is an easy—too easy—explanation for things that we do. But it's true, you know? It's the ocean. Everything in it, and everything that you put in it, and everything you bring in it has to be shared, you know. It's how we are. It's also because many of us are also poor. So, collective work works best when you're poor. You think? Everybody's helping each other out, you know. See? And then, it works the other way around too.

How?

Like, you know, our school is a collective! So, everything in school, we all share. I think it's the same process, you know. Same logic. All school property is shared by everyone. So, whatever the school has, it's shared by everybody. Right?

Collective property, or its logic, was indeed something that many Pacific Islander students, and many others who identified with them, thought of as what explained their attitudes about money (especially about scholarship money), resources, and their school as a whole.[20] Whenever an event was planned, for example, around the visit of a scholar from out of town, and students were enjoined to help in paying for food, accommodations, and the like, they almost always thought about reaching into their own pockets as the first thing they needed to do. They just thought about this as a regular and acceptable thing to do. Or, at least, they used to think this way until I reminded them that the university had funds for these kinds of things. That caught them by surprise.

One time, in planning for food and refreshments during a campus guest's event, many students quickly offered to cook, which staff members and I told them was unnecessary and, actually, not allowed by the school (unless the students obtained official government-issued permission as food handlers). They wanted to make things more personal, and cooking the food themselves was not thought of as something strange to do in such events. For this one, students offered to serve and to clean up, or, at least, one of the older students told them to do so, which they didn't complain much about. Students felt it was just appropriate to pick up the guests arriving at the airport. They offered their apartments for accommodation, which, again, I told them was unnecessary. And they took care of all the invitations, the publicity, the works, by themselves. All in all, they never thought about getting paid for all of their labor. As if this was the best and only way to do things. During the event itself, including all the talks and presentations, food was always present, servers were always ready, and the cleanup crew (usually the youngest students), well, they needed to be reminded of their job. I remember that parents and other community members went to many of these events, including a talk I myself gave on the occasion of a book launch, which Pacific Islander students turned into what they termed as "an islander event." Similar things happened. These meant that students did understand that school events of these kinds were indeed community events. And, as they did during the many other community events that they took part in, students showed the utmost respect to the guests by keeping quiet on the sides, letting only the older students speak up during the question-and-answer sessions. "This is our culture, man," Tavita ruminated with me.

It was the "culture" that made events meaningful to students precisely because they thought of themselves as one with their school, again, understood here as a place that was coexistent with the communities and families from which they came and in which they lived. And it was the same "culture" that had enabled them to pull resources together within the same logic of "what's mine is ours" that seamlessly tied their scholarship or loan money with their family needs, but now appearing in their events most auspiciously as "what's ours is our community's." What a nice symbiosis, I thought, to have had activities that benefited both our campus communities and those communities thought of as outside of ours. I wished, however, that students were made more aware of how special all this was, all these things that they were doing, and their manners of doing them, before some of them left.

"I wish also that somebody taught me how to handle my money," Racquel, a Hawaiian-Sāmoan American student, told me. Racquel was yet another student who had not returned to school ever since she stopped registering for classes in the first quarter of her senior year. She was a campus organization leader, an outstanding student, and someone who was very active in her community. She went on:

> It was just too much! My family bills were piling up. My school bills were piling up. Too much! Sometimes, I wonder why and how this happened. But I know why. I was just too relaxed, too easy, about my money. My adviser told me . . . well, she gave me a warning that I cannot be, I don't know, she said, I cannot be misusing my money for other things. Things were getting dicey. Heck, I paid for our regalia for Poly Day. And I haven't even been paid back! I paid for food for PIPE and PIONEER, and I haven't even been paid back! And then, all these calls that I get, from collectors and all that shit. I hate them! I don't even answer the phone anymore. Hell, I won't even have my phone [service] in a couple of days now 'cause I haven't paid my bill! I don't know. Should I get another loan? I don't think I'm qualified to get one again. Oh well, what can I do? I wanna go back to school. But all these things I have to pay for, I don't

have money for them! So now, I'm not in school. And I don't have a job.
O-M-G. My mom will kill me!

All the students I knew who had quit school did so partly because of some connection to financial troubles.[21] But for them, it was not just a simple lack or scarcity of money or resources. Or it was not the only reason. It was about not knowing where to get money, not knowing how to earn it when it was possible, and not being competent enough to know what to do with it when they were able to get hold of it. Lee, another Sāmoan American student, who left school the earliest, as far as I know—in the middle of his second year—was engulfed in such a cycle of financial aid debt, of receiving money and not being able to pay it back, that he eventually could not take the situation anymore:

I don't know, B, I just don't know how to do all of these things about money. Nobody taught me! At first, I thought I was gonna quit school early because I didn't have anything. I mean, I DID NOT HAVE NOTH-ING! Period! Then, I don't know, just with good luck, I met this adviser who referred me to another guy who was some sort of a financial aid person at the OMA [or Office of Minority Affairs and Diversity], who said I should qualify for some loans or something. OR even FREE MONEY! Wow! I got so excited when I was filling out the forms. They were asking for things like my parent's tax forms. Heck, I don't know. I didn't know about FAFSA way back then.[22] I didn't know [then] about my parents having all these tax forms! I didn't know them at all! So, I called them and got hold of them. And then, yeah, suddenly all this money was in my school account, and then, wow, I was kickin' it! I was hecka splurging and freakin' buying myself all these things like new shoes, new clothes, all these things, man. I was . . . I felt good, man. And then, all of a sudden, poof! They [the monies] were all GONE! And now, I have money that I OWE. Ugh! From having no money to OWING money! Shit, how did that happen? It's the reverse now! I don't understand this!

So you think money is the only reason why you didn't go back to school anymore?

No, I won't say it's the ONLY reason, but it doesn't help that I didn't know these things about money that I should have known before. Ya? Or, that somebody should have helped me, I think. I don't wanna say that money is about everything. I don't really want to blame anybody. Or not see my part in this. Or that everything happened because of money. I don't wanna say that money solves everything. Why? You think so?

Oh no, Lee. I don't think so.

Hmm. I've been thinking about this, you know. 'Cause my mom was telling me that if she comes up with money, then that should make me continue with school, you know. But, I don't want her to do that. That's not good. I don't want her to solve this thing for me.

So what did you tell your mom?

I told her that it's not really about the money. So she shouldn't worry about it. I even said if I have the money . . . well, first of all, we already know that I'm not good with money even if I have it. Then, so, it doesn't matter. When I have money, I don't know how to deal with it anyway.

So what is it?

It's like . . . people don't understand that when we have money, it's for everyone in our family. When I get a scholarship, I think it's not just for me. (*Long pause.*) It's for my family. So, it's not good to get a scholarship, you know? Because they expect me to spend all that for my own self, that's it. They have all these rules. Better to work outside, you know. Because when I get money that way, then I decide how to spend it. With scholarship, you know, there are all these rules and shit.

Oh, I get what you mean, Lee.

A similar story applied to Kani, a student from Fiji who grew up mostly in Washington, but he left school for one quarter during his second year. Kani returned on his third year and then left again at the end of that year. We talked about money too:

Yeah, um, let me see. Money? I don't think it's all about money. But I think it's about things that have to do about money, the way white people see it. With islanders, I don't know, I think it has to do with obligations, you know. It's obligations that can be connected with money. And other stuff that may be not connected with money. It's . . . anyways, really, the bottom line is, I think it's about not understanding our culture. And teachers . . . our school . . . they don't understand our obligations. They don't get it. Teachers don't get it. They expect us to make school our number one priority. Like, when there's a decision between buying a book or helping out in a funeral. Are they kidding me? Don't they understand? Who do you think are we gonna choose? I gotta help my family first, you know. School is second. Am I gonna spend scholarship money on family stuff? If I don't, then I'm a bad islander, you know. If I do, then I'm a bad student. You know what I'm sayin'?

Hmm. Funny, that's how we get into trouble with school, huh? That's when we think school money is family or community money, right?

Hah, I think I know what you're saying! Ha-ha. All these monies that are gone now, huh?

Have you heard? [I was referring to several incidents in which organizational funds somehow disappeared, something I was hesitant to write about in detail here. So I chose not to.]

Well, duh! I think they're being stupid.

What do you mean?

I think it's one thing to say that our money in our culture is collective money, you know. But it's another thing to run away with the students' monies and say that's collective money too, you know. They're using culture to explain their stealing? That's hella stupid. And rude. Stupid shits. They should be arrested, or something, you know?

I guess it's been a running joke for those who have been at UW for half as long as I have that organizational money doesn't stay as organizational money long enough. It disappears! I've only heard stories about such incidents, and since I tried not to get involved with students' financial practices in their organizations, I was not in a position to say for sure if or when they happened or how often they did. I wanted more than an arm's length away from them.

"Ha-ha, you say that 'cause you don't wanna get in trouble, huh?" Ili teased me when I asked him about these incidents of money being stolen. Ili was a Chamorro-Filipino American student whom I had known ever since he was a young student at UW. He had since moved on to graduate school in social work and beyond.

Yeah. I don't want to paint a bad picture of students here.

Well, I think these are very bad students, you're right! It's okay. There are good students and there are bad students too. Don't worry about them. There's bad seeds everywhere. At the same time, I think it's also good to say that, for islanders, we always value the practice of collective work and collective resources. We value this practice about sharing what we have with our family, with our community. But these students, they're doing the opposite! [It's] such a shame, I know. They're doing the opposite of what we value as community and collective sharing. So they give us a bad reputation, you know? Because when they steal, they take from the collective and use the money just for themselves. And that's not being islander. That's not who we are, or who we are supposed to be. That's not how we were raised. They stole. And that is not acceptable. It's not like they're stealing so that the community will partake in what they steal? Not even!

No. I think they're taking money for themselves.

Not that it's okay now to steal if it's for others. I'm not saying that. What I'm saying is that it's wrong to steal, period. But what makes it really bad for us is that these students stole money to benefit themselves! I've seen how they did it! We've seen all these receipts and records showing they paid for a bar tab, or for purchasing alcohol, or for paying a hotel room or something. And then they run away. Never returned our calls! That's not good. That's not islander at all. It gives us a bad name! That's stealing and that's really bad! And it's not good to have people like that in our community, no?

So how do you guys deal with this? How does the community deal with something like this?

Oh, I don't know, we shame them? We don't really do that, because that hurts them, and we don't want that. No bad thing can be repaired by another bad thing. That's what I believe [in]. [Doing] that ultimately hurts all of us, all in the community, when we punish somebody or just focus on the individual act of somebody. What we do is, well, we try to still stick together. We band together to solve this issue collectively. We try contacting the person. We try to reach out to [them]. We look for [them]. Ask [them] what happened? But, really, we don't focus on only that. We look for other resources, other ways of regaining back our money. We try to rebuild our community; we strengthen it, and we use this to teach us and to make our future officers learn from this; what to not do or what to avoid, or what to watch [out] for. Yeah, we don't make things like this destroy us. That would be so . . . so not productive and so negative. We try to keep it together.

Wow, that's something really special.

Kani, the Fijian student, also agreed with me. He was also amazed at how the PSA and other islander students' organizations were able to stick together and persist, despite experiencing such kinds of losses and hardships over the years. What seemed to be key here was a proactive nurturing of an ethos of community whose practice depended on diligent collective work, regardless of whether it manifested as attitude, presence, or commitment. "I swear I'm the last person who will always be depended on to be there to help," Kani once confirmed:

> . . . but I try to go and be present, at least! I know, I know. I cannot be depended on. Why? Ha-ha. Because I'm not dependable, ha-ha. I get carried away, and I just disappear to go somewhere else, you know. That's just me. That's . . . the way I am. But when you said community for us islanders? That hit it on the spot! It's like saying we're in this together. All of us! That's true! That's so fuckin' true. Like, it makes you feel good. And it makes you feel safe. This really becomes truer and truer every day. To have this family around you. In school, of all places! You don't have to be afraid. That's why we all try to make it work. That's why we try to share and do stuff together, right? This is what teachers don't understand. I can see [why]. School people don't really get this. Hey, I have issues, but when it comes down to it, with[in] myself, I know islanders will come to my rescue. I know they'll have my back. And I have theirs too, you know, any way I can. That's something I'm proud to say. And this is the one thing in school that I miss a lot.

So when are you coming back, Kani?

Ha-ha, don't pull a fast one on me, Bonus! Ha-ha-ha. I don't know. I don't know. Not yet, for now. You'll wake up someday and then, I'm thinking . . . huh, watch out, you're gonna see me back in school again! Kani, your boy, back in school! Imagine that?

"WHAT'S THE POINT OF GOING TO SCHOOL? I CAN'T FIND MEANING IN SCHOOL. I CAN'T SUCCEED UNLESS SCHOOL IS MADE MEANINGFUL TO ME."

The phenomenon of school failure that was specific to the voluntary departure of students from the university they were attending—in the cases of students mentioned in this chapter—was complex and much more nuanced than simply being attributed to students' academic underperformance or breakdown, an absence of motivation, or a lack of resources. These students were adamant in attempting to convince me and their school that they were not intellectual failures, that they possessed more than an adequate will to succeed, and that it was not their fault that resources, whenever such were made available to them, were meant to cover less than what they needed to spend for school-related needs. They also thought they were sufficiently integrated into their university: they were proactively engaged, active, and enthusiastic about their college life. If they thought of themselves as failures, as others surely did, there was indeed an acknowledgment that they were personally partly responsible for what had happened to them. But at the same time, they imagined that their individual culpability should be reckoned with in the larger contexts of the structural constraints, demands, and assumptions under which they existed as university students. They had limited access to resources, they were faced with pressures to succeed in an environment that was indifferent toward them (or did not pay much attention to them), and they were not taught the skills and strategies to navigate through a system that was large, complex, and alien to them. Were they simply looking for a justification for their actions? I did not think so. What became clear to me, as I got to know them more deeply, was that they were expressing a structural critique of schooling practices and expectations that stood against their community's ethos of schooling as discovery, as collective work, and as shared resource.

All of these students had very little inclination to pursue a definite career path the moment they entered college, and they did know for sure what they wanted to become even up to their senior year. But that did not deter them from getting excited to find out what lay out there for them to discover as they were proceeding into and all throughout their college experience. They wanted to explore what was out there, so to speak, and, more than anything else, they did not want to get pinned down into a specific major or degree all throughout their college life. They opened their hearts and minds to transformation, or to its exciting possibilities, as they were moving along the college timeline. They leaned more toward imagining and expecting college-level schooling as the pursuit of a particular kind of humanism that was *classic* to the degree that it was anchored to what looked like a traditional Western notion of an "enlightened" education.[23] But this kind of schooling, students felt, was increasingly fading at the time they were attending school, in favor of neoliberal schooling that focused more on the profit potentials of certain careers and the dollar equivalences of completing college courses. They saw this focus in the ways everyone else rabidly competed to get into the most valued major, attain the highest grades, and graduate with more than one degree. They wished their school were free from the constraints of a straightforward capital economy and more open to the possibilities of doing things without worrying about money.[24] Such was a way of thinking that was most commonly desired, pursued, and appreciated by these students who gave up. And it was also this attitude about schooling that they who left school had missed the most.

Community was expected to last forever, and if that community was located in school, it was therefore logical for them to think of school as a permanent place as well, a place to go back to over and over again, as alumni among them had been wont to do. They did not want to forever leave school, or categorically leave the idea of school as a community for them once they graduated from or temporarily left it. Back when they were in it, they desired their school to function like their community, and vice versa, so much so that competing expectations from both ends—between campus life and off-campus life—frequently became intolerable as these drove them to make a choice in a zero-sum calculation. Indeed, when many of them eventually graduated from or stopped attending college, the process of weaning themselves out of this campus community that they so lovingly nurtured and sustained took longer and harder than any one of them expected.

It was mysterious, or rather baffling, to these students that school and the community environs had to be thought of as separate spaces with distinct rules and practices that did not overlap or, at least, have some kind of connection with each other. No wonder, then, that some students who thought this way ended up making the tough decision to pick one over the other. They expected their school to be more organically connected to their communities outside of it, so they were perplexed about these boundaries that had to be imposed, the anxieties that their teachers and classmates expressed regarding these connections, and the seemingly peculiar absence of their culture and their people's histories in their college curricula. In effect, these students did not think of themselves as any different from the rest of those who desired meaningfulness and connection in their education. It is just that the rest made them think they were strange, ignorant, and out of place.

A few of these students who left tried to sever their ties, understandably, from the university community. They faded away from this once significant social field, and they rarely maintained communication with their former schoolmates after leaving. "Everybody thinks that I've wasted my life," Racquel, the Hawaiian-Sāmoan student, once told me. "They think I wasted my time at UW (*crying*), like I wasted my parents' money. And that now that I've gone out of school, they think my life is now such a waste." Days after not showing up during the first few weeks of one school quarter, Racquel knew it was coming. She was going to be a social outcast. No wonder she did not set foot on campus for months on end. But take a look at this letter she wrote to me later:

May 20

Dear Bonus: How are you? You miss me? Just kidding. I just want to say hello and tell you that I'm doing well. I still have money problems going . . . but I'm slowly trying to make things work. I try not to be too negative nelly because I know that's not good. . . . I want to visit you sometime. I want to see everyone before it's too late! Everybody's graduating, right? As for me, I hope I can come back again. And I know [that] the sooner [I do it], the better. But I'm afraid that if I do come back, it's going to be the same. Many times, I ask myself what's the point of going to school? I can't find meaning in it. We talked about this already, right? I can't succeed unless school is made meaningful to me. So, my hope is that by the time I come back, there will be more PI classes to take and that the ones who teach them are qualified, LOL. I also pray that the racists are gone, and those who expect me to be a good girl or a good student, as our teachers would always expect me to be, are more careful not to just throw me under the bus. We should also tell people not to stereotype us islander women . . . we're strong and proud and beautiful! We're not just hula dancers and good cooks. We're warriors! Okay, that's saying too much now. But really, I hope to see you again and when I do, I will give you big hugs and kisses fo sho!

Racquel, indeed, visited us on campus about a month after she e-mailed me this letter. We had an event, actually a protest rally, to argue for a separate Pacific Islander room in the proposed renovation of the Ethnic Cultural Center, where she watched us from the side and then eventually joined us in a forum with school officials. But she chose not to say or do anything. I observed her from a distance and noticed how seemingly at peace she was with her situation. When students like Racquel leave, I thought, we who stay get reminded of the powers and consequences of defiance. In their critique of our schools' attempts to regulate them as proper students who are required to behave well in classrooms, finish the exact amount of required credits on time, and spend their scholarship money only on the strictest terms specified by disbursement regulations, they make us, or at least they make me, wonder at the *constructed* nature of student formation and the narrowly scripted expectations of student obedience. What does it mean to be a good student? What discursive practices, rules, and expectations are deployed to delineate, regularize, and normalize a particular version of a student subject?[25] Who is able to fit this mold? In this instance, Sonny, Teeny, Marie, Daniel, Teo, Senior, Lee, Racquel, and Kani may well provide us with a collective profile of the limits of a universal version or vision of a college student whose formal educational path—the one path paved with curricular requirements, uniform pedagogical practices, and narrow academic expectations—can be singularly deterministic as well as restrictive.

If a student is not able to fit into being what we "regularly" define as a student, what alternatives can we provide? When a student says, "Nobody really understands who we are, what we are" and "whenever our culture is mentioned, it is labeled as 'extracurricular activity'—something outside of what school is," what answer can we and do we provide? Even if my preferred answer is institutional change, as we have done piecemeal on our campus, I am awed at what students—the very people who were at odds with their school's expectations—have been able to do. They proactively wrestled with their fates, determined, though not always successfully, to make their own schooling experience simply meaningful to themselves and their communities by defying curricular timeline protocols, insisting on learning about and researching their cultures and histories on their own, integrating their knowledges into their class projects and essays, paving ways and rooms for collective uplift in spaces that were not there before, and speaking and acting up whenever and wherever they can. I wrote back to Racquel, saying her life was not and has not been wasted, as she swore earlier. In fact, I mentioned, "Your defiance has enriched and transformed the lives of Pacific Islander students and others who have stayed and come after you. Please come back soon!"

4

SCHOOLING OUTSIDE *and* INSIDE

I never ditch class, Bonus! I'm always in school. Always! I never miss practice [for the group's cultural performance]. Ha-ha, yeah? I'm the one who's never late. And I always clean up after these assholes, ha-ha-ha. I'm the last to leave. I should get an A! At the very least! I'm at the top of my game in this one, you see.

. . .

More and more, I think we [the people in the Philippines and the U.S. students in the study abroad program] are so connected. The ocean really connects us, like we're living the same lives, same history and all that. I'm kinda not surprised though, but it's good to experience it firsthand for reals. I wanna do this again! This should be required!

. . .

All of us like this class! It's the first time ever . . . the first time ever that I've been in a class where everyone . . . really, everyone is reading, everyone is paying attention, everyone is involved, you know? It's nice to see it. And I'm proud to be in it. I always get excited with this class. Oh, damn (tearing up), I know, I know . . . I'm gonna miss it when it's all over. I'm gonna cry when it's all done. I'm cryin' already!

. . .

Wha? You kidding me? I didn't know that there were these classes! On Pacific Islanders? Nobody told me, damn it!

. . .

Many teachers and scholars of education have already thought deeply about the positive and productive effects of what are usually called "high-impact educational practices" on college student retention, graduation potential, campus engagement, and overall learning.[1] These practices include programs and activities such as first-year seminars; common intellectual experiences (for example, the ones offered by honors programs, or classes organized around alternative knowledges and pedagogies, as well as multiple learning environments); community service programs (often called service-learning); global learning or study abroad opportunities; and collective learning communities, to which may belong mentorship programs similar to those I wrote about in chapter 2. These programs have, indeed, had an impact insofar as I have seen them in action, and as the first three quotations above, cited from my student interviews and journals, tell us, most emphatically. The first one, shared by Paul, a mixed Hawaiian junior, was an attempt to play smart-alecky with me, because I called him out on his school absences one time. Or so I thought at first. But he did make sense to me quite abruptly after he uttered his semi-serious jokes about truancy out loud; those "classes" that he claimed he never missed were the dance practices his student group organized (including the cleanup at the end of such practices), which he suggested were far more important—and meaningful—to his life as a student. The second quotation, from Junior, our mixed Sāmoan and Filipino American student who was a junior student at that time, is taken from a study abroad class I conducted in the Philippines, where a good number of students, Pacific Islander and others, felt a distinct connection with the country and its people, especially in terms of common histories, values, and struggles. We frequently reflected on our study abroad experiences on-site, through journaling and group conversations, and this excerpt is from one of those talks. As I look back on my records of them, it was certainly illuminating for me and the students to see how learning that was facilitated by and productive of "experienced" connections was made to occur in spaces outside of the regular classrooms.

The third passage is from Deana, also a Sāmoan American student, a sophomore, who attended what was then the first-ever U.S. Pacific Islander History and Culture class on campus, which not only was taught by a Pacific Islander scholar but was pointedly designed to facilitate a "common intellectual experience" by way of pedagogical practices that were collaborative as well as organically driven with respect to indigenous islander ways of learning. In my observations of this class, oftentimes called "the ocean" by its teacher and participants, I found the students to be truly engaged and invested; it was indeed a high-impact educational experience for them, as they noted in their conversations with me. Courses such as this strongly demonstrate the remarkable excitement and overall power of alternative learning techniques and environments. And many scholars have definitively touted their benefits, as such experiences "highly correlate to the most powerful learning outcomes," and "students' participation in one or more of these practices [has] had the greatest impact on success, on retention, on graduation, on transfer, and on other measures of learning."[2] According to George Kuh, in his book *High-Impact Educational Practices: What They Are, Who Has Access to Them, and Why They Matter*, these types of courses "have been widely known to be beneficial for college students from many backgrounds."[3]

I am not suggesting here that only so-called high-impact educational practices such as study abroad, experience-based curricula, and mentorship programs are the only ones that should matter in enabling students to succeed in their college schooling. But even though I will not shy away from making a strong case in advocating for them, I would rather emphasize more what many students have otherwise told me time and time again. And that is, it is not about imagining these programs as courses that college students can simply check on a list of things they have to do in the course of their lives as students. It is not about courses that apply a strict formula in their curricula or students automatically picking courses with a particular label as they anticipate a set of predetermined recipes that might guarantee their success. Instead, it is about valuing and highlighting these courses and programs that were central to students' lives rather than peripheral or extracurricular to their course of study in the university.[4] It is about constituting these courses within and outside of campus as organically, constitutively, and holistically linked to the students' overall educational experiences. And it is about purposefully designing these programs in ways that recognize and engage with the students' particular histories and contemporary conditions. In other words, the claim that is being made here is that if these types of classes are labeled as "high impact," then why not offer college classes in these modes? Why not make all classes meaningfully historical and relevant to the lives of the students who are in them? How can students be active participants of their own learning, how can they experience and value collaborative meaning-making in the classroom and outside of it, and how can schooling in general be relevant to each of them?

The nuanced answers to these questions form the bulk of this chapter. But the spirit behind them is not to offer universal blueprints for college success, akin to "lessons learned" from experimenting with course plans for underrepresented students and others, and in view of developing high-impact courses for all students. The students in this study did not plot these programs together with me for such reasons, nor did they initially intend to develop templates for meaningful schooling that would somehow end up in some unknown teachers' bag of generic tricks. They were not looking toward having these programs be applied across the board. Students engaged in these selected programs, and enrolled in a particular course, without expecting that they would change how they viewed their schooling experience, how they would end up finding meaning in the process, and how their life would be positively altered altogether by the time school ended. They discovered these sites of learning by themselves and upon the prodding of their friends, and they organically acted in co-constructing their activities (with the help and support of their teachers and mentors, of course), responding to the conditions that they faced, the limitations they wanted to overcome, and the possibilities that they imagined. The advocacies that students eventually pushed forward—transformative meaning-making in a "cultural event," an outreach/recruitment project, a study abroad program, and an "islander"-inspired course—were both serendipitous and thought out in progression. But such advocacies were fueled fundamentally by a great deal of struggle regarding finding meaning in what they were doing in school, looking for alternatives to being and becoming "successful" students, and searching for as well as recognizing their and their community's value in multiple educational settings. These are their stories, expressed through conversations, letters, and journal entries shared with me, of being in and experiencing their university, both inside and outside of its classrooms.

POLY DAY

It is 8 in the morning and I'm so relieved and happy that the sun is shining. Yes! Last year, it was raining a bit at this time and, what a bummer, everything was just gray and gloomy. What a bummer! And then, of course, there's that other year when it was so blazing hot the dancers' feet were literally burning [as they were dancing onstage]. That was painful— I'm sure—for all of them! I hope it doesn't turn out that way today. It's just 8 in the morning, so who knows? I better get to the ECC [the Ethnic Cultural Center] to meet the kids.

. . .

I wrote this partial journey entry on the day we marked on campus as Poly Day. Poly Day, short for what is implicitly regarded as Polynesia Day or Polynesian Heritage Day, was an almost daylong set of events usually held in April and led by members of the Polynesian Student Alliance (PSA) that celebrated Polynesian history and culture for an audience that included both the on-campus student body and college student recruits from nearby high schools. Poly Day was mostly student-led and student-organized, as well as student-participated, so much so that many students, islander or not, supported it by coming in droves to Red Square, a large open-air gathering space on the UW campus. Like a well-intentioned and group-empowering gesture, Poly Day's highlight was its hour-and-a-half-long show or cultural program held on an uncovered stage, around noontime, that presented songs, dances, and tidbits of historical information about Polynesian culture. These were what the public saw: usually Hawaiian, Tahitian, Māori, Fijian, Tongan, and Sāmoan dances (in other years, performances from less well-known places such as Tokelau and Tuvalu had also been included; occasionally, a Filipino dance number or two were also incorporated into the lineup); some opening chants or songs; the well-regarded haka (traditional ancestral war cry or chant); and the much-awaited Sāmoan finale dance performance called Taualuga, featuring the year's *taupou* (a performer who traditionally represented the daughter or son of a high chief, in Sāmoan culture). Interspersed throughout the program were some historical and descriptive notes regarding the performances as narrated by the student emcees, some audience-participated games with small prize tokens, yells and whistling from both sides of the stage, and the throwing of money into the air, onto the floor, or onto the bodies of the performers, in recognition of their skill and presence onstage. On many levels, Poly Day was, and has been, a joyous and high-energy event.[5]

Dancers slapped hands on chest and thighs while chanting:

Kia whakaronga, kia mau!	Listen up now! Take your stance!
Ringaringa e torona	Arms outstretched
Kei waho hoki mai!	Out and back!
Taka takahia! Hi!	Get ready to move!
Taka takahia! Hi!	Get ready to move!
Taka takahia! Hi!	Get ready to move!
Torona titaha!	Slap your knees!
Kss! Kss! Kss! Kss!	
Aue tika tonu!	What is right is always right!
U-e!	In-deed!
Aue tika tonu!	What is right is always right!
U-e!	Ah—yes!
Ka mate, ka mate	I may die, I may die
Ka ora, ka ora	I may live, I may live

Ka mate, ka mate	I may die, I may die
Ka ora, ka ora	I may live, I may live
Tenei te tangata puhuruhuru	This is the hairy man
Nana i tiki mai whakawhiti te ra	Who brought the sun to shine again
A upane, ka upane	Step up, another step up
A upane, ka upane	Step up, another step up
Whiti te ra, hi!	The sun shines! Rise!

(Excerpts from Māori traditional ancestral war cry attributed to Waimarama Puhara, a tribal chief, and, for the last verse, Te Rauparaha, also a chief and war leader of the Ngati Toa tribe; courtesy of Malaelupe Samifua; performed by UW students.)

Occasionally, there was impromptu dancing from a few members of the audience; that's why there was always a wide empty space allotted in front of the stage, just in case people wanted to "contribute" their own share of the performances going on or simply get into the spirit of the dances. I knew at least five high school students who stood out doing spur-of-the-moment dancing in several Poly Days, and later on they became college students themselves at UW. They actually ended up as students I got to mentor and who became student leaders later on as well. And then, at the very end—and this had been happening for about seven years already—when the emcees had said their thank-yous and good-byes, everybody was enjoined to dance altogether the "electric slide." Yes, a country-western-inspired line dance to top off a Pacific Islander event! This was not a big surprise to everyone, I think, since this line dance had been de rigueur in most Pacific Islander and Filipino family or community parties. At the program's closing, just at the moment when the cleanup crew was about to commence its takedown of the stage and sound equipment, a group photo was usually taken, marking the collective work and collective success of Poly Day. I myself took pictures with the students. I also mingled with the parents, community folks, and the rest of the audience all too often. Students usually had this totally exhausted look on their faces by the time we were done. They didn't want to think of anything else but to just lay down somewhere and possibly have a drink or two. They had worked very hard for this *one day* of the year when their culture was showcased in such a public space right on their own campus, scripted and performed by no one else but themselves, and witnessed admirably by hundreds. Later, I wrote in my journal:

OMG, I'm so glad it's over! Kids were not in sync sometimes, but the dances were actually good, I think, considering that they were not able to practice a lot. And some of them, without any practice at all! Ha-ha. Spent some time staffing the booth to sell the shirts with Deana [a Sāmoan American student leader, junior]. I'm not gonna complain about this. Hey, we raised about $200 easy. That'll be good for the students. But I wanna think more about what Deana told me as we were watching the show. She says it's funny that we keep on saying that we hate stereo-types and we don't like it when people see islanders only as people danc-ing the hula or whatever, or as football players. And then, in the show, we just saw football players dancing the hula. Hah! That's ironic indeed. I smiled back at her and told her something in response to her comment, like what she said was just a remarkable thing to express. So I asked her what she thought about what she said. To which she replied, "I don't know. We want to honor our cultures and we want to do this in public. It's kinda risking it, you know? But what can we do? Better than not doing anything." Or, for me, better than doing it badly. So, yeah, these students do take the risk of . . . well . . . reinforcing some stereotypes!

What the audience did not see were the two tents at the back of the stage, both covered on all sides, one for women and the other for men, used for chang-ing costumes and for safekeeping their backpacks and other possessions. Stu-dent leaders and family members walked around these tents, guarding them against looters or any other kind of troublemakers. There had been incidents of theft before, and there were other times when some creepy person or two would gawk at performers changing for the next set. So, student organizers became more vigilant over the years. I would assume that the audience also did not see the roving security patrols wandering about and checking for any "suspicious activity," just to use a police parlance here. Some volunteers did wear T-shirts marked "SECURITY" boldly in the back, but I doubted if anyone really paid attention to them. Perhaps they did, but only when real security in-cidents happened, as they did every now and then. High school kids from rival gangs mean-mugged each other several times, brandishing weapons of some sort, or actually starting fights—these occurrences had dented a bit the spirit of the day's activities these few times before, but they had always been swiftly quelled. Some of the UW students would be very upset and scream at them and everyone, thinking that episodes like this reinforced nasty assumptions or stereotypes of Pacific Islanders as violence-prone people. These student leaders would bust out yelling at these troublemakers, chasing them away, out of the campus. But the rest just brushed them off. Many high school kids, they said, always did silly and shallow things; we shouldn't even bother with their antics.

It was the high school kids, however, who were always at the *center* of Poly Day. Supposedly. Those who were not familiar with the inner workings of Poly Day most probably did not notice this, but the biggest reason why this event was put up, and why this event still mattered into the present especially for those students who put them up, was to recruit high school students into college. Early on, the inaugural organizers of Poly Day thought, what better way to entice students to go to college (or consider applying to and entering this particular university) than to send them a message—through a celebration of culture—that they could *indeed* be college students and that they could practice their own culture while in college?[6] Many people usually forgot this, or did not notice this when they attended, but the stage performance, although it was always the centerpiece of Poly Day, was but only a segment of the day-long set of activities whose parts were all systematically designed technically and purposefully for outreach and recruitment. Indeed, many students often-times lamented the heavy focus given by most members of the audience on the "entertainment" they saw onstage.

High school kids from many parts of the state, varying in numbers every year from about two hundred to as many as five hundred to six hundred, were bused into the campus as early as 8:30 AM. They began with getting to know one another in an introductory caucus, moved into several small workshops, toured parts of the campus when time permitted, ate lunch together, and then finally attended the stage performance in the afternoon. Morning work-shops ranged from lessons in Pacific Islander history and culture to strategies for applying to college. I helped out in some of these workshops, but most of them were intentionally student-led so that bonds between younger high school and older college students could be initiated and hopefully sustained. Some alumni, community members, and Pacific Islander college students from other local campuses also participated or were consulted from time to time. This question of why culture was showcased, along with why it was important and what needed to be done, was intimately and tightly woven into the UW students' desire to bring the high school Pacific Islander youth into their fold by enabling the possibility of their thinking of college, at the very least, as a potential option once high school was over.[7] That was why it was imperative that these college student recruitment organizers express to their high school visitors that the possibility of going to and being in college was real. They did not need to be just islanders or mere college students; they could be *Pacific Islander college students*, not one or the other. They could be Pacific Islander college students who felt proud of their culture and were actually proudly practicing their culture on a college campus, as opposed to students who had to leave their culture at home, so to speak. This was their line. This was what I was always reminded of every time I attended, helped organize, or participated in Poly Day, ever since I remember doing so way back in 2002.[8]

Today, we had a debriefing session on last week's Poly Day, and I did bring up the situation regarding rowdy and rude high school students during the two workshops I conducted. I get upset too quickly when the [high school] students either don't pay attention or refuse to participate. And I told them I was glad that Apala [a Sāmoan American student leader, transfer student, senior] was there to yell at the kids. I was losing my voice anyway. But Apala was also quick to remind me that high school kids will just be high school kids. Some of them will just misbehave no matter what. And that, still, a good majority of them, she said, will not realize the important lessons during the moment of them doing this. They're just too young and involved in other things, she said. They will realize our lessons we give them: of the importance of culture, of the critical importance of education, and the importance of knowledge as power at a time later, after this workshop is way over. I want to think more about this. I think this is important. Apala's right, I guess. She said she herself didn't know about all of these things when she was in their shoes, until later on when she stepped into college, when many things [eventually] made sense to her. The same thing will happen to these kids, I hope.

(Later)

What Apala told me earlier, about working with rowdy high school kids, I thought, makes sense to me as I now think about the risk that Deana was saying [about stereotypes]. Sure, we take risks in displaying our culture. [This is] much the same as taking risks when bringing the high school kids to our campus, giving them a short workshop on the connections between culture knowledge, and power, and then expecting them all to get everything right just like that. . . . That's a tall order! Such high expectations we have. I think it's enough that we do all of these things, plan them carefully, and do them with good thinking, and then have the [high school] kids take all of these back home, [at] their own pace, without us feeling so bad if they didn't get it for the first time, or if they don't get it all right now, or seemed to be not aware that they were getting it. Yeah, this is a good risk to take after all.

Poly Day was an event centered on the objective of recruiting high school students, but its strategy centered "culture" as the main subject of its recruitment. And because "culture," or at least, its importance, needed to be legible in particular ways for the high school students, UW students made a calculated choice to put forward a representation of what they considered as islander cultures appropriate to their objectives. Of course, this was never a clean and stable process of selection. What should be the "right" Pacific Islander culture to stage? What should this culture look like? What impressions about their culture should we or do we leave with the students? Poly Day organizers and performers regularly had heated debates about the choice of the dances; the order of the dances (which group should come first, why are Sāmoans always the last to perform, why should they always be the finale, and are they the only ones who are important?); the logic of the dances themselves (why always the sexy dances, why dance the dances with overly masculine aggressive moves, and why do women need to show those very feminine dances all the time?); and the variations on the dance steps and routines (why do the dance in the traditional way, who said this was the tradition, why can't we change tradition, and why can't we improvise?). It was an informal memory among the various groups that Sāmoans always took the lead on many aspects of Poly Day (including Poly Day as a whole and the PSA in specific), so others called them out on their apparent dominance. I had heard others refer to this as the Sāmoan hegemony within Polynesia. What about the Hawaiians? Why were they usually not visible? Or prominent? Or, at least, why should they not be as equally important as the others?

> This issue about Hawaiians being sidetracked has some history to it, I heard from Tavita. He showed me this video they made, called *Forward: A Story about Pacific Islanders.*[9] And it does explain some controversy about some islanders joining the Hawai'i Club [Hui Hoaloha 'Ulana] way back when [around 1999–2000] and then getting disappointed at the lack of indigenous representation there, or otherwise being shocked at the large presence of nonindigenous but "local" Hawai'i-based students in the organization. Lani [a Sāmoan-Hawaiian student, junior] talked to me about these issues yesterday and she said it was right about the time I was getting hired. She wrote a letter to the *Daily* [the campus student newspaper] complaining about the lack of Pacific Islander presence not just in the Hawaiian organization, but on the campus as a whole, and the disrespectful ways in which students performed Pacific Islander culture during events like the club's luau. And then, other students answered

back and many of them castigated her for hating on the [Hui] club and what they do. Sounds like a local version of identity politics being played out here. Indigenous or native students versus settler or immigrant students? No wonder the Hui don't [*sic*] participate [in Poly Day] as much. They just come in to dance a segment or two, and then they leave right away. They don't stay. They don't even socialize with others, or participate in running the workshops. Or even help a bit in planning and organizing. And then, there are times when they're not even around at all! I wonder how this will all pan out later.

Poly Day student organizers, over the years, did try their best to be inclusive, despite and because of this unfortunate history with the Hawaiian students (or, specifically, those who were members of the club), but their open-mindedness here and elsewhere in, say, allowing a little bit of modification in dance steps had also been met with mixed reviews. There was talk among elders in the community who expressed dissatisfaction and dismay upon seeing certain indigenous dances changed or infused with Western elements such as hip-hop and country, or when conventional male and female roles and expectations were reversed or disobeyed. Or when Hawaiian dances were missing. Some of them would be heard to occasionally claim that many of the dance steps that were performed were wrong, or were done improperly. I was not able to verify these by talking to the elders directly, but for sure, there would always be members of any community who would be against any kind of change or variation from the norm, I thought. Students, however, oftentimes seemed to revel at their capacity to mix old and new while keeping vigilant about the public nature of their performances, the presence of elders in the audience (who expected a certain kind of "authenticity" in their choreography), and their desire to entertain, please, respect, and educate all the members of their audience about the cultures they were proud to display, in the ways they chose to construct and represent them. "There's no way we can expect everyone to dance in very authentic ways and to make sure every step is legit," said Apala in a Poly Day planning meeting. "But we should try to be true to our culture, our dances, at least."

Every "cultural" performance breaks from tradition in varying degrees, and "tradition" is itself a construction of the past that can never be clean, exact, or pure.[10] Choreographers involved in Poly Day, whether they were students, professional volunteer teachers, or community members, taught students what they knew, and whatever they knew was surely sourced from different sites of prior instruction, expertise, archival material, memory, creativity, and imagination.

It is not this narrative's mission to dissect the intricate ways in which Poly Day performances were invented and reinvented—and what they all deeply meant—but as for the students who participated in the performances, they tried what they could and they also opted not to be overly consumed by questions of cultural tradition, invention, and change. They thought that questioning and considering so many things would have been quite immobilizing. "We just try to sing and dance the best way we can," I overheard one student say one time. "We trust our teachers, so the important thing is to just perform well. Respect and represent, and appreciate, and value, you know."

Indeed, to represent culture with respect and with pride as well was always a top goal of many students during Poly Day. And to be among those chosen to represent—dancers numbered fewer than thirty, most years—was something to brag about. They were going to be onstage, and they would be the ones who were going to be applauded. Their parents, family members, and other important members of the community would be there during the event, so they wanted to shine and be noticed. And to do their job well. They wanted their community to be proud of them, and they wanted the high school students to be impressed by their bodies and their moves. Oftentimes, there would be stiff angling for spots in the front of the stage, especially in a dance number that would have more than twenty dancers in it. "You can't be seen if you're dancing in the back, of course," a female dancer/teacher insisted to me several times. "So, everyone, just everyone, wants to be in the front. And if you're in the back, you try to move a little bit up front, you elbow others up while others elbow you out too, so that they move a little bit away from you, or you tippy-toe so that you stand out against those in front of you. Everybody wants to be noticed during Poly Day! Everybody wants to be the star!"

In my journal, I wrote:

I'm a little bit weirded out by the over-focus on the body during Poly Day, and I wonder how the kids feel about this. On one hand, they're proud to show themselves and all their talent and grace and looks and all that. But on the other, isn't [doing] this feeding into the stereotype too? Like, are the kids helping in portraying island culture as just only about the body? I don't think they'd say they're doing this, though. But it's something to think about. It's part of the risk they take.

From another Poly Day event, I asked:

Queerness on stage? This Poly Day is the first time I saw a queer [islander] student dancing with the boys. Wow, that was fantastic; I was so proud of Jan [a Filipino/a American, sophomore]. Not one of the dancers, boy or girl, made a big stink out of it, so that was good, considering how homophobic some students and community members can be. But I heard some audience members, maybe some elders, who were not happy at all. Did they think this was a no-no? Well, maybe they were just surprised to see a "boy" dancing a male dance, but [one] who did not look like a "boy" to them. Something unexpected happened. Did Jan care? Maybe. But Jan still performed in the best ways . . . even better than some of the other dancers. Jan didn't want to stand out, but everyone seemed to notice, not the way Jan looked per se, but I think the way Jan was giving it all, showing how much Jan worked hard to do this despite not looking like how "boys" were expected to be. Way to go, Jan!

The most coveted spot for dancing during Poly Day would have to be the taupou, the female, sometimes male, lead in the finale centerpiece number mostly adapted from the Sāmoan Taualuga.[11] This person always wore the most elaborately decorated headdress, made especially for the occasion, with feathers, hair, shells, tiny mirrors, and other decorative items. She would be dressed in the most beautiful regalia, sashed with tapa and layers of mat around her body, and bedecked with necklaces and armbands strewn with shells. And her face, arms, and other parts of her body would be color-marked with islander-inspired geometric lines and figures. She would carry with care what looked like a sword or a large-hooked blade while she danced onstage ever so gracefully, as other performers and audience members flocked to her, screaming, dancing, and tossing money at her feet or sticking it to her body, all in recognition and appreciation of her status and dancing skill. It was amazing that, over the years, I hadn't heard of anyone fighting adamantly over who got to be the taupou for the year; it just worked out that there was always someone who stood out and could do the job ably and without debate.

Women dominated the dances, as well as the organization of Poly Day as a whole. They always outnumbered men especially in terms of commitment to regular practice or simply in their willingness and ability to dance and lead the workshops. Organizers scoffed at other non-active members of the PSA and some members of allied student organizations who volunteered to dance, for they worried that these dancers were not as familiar with islander culture and therefore did not value the dances properly or did not see the point of the performances vis-à-vis their high school outreach efforts. "Not me," said Mork, our senior Khmer American student. "I know and respect island culture, you know. I see a lot of . . . I don't know . . . connections and similarities with my own culture. But the others? They just want to perform just to be onstage and be seen by everyone." To mitigate this, PSA officers at some point decided to require the payment of PSA membership dues for all dancers (to ensure their commitment to the organization), mandated regular attendance at their meetings, and obligated absolute presence in all of their posted rehearsals. Said one PSA officer, "These dancers just want to be onstage and show off their hula that they learn from their [private] teachers here for free. Or that they learn from us! For free too! They're not here as Pacific Islanders with a mission. They don't even know that. They just want to show off." "What's your mission?" I asked. "Huh! You don't know? How could you not know?" she half screamed and rolled her eyes at me.

I did know that the mission was to stage all of this as part of outreaching to and recruiting of high school kids. But I also knew that it was easy for many students and audience members to forget this amid all the spectacle and flurry of Poly Day, including its planning beforehand. Even the performers themselves, in their desire to represent well their heritage by dancing flawlessly—hopefully—oftentimes got so entangled in the hectic pace of rehearsals leading up to the actual day that they behaved testily with one another, complained about exhaustion, focused too much on weight reduction, and eventually neglected their studies. For a teacher like me, and because many of them were my students during the school quarter when Poly Days were held, around April, this became also a most dreadful occurrence. One could keep reminding the students that they were first and foremost college students, and that all of these activities were simply "add-ons" to their lives on campus, but no determined and passionate student/performer paid this, or someone like me, any serious attention most of the time. That is why I say that this was dreadful, the most dreadful part of Poly Day to me. Many students flunked their classes during this quarter or obtained very low grades, at the very least. So, one of the strategies we suggested over and over was for performers and organizers to register for an "independent study" class with me so that they could count their Poly Day activities as part of their academic work. They were then asked to perform some kind of research in the process of preparing for their cultural activities, and then were required to eventually write an essay that would be meaningfully and relevantly thought out, written, and presented. Many students availed themselves of this opportunity, and at least one other professor on campus integrated Poly Day–related work into a course on Pacific Islander history and culture.[12] Students appreciated that.

What did students learn from Poly Day? Students of Polynesian descent, and those few others who were allied with them, such as Mork, constituted the most dedicated and committed organizers and performers of this event. Months of planning went into Poly Day, and a huge dose of sacrifice, patience, and hard work was invested in it. I'm thinking of the nightly rigors of rehearsals at least three or four times a week, and then daily once Poly Day inched closer. I'm also reminded of all the fund-raising the students had to do; the contacting of stage and sound engineers; the applications for permits for holding a public performance at UW; the coordination with the high school principals, teachers, and chaperones; and the arrangements with the campus police, the caterers, vendors, campus administrators, sponsors, community leaders, allied student organizations, workshop leaders, scriptwriters, and stagehands. There were so many things to worry about. Students had a very long list, indeed. It would have been better had students thought of writing and publishing a manual for running it. But, alas, every year, the wheel was reinvented, so to speak. As far as I know, I was the only one who was consistently present over the years, since Poly Day was in its infancy. I generally kept my hands off in its planning and organizing, offering to help only when students asked for it (which was not frequent), so I saw many students go through the ropes each time, as if it was their first time to do it. And usually, it was. So, at the very least, students learned how to organize a large event successfully, from coordinating with school authorities in reserving the place, handling permits and logistics, and booking technicians and stage help, all the way to drafting and fine-tuning the goals, drawing and revising the program, writing and editing the script, and arranging rehearsals. During those years when high school kids volunteered to perform, additional time was given to teaching them intensively. And that was just the performances. As was mentioned already, the centerpiece of Poly Day was supposed to be the high school students. To fulfill this mission, UW students had to start way earlier, even months before Poly Day, so that they got to know and decide which high schools to target, which principals and teachers to go to, which students needed to be identified and contacted, and which parents needed to be phoned for permissions and such. These students would have to be bused, they would have to be chaperoned by a school-sanctioned or recognized person, and they would have to be fed. And of course, since they were all minors, they would have to be secured and protected on campus. The sighs of relief came from UW students only when all the high school kids ended up back in their campuses and homes safely, once Poly Day was over.

The bonding that happened on the road to Poly Day could not be adequately measured and appreciated, from my perspective, by looking merely at its final product. Even then, the presumed consequences or benefits of a one-day event like this could not be tracked simply by noting how many Pacific Islander students felt less isolated on campus, how many of them learned more about their ancestors' histories and traditions, or how many audience members changed their minds about Pacific Islander stereotypes. We also did not simply count how many of the visiting high school kids applied to and eventually got into college, how many of them felt better about themselves and their heritage, or how many of them improved their prospects of seriously considering a degree and a career well beyond high school and college. Even though someone suggested to us to do it, we did not compare college kids' grades before and after Poly Day. I thought that was absurd, considering that students rarely earned grades specifically for participating and working hard in this event, nor was the prospect of earning good or better grades their ulterior motive for planning and doing Poly Day. If they had a choice, they would have probably considered being graded for the work they did (as few of them did, in independent studies with me, as I mentioned earlier), but that would have been just icing on the cake, a small and simple reward, and not the principal reason for dancing, working with, or teaching and hosting the high school students.

If I were made to choose one big thing that stood out for me, it was the exuberance, or what looked like a mixture of stress and pride, that UW Polynesian students and their allies experienced before, during, and after Poly Day. Performing high school outreach in the name of cultural uplift was something many other organizations did, but to have the Pacific—the *ocean*—represented so publicly on campus, and so wrapped around a sea of brown bodies, young and old, despite and in spite of their being so marginal, remote, unfamiliar, and unexpectedly visible to many others, was so profoundly important to the students. Instead of doing nothing, as many of them said repeatedly to me, they preferred putting up with the heavy costs of mounting the event, and not just in the financing of it, but in expending the enormous energy required for learning the dances and chants, and, more importantly, in preparing for the high school outreach workshops. It was also about begging for support from a variety of campus units and community organizations (many of which indeed gave to them), rounding up and keeping an eye on rowdy high school kids, and making sure everything and everyone was on track before, during, and after the event. And then, it was also about coordinating with the other "islander" events on the campus during the spring quarter season—the busiest time for all these students—when the Filipino cultural night (sometimes, *two* nights!) and the Micronesian Islands Club (MIC) fiesta or cultural event were also held. Both could be and, on many occasions, were as equally elaborate as Poly Day. Polynesian students helped out and participated in these events too, and, of course, nobody wanted to have conflicting engagements. So, dates had to be negotiated and decided very early on. "It's a lot of work," Apala said to me as she was decompressing with her peers after a performance. "But it sure is . . . a lot of . . . love." She continued: "Just think about it, there's nothing here that's not about love . . . love for our culture. For our people. For our ocean. These are all love . . . and pride . . . and, damn it, more love, ha-ha! I can't believe we're done. So, yeah, I don't wanna think of next year even! I just wanna take it all in for now. Just sit back and take it all in. I'm feeling good and feeling like . . . I'm so proud and happy for all of us!"

PIONEER!

It was a cold, wet, and windy day in the city of Tukwila, some eleven miles south of Seattle, and all I could remember that autumn was that I was complaining in my head the whole time about having to help out in doing student outreach at Foster High School there, instead of doing something else, like resting at home. It was a Saturday too, so that didn't help much in my grumbling. The only thing that kept me there was that four of my own students were present. And more were coming. High school students were coming! It would have been a gigantic shame if I just decided to walk away. So stay I did.

BENNY (a Sāmoan student leader, junior): Hello, everyone! Welcome to this fine sunshiny Saturday! Hello! Hello!

The irony didn't hit the students. Or, not yet. The nine high school students—five males and four females—appeared to be barely awake.

BENNY: O-K! Well, welcome to PIONEER! Does anyone know what PIONEER means? Anyone want to give it a try? What PIONEER stands for? Anyone?

Students were still silent. Their heads were mostly bowed down.

BENNY: All . . . righty! (*Voice getting louder.*) Ahem! PIONEER stands for the Pacific Islander Opportunity Network for . . . (*eyes closing intently*) . . . Educational Equality and . . . Representation! (*Eyes opening wide now.*) Wow! I almost didn't get that right. Whew! My name is Benny. And I'm a student at UW. And I'm a junior, studying American ethnic studies. Okay? Let's get things going now. Everyone, stand up! Chop-chop! Come on! (*Hands clapping.*) Let's do some warm-up, some icebreakers! (*Arms gesturing.*) Everyone stand up! Come on!

Students got up, some reluctantly, stretched a bit, and then checked one another out by looking around, trying to do it imperceptibly. I scanned around too. There were indeed a handful of these high school students in the audience; we were not expecting many. And there were six students from college, sitting in the back, all PIONEER volunteers who, for the second Saturday already in their fall quarter, were also checking out the high school kids. They wondered who would make it to college, I'm sure. Or, at least, who was more awake than others, and who was glad to be there. But their goals were much larger and deeper than that. In the invitational letter they gave out to precollege students, they wrote about how PIONEER was "geared toward high school students interested in attending the University of Washington." But Benny was always the first to clarify this. "You don't have to go to UW for college, you know," he always said to the high schoolers during his welcoming speech. "You can go to any college you want, any one college, as long as you go to college. Period."

The letter continued: PIONEER will "introduce you to all the exciting opportunities on our campus, teach leadership skills and academic/college planning, as well as help navigate you through our rigorous admissions application process." This was surely a workout, this PIONEER, I heard many students say. And was it all worth it? The college students I knew who had been involved with PIONEER just shrugged their shoulders sometimes.

JUNIOR: It is about numbers. And it is not. I mean, it's nice to bring up the Pacific Islander student numbers on campus, but we don't want to make that as the . . . what do you call that? The end all and be all of PIONEER. No. We just want to try, to do our best, and to get to know these high school kids who are going to be with us. Or join us. Or be like us. We want to connect with them. And we want them to connect with us. That's the most important thing. To build community with them. The rest is just, you know, for show, you know. I did not know this before, but, more and more, I realized that [this] is so.

DEANA: Yeah. This thing about numbers can be so blown up, you know. It can be distracting, I think. Hmm. If we care too much about how many, then everyone becomes a statistic, like they just matter only when they get counted. That's not good, you know. We try to get to know every person here, every high school student. Every student. We try to, you know, make them know their history, value their culture, find their way into college, hopefully, and make their lives better for them . . . and better for their family and their community. Better for all of us.

APALA: We try to make them be closer to their culture, to be who they are. So, when they get to UW, they don't need to feel like they're out of touch, you know. Or that they have to give it up, feel shame, or something whatever. That's really stupid. Or silly, I think. Or that they feel like they have to act white or act so . . . so different from who they are as a people, as islanders. We want them to learn how to appreciate their culture. To know it, and be proud of it. To share it too. All of these are connected, you know? Culture, college, and community. And self and identity! I did not experience this before, coming in, so I want to change it for our future students.

Back to the workshop . . .

BENNY: Okay, let's do some icebreakers! Everyone form a circle! We're gonna play "two truths and one lie!" Two truths . . . and a freakin' lie!

Someone from the audience, one of the high school kids: Oh. My. God.

BENNY: Yup! Oh . . . my . . . God, you too! This is gonna be a good getting-to-know-you game, yeah? So? Everyone? Think up of two things about you that are true and one thing about you that's a lie, okay? Say your name first, where you're from, what high school or college you go to, and then tell us the three things about you.

Another one from the audience: For reals? I don't think this is gonna be fun. (*Sulking.*)

BENNY, *disregarding the comment and ignoring the sulk*: Yup, it's gonna be fun, fun, fun! Yeah? And then, after you say these things, you point at someone else to guess what's the lie. And then, that person does the introductions next. Then, someone says which one's true and which one's lies. And so forth and so on. All right? Did everyone get that? Come on! Let's play!

Grumbling from the audience. But excitement too, since many others were grinning and looking up to probably think of what their truths and lies would be.

BENNY: All right! Let me start! Hello, my name is Benny, I'm from Tukwila, and I go to UW. I study American ethnic studies. That's my major. Okay? You! (*Pointing at someone directly in front of him.*)

Student who was pointed at: What?

BENNY: Hmm? Yes, you! Your turn! Two truths and one lie.

Student who was pointed at: But you haven't done yours yet!

Audience opening up, hissing and laughing hysterically, all of a sudden.

BENNY: Oh! Okay, okay! Um, let me see. Okay, here it is, listen up! I've been to study abroad in the Pacific twice, I do not eat pizza, and I can play the ukulele.

STUDENT: All lies! All lies!

Everyone laughed even more hysterically.

BENNY: No way! Only one of them is a lie! That's the game!

STUDENT: You don't play the ukulele!

Everyone laughed again.

BENNY: I do! I do! That's not a lie! That's the truth!

If there was anything that PIONEER student mentors were really good at, or at least one thing that they did best, it was that they knew how to build community with their students. But it was not as easy as it seemed over the years. Pacific Islander students at UW were heavily involved, just as other students were who worked with younger kids in many other college programs on campus. But these students, I thought, invested more than enough amounts of time, money, and energy beyond their studies when they chose to commit themselves to such activities that did not necessarily earn them grades. They were all in an environment in which they had to contend with ignorance, racism, and invisibility. And they felt the obligation to serve their communities, something that they thought many other regular college students did not have to deal with. In one of the PIONEER mentor meetings that I participated in, students talked to one another about the challenges of "giving back" as reminders of how some of them were indeed PIONEER kids themselves when they were in high school. They were helped out before. And now was the time to show gratitude by being PIONEER mentors themselves. It was their turn. It was a good motivation, I saw and felt, and something that built upon the students' perception of the larger contexts of the historical invisibility of Pacific Islanders on campus. It also helped in making sense of why things needed to get done, why going to college was not just about being a student, and why building community was somehow a responsibility. Junior shared with me a few thoughts about this logic:

Well, it kinda doesn't make complete sense if we go to these high schools to do PIONEER just to help out. It's not just to help out these kids [as individuals or as mere students]. It's about building and helping a community of many more PIs to go to after high school. That's why we help out. You know what I'm saying? That's our commitment. Like, I didn't start all of [this]. Someone else did. Some islanders already started this. Way before me. So we just continue the work that was started before. That's our duty. Or else, all that hard work from before [is] just gonna go up in [the] air. What a waste!

These connections across history and community were always made clear to all students, to both college mentors and the high school students themselves. In one of the pre-PIONEER workshops that we did on campus, college student volunteers collectively listed "building and sustaining a community of love and support" as a top goal they wanted to work on for the coming school year. This was not a surprise to me, having felt a strong sense from every student over the years that PIONEER was indeed about building relationships with future college students very early on, instead of waiting until these high school students got into college.

BENNY: All right! Thanks, everyone! That was a good icebreaker, huh? And good introductions too! Now, we know everyone! Okay, now, we're gonna have a little exercise . . . or . . . a presentation in getting to know more about PIONEER. It's gonna be a short one, don't worry. All right? And then, after that, we're gonna ask you to fill up some forms, okay? And then, lunch! So, did you hear that? Lunch! We're gonna eat! Yay!

AUDIENCE: Yay! Let's go!

BENNY: Everyone, stand up, form a circle, hold hands. Bow down, and close your eyes!

AUDIENCE: Wha? Huh?

BENNY: Dear Heavenly Father . . .

DEANA: . . . and Mother!

BENNY, *looking at Deana, then closing eyes*: Um-hum . . . um-hum . . . yes, thank you, Deana. Dear Heavenly Father and Mother, bless the food we're about to eat. Bless the hands that made the food. Bless all of us who need to bow their heads and close their eyes. . . .

(Audience members, giggling, bow as Benny instructed, then close their eyes, trying to be quiet and serious.)

BENNY: Bless our dear PIONEER peeps. Help us get through the day with our workshops and activities. That we may be enriched and prepared to go to college. Bless those who are in need. Bless those who are not able to eat. And thank God . . . thank you for all the blessings you give us. In Jesus's name, O Lord, amen!

AUDIENCE, *in unison*: Amen!

In the pamphlet that the students wrote and gave out as copies to the students, it was the year 2001 when:

> *Pacific Islander (PI) students from the University of Washington (UW) responded to the alarming percentages of PI dropout rates and the low percentage of PI college admission by creating a one-of-a-kind outreach and recruitment mentorship program that could help promote the importance of school and culture. They dubbed it the Pacific Islander Opportunity and Network for Educational Equality and Representation, or PIONEER. Their goals for the program are to:*
> - *increase PI admission into the UW*
> - *provide resources for students to access college/scholarships*
> - *learn and value PI history and culture*
> - *create communities of love and support*
> - *and teach students to give back to their communities.*
> *With these goals written in ink, they set out to build a community for Pacific Islanders.*[13]

Since the leadership of PIONEER changed every year, certain elements got added, deleted, or modified. But the fundamentals stayed the same. Some directors chose to focus on college applications all of the time, rather than have students divide their energies learning a dance for Poly Day and participating in a leadership or history workshop, on top of dealing with their applications. Sometimes, a student director just focused on a handful of schools rather than reaching out to high schoolers from a variety of locations. Some added a field trip or two, or a workshop on health, sexuality, or time management, to make things different from the usual. Others had to deal with unexpected conditions during their term. One year, for example, Junior added a "subtitle" to the program, *Finafinau* (Sāmoan for "perseverance"; he later wrote an independent study paper on how finafinau related to the program), to represent and focus on what he intended to achieve collectively during his term. It was because he was facing a challenging year when PIONEER had to weather budget cuts and student nonavailability. Funding reductions made students limit their bus trips to pick up and take kids back to their schools, reduced their ability to provide food, and caused them to cancel several workshop sessions. This was such a far cry from what Migetu and Tavita were used to when they ran the program early on, when PIONEER was just starting to grow. They were PIONEER's founding directors, and they went all out when they did it for the first time. I remember we had full-day activities and elaborately conducted sessions, and the college and high school kids were energetically pumped up all the time. Well, it was not as if students were consistently involved and able to participate fully every year that PIONEER was active. The ebb and flow of school support, student struggles, and all the varying circumstances of availability, necessity, and timing actually made the program slightly different each year. It was also during Junior's time as director that PIONEER almost folded up, mainly for what he seriously considered as a lack in student initiative. A part of an "urgent" memo he wrote and distributed to the students stated:

Our last PIONEER meeting that was canceled made us realize the grave state of our program. Our volunteer numbers have dwindled throughout the years and in our last meeting, we saw the same group of mentors who have shown up for the past years in attendance. It has come to my attention that we have only three options for PIONEER this year and it requires a group meeting in order make a decision for PIONEER. The three options that the mentors came up [with] in our last meeting [were] 1) we cancel PIONEER for this year due to the time constraints in our community, 2) we have PIONEER but only twice a quarter, or 3) continue with the program with the same consistent volunteers and hope for the best.

The PIONEER program was eventually not canceled. It ran, but on a shoestring budget and with very limited participation of both mentors and high schoolers. "Oh well," Junior told me subsequently, "at least we hung on." Like many other student-run programs, it took the will and the commitment of their participants to enable such programs to run and be sustained. Junior went on: "Funny that all these goals to bring up PI numbers in school . . . depend on us college students to work on. It's like . . . we have to work personally to get our numbers up. Sure, the school helps us. But only a bit. And if we don't do it, we get blamed. It's our fault. When we don't do it well, or the numbers are not there, we're the ones who are bad or lazy. So, we're pressured a lot. Like, these things [solely] depend on us! It's unfair!"

BENNY: Okay, okay! Now that we've finished eating, please don't forget to clean up. Recycle, okay? Let's move on! Let's get on to . . . what is it, now? (*Looking at Apala.*) Oh, yes, our college applications workshop. Apala! Let's go do it! How are we gonna do this?

APALA, *bolting from the floor to stand up*: Okay! Let's help each other in filling out our applications forms, okay? Our college apps! We'll just use the mock-ups, so it's okay to make mistakes. Let's divide . . . into . . . how many do we have? Oh, we have eight . . . nine . . . kids. Let's do four groups. Yes, four groups! Each group will have two or three high school kids and two college kids . . . so that we can work in pairs. Pair up, everyone! (*Clapping.*) One college mentor with one high school student. Let's pair up! Let's go! (*Clapping.*) Everyone grab a pencil and a form! We have them right here! Here you go! Pencils and forms!

It was the beginning of the fall quarter then, just the perfect time to work on college and scholarship applications, the deadlines of which would be toward the end of the year, or the early part of the following year. But not only were many high schoolers unmotivated to go to college, they were also unfamiliar with the process of applying to college. Lusse, another Sāmoan-Filipina student, who was also Junior's sister, and who had graduated already and was now a college recruitment counselor specifically for Pacific Islander students, explained how crucial this work was:

Many kids are [the] first generation in their families to go to college. That means they didn't have parents and other relatives who've been to college. Or they've been to college, but somewhere else, like in the islands, which most probably [has] a different system than in the mainland. This also means these kids didn't have the benefit of even hearing about going to college, unlike many other families whose dinner table conversations included going to college. Or that uncle this or auntie that went to Harvard or Yale or something. These kids don't have that benefit at all. They're clueless about scholarships, or just the simple . . . even far possibility that their college education could be paid for by someone else. So, just imagine, if they didn't have these [benefits], how could we expect them to know how to apply, what to look for, how to properly fill out the forms and represent themselves well so that they stand a good chance [at] getting into college? And be excited about it? They don't even get the benefit of being encouraged to go to college by anyone close to them. They don't have counselors in their school who remind them of deadlines and forms and stuff like that. Man, the list is long. It's so bad!

Applying by filling out forms appeared basic to many, but not to these high school students. This was the reason why PIONEER had a practice of pairing up with students one-on-one, right from page one of the form and all the way to financial aid applications, scholarship applications, and especially essay writing. This was serious work, and it needed focused and careful attention to detail. Here's Ellen, another islander student turned counselor:

> The essay, I think, is the most important part. And there's actually more than one essay! This is where students get the chance to explain them-selves in a way that they come out as persons . . . as human beings . . . not just someone who filled [in] the blanks and all. They can clarify things here, they can show their creativity, they can talk about their unique expe-riences that are not . . . captured . . . by the forms. But, they should also be well written! Like, [there should be] no mistakes, no typos, nothing that's gonna look bad. This is their chance, so it's important that they get help!

> (*Apala stands up, reaches for her laptop, punches a few buttons, then slowly cranks up islander music.*)

> BENNY, *whispers toward Apala*: What are YOU doing?

> APALA, *whispering too*: I AM PLAYING some MUSIC. (*Rolls her eyes.*)

> BENNY: Huh? But why? (*Rolling his eyes too.*)

> APALA, *louder than a whisper*: 'Cause I'm bored! Hmmmph!

> (*Students began snickering, distracted for a while. Then, they go back to their business.*)

Indeed, sessions like these could seem so uneventful and dry. That was all the more reason for the college mentors to get on with this work as quickly or as efficiently as they could, so they could proceed to other more lively and engaging activities. So, when they got the creative juices going, they turned to exercises that veered away from the usual monotony of writing in pairs, such as facilitating group discussions "to talk out" potential answers to an essay prompt, or writing out applicants' responses on paper or on a board, including starting "wish lists" for what to major in college and what careers to pursue, in letter form. These letters would be sealed and given to me, and the plan was for me to keep them until they were opened at a later date, when the high school letter writer would presumably land in my office as a UW college student. I was always moved when a handful of students eventually did this. But I still have many of these letters, waiting to be opened soon by an incoming college student, hopefully.

Many college mentors got even more excited when PIONEER days proceeded into the part when "identity" workshops were held, for this was when they availed of the chance to be the "knowledge facilitators" of their own cultures and traditions, as well as the discussants of their own contemporary experiences and struggles. To them, it was not that difficult to connect cultural enrichment with the college applications process for their high school mentees, for they knew already from Poly Day and PIPE, and in their fundamental political consciousness, that both identities—of being a college student and a Pacific Islander—were, in many ways, two sides of one coin. One did not have to be given up for the other, neither should take precedence over the other, and both had to exist in tandem for meaning and success to be found as a Pacific Islander college student. These workshops were then designed to fulfill any one or a combination of the following: familiarizing students with some basic thoughts and theories about knowing one's self and one's community; teaching them lessons regarding indigenous cultures, colonization histories, and resistance movements that they might not have known; and strengthening their views regarding the holistic integration of the values that came from their heritage as Pacific Islanders into their lives as students and community workers. Oftentimes, there would be long conversations about relevant topics such as racism on campus and in their everyday lives, sexism, gender, feminism, mental health, sex and sexuality, homophobia, and their common histories and experiences with other groups, including the significance of the ocean in their lives. Over the years, different mentors experimented with various kinds of workshops, ranging from traditional lecture-style presentations to art, singing, or language lessons that were more interactive and therefore engaging on so many levels.

BENNY, *standing up slowly and stretching*: Okay, everyone! Time's up! Come on! I guess some of you have your rides waiting for you outside? Huh? Some of you need to be driven back home? All right? Let's all get ready then. Everyone, make sure you write this down somewhere, or put it on your phone, or calendar. Our next meeting will be two Saturdays from now. Okay? Mark that down, everyone. We're gonna continue with our workshops and meetings, okay? This is not the end of it! (*Shaking his head.*) There's many more to come! So mark these dates!

APALA: Benny's right, people! Our next meeting will be here, same time, same place. We're gonna coordinate and find out who needs to be picked up, who needs a ride, who doesn't. Yeah? Make sure you tell your mentor what you need. Coordinate with them, okay?

BENNY: Okay, so at this point, we're gonna say thank you to everyone, yeah? Thank you guys for coming over, thanks for spending part of your weekend with us. Thank you to the mentors, who gave up part of their weekend for us. Thank you to our teachers and volunteers. Thank you, everyone!

APALA: And, as is our tradition, we're gonna do our solidarity clap, okay? Everyone! Let's do this! Let's form a circle! (*Clapping.*) And follow me! If you still don't know this. . . . And make sure you remember this . . . memorize this! Yeah? Because we're gonna do this again next time. And we're gonna do this every time we meet, okay?

BENNY: Wait! We have to explain this to the first-time students, ya? Who wants to do this? Who? (*Looks around, and quickly spots Junior.*) Junior, you go do it! Junior!

JUNIOR, *at first, reluctantly walking into the middle of the circle*: Huh? Me? Sure. Okay! Let me explain! (*Goes to the center of the circle.*) Okay, everyone, this is called our solidarity clap, okay? Our solidarity clap! Our solidarity clap is used to unite all Pacific Islanders and our supporters, and we always do this before and after our workshops . . . in order to bring a sense of unity . . . and respect for all of our PI cultures. Okay? All for unity. So, first, we do the MEChA clap! You know what MEChA is? It's Movimiento Estudiantil Chicanos/Chicanas de Aztlan. We borrow this from our Chicano and Chicana brothers and sisters. It's a call to solidarity. Like, calling everyone to join us and be with us as one. Let's bring us all together! Let's clap! Slowly first. Then going faster and louder!

(*Slow clap, progressing into a faster and louder clap.*)

Okay, now let's rub our hands together!

(*Hands together, vigorously rubbing.*)

Mili, mili, mili! . . . Mili means "getting ready." We're preparing for unity, getting ourselves ready. Mili, mili, mili.

Then, I say *patia*! Patia means "one clap"! It means attention!

Patia! (*One clap.*)

Patia! (*One clap.*)

Then, I say *lu'a mai*. It means "two claps"! More attention!

(*People giggling, but becoming more serious.*)

Lu'a mai! (*Two claps.*)

Lu'a mai! (*Two claps.*)

Then, I say *lu'a mai mala* PIONEER! It means "two claps for PIONEER"! You clap twice and then yell out PIONEER!

Lu'a mai mala PIONEER! (*Two claps.*)

(*Everyone yelling.*) PIONEER!

I say lu'a mai mala UW! Two claps for UW!

Lu'a mai mala UW! (*Two claps.*)

(*Everyone yelling.*) UW!

Then, I yell out *isang bagsak*! Isang bagsak means "one foot down"! Or "one step down." We borrow this from our Filipino brothers and sisters, from Filipino political activists. It means solidarity! Like, one for all! And all for one! So, when I yell out isang bagsak, everyone stomp one foot down, okay?

Isang bagsak! (*Altogether, one foot stomp from everybody.*)

Then, lastly! Here's the last one! I'll say *i'sa*! It means "unity" in Tongan. I say i'sa, then everyone points a finger toward the sky. I'sa!

I-sa! (*Everyone's forefingers pointing at the roof.*)

Let's all do it! Everyone clap![14]

Technically, these PIONEER sessions that were held on a set of Saturdays during the school year concluded at around 4:00 PM, almost always never after 5:00 PM, for the high school kids had to be brought home or had to be picked up safely by their parents or guardians before dark. But the world that the high school students had been introduced to in PIONEER did not end there. It was part of a string of programs and events that altogether offered participants a range of opportunities and possibilities to build community with as many college students as possible and among themselves, all throughout the year (or several years for some). These included the annual Readiness for Islander Success in Education (RISE) one-day program that specifically targeted (but was not completely exclusive to) Pacific Islander high school seniors; Poly Day; the Micronesian Islands Club Night; the Filipino Nite (or Fil Nite); and a host of a variety of activities that were conducted under the auspices of student and community organizations such as the Polynesian Student Alliance (PSA), the Micronesian Islands Club (MIC), the Pacific Islander Student Commission (PISC), the Filipino American Student Association (FASA), the Polynesian Outreach Program (POP), and the Northwest Association of Pacific Americans (NAPA). Other similar program entities that students reached out to included: the Adelante Con Educación (ACE) conference; the Encouraging Minority People to Overcome with Education and Respect program (also called EMPOWER for a time); the Essence of Success Program; the Native American Student Day; and the Esperanza en Educación (EEE) conference.

Later, the dreaded month of March eventually rolled in; dreaded because that was usually the time when the high school kids got their acceptance or denial (or conditional acceptance) letters. It was always a time of great anxiety, but also a moment of big and small celebrations, depending on who you talked to. And then, Poly Day kicked in around the second-to-the-last week of April. Here, some of the PIONEER kids got to showcase their newly learned and mastered dance steps in a program slot all to their own and onstage for a supportive audience. They got big applauses and were usually introduced as the young'uns who had been prepped well by their college counterparts, now very proud to see them represent for their communities. These high school students then got their taste of performing in public, on a campus that some of them would end up attending later as college students. In such a double treat, it was not hard for them to think seriously about the meaningfulness of what they had just gone through and worked hard for—all the work of college applications and the identity workshops, the van rides and the pickups, the dreary Saturday sessions, and the annoying check-ins that their mentors regularly peppered them with throughout the year—now finally bearing fruit. What used to be imagined just as possibilities, had now turned into realities and greater potentials. And fortunately, they were not starting from square one. All these things they had learned, all the tools they had been exposed to, and especially all the networks of brothers and sisters they now counted as friends and supporters and soon-to-be classmates were now ready to be availed of as well as partnered with. They would now have to think of ways to make this all worth the trouble, but regardless of what they did and would do, they were surely expected to be called upon at some point to give back.

Yes, eventually, sometime before the school year ended, and at a time when everyone would have been most definitely exhausted, UW students had to think about and name the next director of PIONEER, get ready with the outreach and recruitment processes once again, attend to its promotion in career and college fairs, coordinate with counselors and parents to fill out student permission slips, hunt for and sign up volunteers, and call or e-mail continuing and prospective high school students. To many UW students, these seemed like a never-ending set of activities, stopping only when one graduated, even though a good handful of alumni indeed returned to help out every now and then. Many Pacific Islander students at UW always thought about the next step, the next leaders, the next generation of students, not so much to strictly replicate the programs or simply reproduce themselves, but to remind one another to continue the work that others before them had started already, to call on one another to continue serving the very communities they were a part of, and to take action because of a strong belief and apprehension that no one else would except them. I noticed how this kind of attitude persisted over the years. New students were never really entirely new, for they had already had the PIONEER experience way before they got into the university. There would be a few true newcomers, including out-of-state students and students who happened to pass by our recruitment tables during freshman orientation events. But these students were quickly plugged into the politics of being a Pacific Islander student on campus by the more senior students they met. Somebody told Matthew, a Tongan student from the suburbs, to simply approach our group and introduce himself to us. He was quiet at first when he came to one of our PIPE tabling events, I remember, but he soon blossomed into a student whom I later admired and cared for because of how he reminded me of others. He later became PIPE codirector, along with Turtle, a Vietnamese American student who hung out with Pacific Islanders during his high school days and even learned some Polynesian dances that he performed during Pacific Islander events, while becoming my devoted mentee in PIPE and a high-performing student in my classes. They both would soon mentor a bright Sāmoan student named Richmond, from the same high school Matthew came from, and someone who was an accomplished Pacific Islander dancer as well. I knew him through his brother and sister, both UW students and children of active community members. Richmond became a mentee of mine as soon as he stepped into college, and he was closely watched as a young student by many other Pacific Islander students and staff as he was progressing. Matthew and Turtle even took him in, accepting him into their campus apartment his first year, when Richmond did a lot of commuting. Old groups trained younger ones, and so on and so forth, passing on an ocean full of practices, networks, unwritten tricks to doing well, lists of classes and teachers to avoid, stories of wins and losses. This was how traditions were passed down, revised, and transformed.

(*Slow clap, progressing into a faster clap.*)
Mili, mili, mili! . . . (*Rubbing hands together.*)
Patia! (*One clap.*)
Patia! (*One clap.*)
Lu'a mai! (*Two claps.*)
Lu'a mai! (*Two claps.*)
Lu'a mai mala PIONEER! (*Two claps, then PIONEER!*)
Lu'a mai mala UW! (*Two claps, then UW!*)
Isang bagsak! (*One foot stomp.*)
I-sa! (*Fingers pointing at sky.*)
Che-hoo! (*Clapping.*)

STUDY ABROAD

I have heard many students tell me how lucky they were to have been on a study abroad trip with me or with other professors. And I have always responded to them by similarly saying how lucky it has been for me to travel and study with them, especially because these trips were one-of-a-kind experiences. The study abroad classes that I organized and led were meticulously planned, carefully directed, and intensely executed. But even though they were, at the same time, also unpredictable, chaotic, and exhausting, a good majority of students and I regarded these trips with much fondness and joy. Sure, we had our rough moments here and there, but, overall, we bonded well, we were able to do something good with our hosts, and we were transformed for the better. No on-campus classroom could replicate what these trips produced. We learned and experienced important lessons on site, outside of our usual comfort zones, and well beyond what any of us expected. Luck should not be the basis for making it to these trips, I thought. And many students concurred with me. Such study abroad experiences should be required of every student. To express and prove this, I detail some excerpts from my own journal entries as well as those entries from the study abroad students who were in my trips.[15]

ALANA, a Sāmoan student: I'm walking here [in Manila] this morning and all I could think of was that this place feels like home to me. The vibe here is really weird, but not in a bad way. I mean, for whatever reason, I feel like everything's so familiar and comfy, and yet this is my first time here. I feel connected. The people look like me, they behave like me, they kinda smell like me. And the air is like my neighborhood. The people around are like my family or neighbors even. They smile at each other, yell at each other, I don't know, the sounds are just too familiar. Like I never left home. The ocean really connects, as you told us before this trip. Now I understand. Weird, no?

PAUL, a Hawaiian student: At first I thought study abroad classes are just regular classes that you just took somewhere else. Now I realize I'm so mistaken. I'm glad I picked your class. Because when we study things like history, and colonization, slavery, freedom, it's not enough that you read [about] them. It's really important to actually feel them or go on-site to where they happened. Right? So, like now, when we were reading about the impact of U.S. colonization of the Philippines, we get a visual of that here, like all the McDonalds and the Starbucks all over, and everyone speaking English, and everything looking so American. No wonder many of us feel like home, because everything looks so American. It's kinda sad, you know, but it's also like this in many places, I think. We are connected but that is the reality of the global world we're living in. What do you think?

JUSTICE, a student from Saipan: How are we going to be graded for this class? I mean, you can't really be absent or late, because we live in the same place and we go to our classroom at the same time, LOL. If we're going to be graded on something, would that be our participation in the activities? How do you grade that? Like, how will you judge us on how we interact with others? We should smile and be nice all the time? I'm just kidding. But I just want to know. I wanna give you a hard time, LOL.

RICHIE, a white student: Thanks for the opportunity to submit the art-work I did and that I'm very proud of. Please read the essay that is a companion to my painting. I don't want to explain too much because I want you to find thoughts and messages in the painting without me telling you. That's art, you know. Thank you for my grade too.

JUNIOR, a Sāmoan-Filipino student: I chose this program in particular because I believe it will help me with my own personal identity. I was born and raised in American Sāmoa and I am half Sāmoan and Filipino. Actually, no. I'm full Sāmoan and full Filipino. Get it? Ha-ha. All my life I was taught . . . all about my Sāmoan culture and knew nothing about my Filipino side. So with this exploration seminar, I will be able to learn more about a culture that has been distant to me. With this seminar I will be able to understand more of the Filipino culture and their way of life. This program will also help me put a new perspective in learning because I will actually be experiencing my education and not just reading about it in a textbook. I understand some of the history that the Philippines and Sāmoa went through as a result of the U.S expansion in the west and I believe that this program will open my eyes to see some of the historical footprints that the United States and other colonizers, such as Spain, have left on the culture and people. I am interested in finding out how those cultures have blended together and would like an opportunity to explore the various aspects of people that live in the Philippines. This will not only expand my knowledge as a global citizen but it will also allow me to be more conscientious of my position of power because of the fact that I am an American and I do not get to realize how privileged I am because everything is so easy to get here in the states, and not so easily obtained by other people in third world nations such as the Philippines.

CARSON, a Khmer student: I wish school was regularly like this. [If it were so,] I'd be coming to class all the time and not missing a beat. I've done all the readings because they're so interesting. And they're like reading and experiencing at the same time. And I also like that we are here for community service. It's good to do that because we don't want to come here and be [treated] like guests. We are here to work and be useful to others. That's the least we can do to make up for all the colonization our country did. And all the poverty that it caused! We are lucky to be on the other side of the equation that our ancestors were responsible for. But we should not be too smug about it. We need to give back. If there's one thing we should all learn from a class like this, it should be about giving back. What other course will do this requirement for students?

Excerpts from my introductory letter to students, shown to the participating students before our study abroad trip:

I come from several places and I go home to several homes. I was born in the Philippines, I was raised in Manila and Quezon City (two of the cities we're visiting), and I've spent many years studying and working in the United States. Becoming an adult was both a painful and exhilarating experience for me. I traveled back and forth, I attended different schools, and I was many times separated from my family. I also relished our multiple moves. Every time we changed residences, I felt like starting fresh, becoming a new person. It sounds like a life of privilege, but it is also one that was lived out of necessity. Both my parents were looking for better lives in the United States and they tried hard to make them better here. I'm very excited about this trip, I'm very energized by what's been planned, and I am so filled with both anxiety and joy all bundled up incoherently, like how it was before when I was about to change homes once again, right at the cusp of closing a door and turning around to face what's about to come next. In the Philippines, I encourage everyone to find a home. And to help others find theirs, in whatever way it can be imagined and defined.

Along with searching for home, I'm very interested in studying those who cannot "fit." As a young man, I've often wondered why I myself couldn't fit in many places I was supposed to. So in my research, I study why and how groups of people—Filipino immigrants, Pacific Islander Americans, underrepresented students—are excluded, devalued, and misunderstood, and how these groups, in turn, struggle with such treatment. I argue that these struggles offer us remarkable ways on how lives can be transformed in the face of despair. So, in our trip, do try to keep an eye on these things: finding homes, struggling to "fit," and transforming selves, others, and society.

TANIELU, a Sāmoan-Filipino student: Thank you for taking me into your study abroad class, Bonus. This is really something that I won't forget. I was able to see my relatives, but really, I was able to see my other home, and I was able to be of service to the people here. I know you were mad at me many times for being naughty and all, but you know I don't mean to disrespect you. I just have too much fun sometimes, and I get carried away. Our class did not feel like a regular class at all, but not in a bad way. I just feel like we were having so much fun going to different places and meeting people, and learning about everything, that I forgot that we were in a class. I wish our other classes were like this. How will you test us now? Ha-ha. Well, as you know, I am going to Tahiti after this. So, it will be another class that's going to be not a class, I hope. I have not been there before, but I have heard so much about it. I wish you and others [could] come with me. It will not be the same. Again, thank you for everything and God bless.

KABRU, a black student: What stood out most to me during our study abroad to the Philippines was getting to see firsthand the manifestations of postcolonial resistance. One of the main ways I saw such resistance was at our host campus. [We saw their teachers] leading an effort to reclaim indigenous musical practices. They were working on reclaiming indigenous and non-Western ways of learning. I remember her discussion about oral and written traditions and about how indigenous musical practices operated in the former, which presented inherent contradictions in the writing down of indigenous music. This was really interesting to me because it sparked questions of authenticity and of how one negotiates reclaiming culture with the inherent contradictions that emerge in the process. We also saw how colonization is being resisted and negotiated through the revival of indigenous Philippine folk traditions as a part of modern Filipino identity.

But the most impactful part of our [2011 Philippines] study abroad trip for me came through the friendships I was fortunate to gain with my fellow classmates in the program, the people we met through the program, and especially with Prof. Bonus. I knew a few other students in the program when we first started, but by the end many of us became very close, and have become a part of each other's lives since. Prof. Bonus in particular has become like family to me. Prior to the trip he helped me apply successfully to graduate school, and in this program modeled for me the type of professor I one day hope to be. Being mentored by him created the desire within me to pursue graduate school in ethnic studies, with a dream to one day teach and lead study abroad programs of my own. In particular, I want to be a teacher like Prof. Bonus who moves students beyond the classroom, to serve among activists and workers, engaging alongside them in service-based projects that empower students to become agents of change, while being critically aware of their own positionalities and privileges. During moments of collective reflection, through our course assignments, and in our social downtimes, this dream was reaffirmed for me. Needless to say, this trip was incredibly meaningful and impactful toward my intellectual and personal development.

JENNIFER, a Filipina student: I didn't like that we went to the red light district! Well, some of us went, and some of us did not! I did not! I thought that that was insulting and did not give us any real lesson that we didn't know before. I did not like our conversations about it after. I thought [name of student] was rude and did not know what he was talking about. He was also very insensitive about dealing with these women. He did not learn his lesson at all! But my favorite part was when we had our day with the orphans and our day with the senior folks. I thought that our presence was our service and it was our lesson. I liked that we interacted with the kids and we were not there only to give them money or goodies. What I liked was that we spent quality time with them. It was a good opportunity to combine our readings about poverty and the effects of colonization with our interactions with those who have been dispossessed. Our kids and older people liked us, I think, and they did us a great big favor when they taught us the value of being human . . . in the face of all these bad histories and current poverty and being an orphan and being old and alone.

MYRA, a Filipina student: I truly think this class changed me. I know your word is "transformation." So, I'm just gonna say that. I've been transformed!

DEANA, a Sāmoan student: When I came home from the Philippines, I was humbled from my experience, and more determined to practice having critical lenses about the privileges I carry as a student, and how I interact in spaces that I occupy. It made me more aware of the need for indigenous students who carry these deep reflections and practices to occupy spaces that weren't meant for us, such as higher education. Being able to share my learning experience with a great professor and cohort was an experience of a lifetime that I will always cherish. We all came from different journeys [and] being able to share them and learn from each other was an experience I could never find in a classroom. I'm grateful for the experience and humbled by the Filipino people who took their time to host us, to share with us, and to bless us with their stories.

SUFI, a Tongan student: Gosh, this is really the case where the ocean separates us and connects us! Not one or the other. We really feel it here. I'm so lucky to have been on both sides of the big ocean, on so many islands in the Pacific now, on many parts of our Oceania! Unbelievable!

TAVITA'S CLASS

"Their world has opened up big time. It's a bigger world this time for them, you know? Our ocean." These were the first words Tavita told me when I asked about how his students were doing in the class that he was teaching. The fall quarter had just started its third week of ten, with Tavita teaching the first-ever foundational Pacific Islander studies class my department had offered.[16] This survey course was the result of our collective attempt to put out something that we had never done before, even though our department and other academic units on campus had already offered Pacific Islander classes before that were focused on one ethnic group or a specific topic, not a survey course like this one. But more special than having a foundational course, this class was somehow extra significant for many of us, teachers and students, because we looked to Tavita as someone who was one of ours, trained in the specific study of Pacific Islanders within an ethnic studies graduate program, now grown up, and teaching a class at the institution where he obtained his bachelor's degree. He was local. It was here at UW where he "discovered" his calling as a scholar, in quite unexpected and convoluted ways, as we usually said to each other whenever we had time to reminisce. Our ocean brought us together, despite and *because* of the separating distances of our origins and routes. "We've traveled a long way, B," he mused, "and we've come back! Back to where we started."

I told Tavita I was proud of him. But he always seemed hesitant to accept compliments, and I understood that, so he just grinned widely, offered me a long hug, then quickly moved to another topic.

That move of his was short-lived, however, for I swiftly pulled him back to the business of his new class, in a way, to signal to him that it was okay, and that he deserved an acknowledgment that he was doing a more-than-good-enough job, I thought. I wanted to know the mood within his class, in preparation for a guest lecture he asked me to give, so that I could tweak my plans if needed. I was both apprehensive and excited; I was afraid I might underperform in front of a class of what I heard were super enthusiastic and smart students, but I was also eager to be in a class I wished I had taken myself when I was in college. This was incredibly exciting to me, and saying yes to this guest lectureship was secretly my ploy to get into Tavita's classroom, for sure. I didn't want to just sit in, for that would have been so distracting to everyone, and would have made Tavita unnecessarily and unfairly anxious. But I also wanted to observe everybody, so the guest lecture eventually became my one and only chance to do so.

Tavita told me his students were ready for me. They had been introduced to the study of the ocean on so many levels already, from thinking about it as a physical geographical entity to imagining it as an open space of ideas and practices, as a metaphor for a variety of meanings and expressions, and as a source of indigenous knowledge or ways to understand the world. "We already familiarized ourselves with the big map, you know," continued Tavita. "Funny how the map of the Pacific is so huge it occupies so much of the earth, yet so many are so unfamiliar with it! Yeah? I had to study hard to identify each island, hah! Kinda tough. And I showed them a Pacific-centered map too! That was fun!" It was my first time to see a map configured this way, so it was something new I learned as well. We both remarked that showing a map that decentered every continent and then purposefully presented the Pacific in full, not cut in half as most other flat maps did, was refreshingly unusual. It was also eye-opening for students, Tavita reported, after he asked them to view the map up close so they could see each and every one of the islands better and in their full form now that they were not as tiny as most maps would have drawn them. This was his way of illustrating for his class the power of illusions, the benefits of learning competing perspectives, and the social constructions of "smallness," which their Hauʻofa reading invited them to question.[17] Smallness is indeed a state of mind.

"Smallness" as a descriptor for the Pacific was also something that Tavita deployed in introducing his students to the field of Pacific Islander studies, noting for them the ways in which the field of study had been ignored, denied legitimacy, and undervalued precisely because of how tiny and inconsequential the islands had been perceived to be. Tavita opined: "I think this has made our students see the ocean in a different way. They see its larger contexts of things like colonization and its aftereffects, you know? Colonization made us feel unimportant. Made others see us small."

Then I asked, "So how are your students resisting this? Have you talked about that already?"

Oh, right from day one, from the very beginning, hah! I told them, from now on, let's see how things that we say and do can be things that we say and do to actually resist this bad history. Yeah? To resist colonization. Yeah?

Tell me!

Well, I made sure we read a chant on day one and then we sang a song on day two. Right at the top of the class. I said, okay, let's do this piece by piece. One by one. You see, this chant . . . this chant is old. It is ancient, I told them. And it is sacred. It means so-and-so, and this and that, I told them. And our colonizers banned this from being said out loud by our people . . . practically outlawed it! So now that we have it, we have it back from that time, we're gonna try to bring it back, yeah? So, see, this mere attempt to bring it back to our presence now . . . in the class-room . . . this is . . . a form of resistance, yeah? We resist what the colonizers did. We bring back what they tried to . . . you know . . . suppress. So, here we are! We're performing the chant, we're doing it out loud . . . so we're practically performing an act of resistance. Yeah? Get it?

Later on, I spoke to one of the students who was in this class. Here's Debbie, a Sāmoan, responding to my questions about colonization and Pacific Islanders:

I'm still trying to figure it out, but now I see more and more the bigger picture, you know. Like, I see how pieces are fitting together, ya? Like, why our class has never been offered before, why only now, why it took us to beg for this class, why we don't hear about islanders being talked about in other classes, why our histories are never told. All these whys, you know? And then, yeah, in class, now that we have our own, I see how things come together, you know? Like, we don't only study our history and our experiences with colonization. We also look for ways to do things differently, you know? Like, doing songs . . . singing in class . . . other people will find that strange, you know? We don't do these things in our regular classes. But with us, that's our culture! That's who we are. So we do it in class, of course! How else? We learn from songs and from dances, and from chants. That's where our history is, and all these messages about who we are. Ya?

And then, here's something to connect Debbie's thoughts with those of Tavita, who said this to me later on, as the school's term was coming to a close:

Well, we try to do things a bit different here. I try to inject some islander stuff everywhere in class. You know how we do this? We start with a prayer, we end with a prayer. We do these songs and dances. I teach them a particular form of storytelling too. Like, we talk about tapas . . . about mats . . . and how they are storybooks in a way, you know? We lay them out on the floor, like, we spread them out so that everyone can see them all laid out. And then we tell stories, we read stories to each other. We follow the flows of the tapa. We try to be islander in doing things, like reading together, singing together, studying together. Ya? We bring food, we eat together, we share what we have, you know?

Once, this is funny, listen. . . . The other week, I noticed that students were kinda not doing their homework, they were sliding down, like, they were coming to class unprepared. So, you know what I did? I scolded them. But to do this, I told all of them first to sit on the floor, form a circle, gather around each other, with me sitting down with them too, you know? I said, okay, let's all level with each other, ya? Let's talk, eye to eye, face to face. What's going on? they asked. But I told them to just sit down and sit together. I started the conversation. They got it. They were snickering at first. But after a few seconds, they knew what was going to happen. They've seen their elders do this. They've seen their communities do this. They became serious . . . more serious about it. It turned out to be a great session, you know? Students explained their struggles. They talked, you know. We aired our beef with each other. That's the islander way of dealing with stuff, ya? We did that in class! We did what a normal Pacific Islander community would do. Isn't that awesome?

Tavita indeed made sure to turn his classroom space into a community space, befitting how we did so in all of our oceanic-inflected lives on campus. On the day I guest lectured, I was told to stay put in my office. "Someone's going to pick you up," he instructed, "but, can we use your car?" We laughed out loud on the phone. "Tanielu will pick you up. He volunteered. He said he'd be honored to drive you." I said, "Of course!"

Tanielu, our Sāmoan-Filipino student, arrived way ahead of time. He said it was because we needed to pick up the food first. I half smiled, wondering aloud to him if there was going to be a party of some sort. Anything elaborate would really be unnecessary. I hoped this would end up as nothing eventful at all. But then he said: "Why, yes, of course! It will be an event, Professor Bonus. This is our community event, ya? It's a good day. You're teaching us today!"

I soon got nervous, but then Tanielu behaved as if it was just going to be one of those days. As if this was the usual thing for their class. I shrugged my shoulders. By the time we neared their classroom, my nervousness escalated a bit. There was a good-size crowd gathered in the hallway. And when I entered the room, I noticed how unexpectedly large the class was. "I didn't know you have this many students, Tavita," I whispered to him, as he hugged and greeted me by the door. We both walked into the room, toward the front, where a mini lectern and chair were waiting for me. "Oh no," he quickly muttered, "a lot of the people here are guests." "Huh?" I said. "You have guests?"

Yeah, I invited some people, you know, ha-ha, and then students invited their guests too, you know. Look! Let's see . . . hmm . . . there, you see (*motioning with his head in different directions across the room*) . . . there's [name] from the OMA [Office of Minority Affairs and Diversity], there's [name] from advising, [name] from athletics, and then, yeah, Migetu over there. You see him? He's always here; he always shows support; that's good! And then, look, over there . . . there's [name] sister, [name] cousin, and [name] boyfriend, I think. We always run out of chairs, you know. It's like a community event! Every time we have class, ha-ha. But today is even more special, 'cause you're teaching!

My notes from that day were scribbled fast, for I was trying to capture the class's collective positive energy, which I had rarely experienced or observed in most classes I had been in. But despite many years hence, I could easily recall observations that I didn't even write down. I remember telling myself how it was so obvious to me and to anyone else who would care to think about it, that students in a class like this performed much better than usual. They came to class prepared and ready to interact with me, they were attentive and serious in their engagement with me and with one another, and they were able to draw connections so naturally, as it appeared to me, between their course materials and their personal lives. They were quite adept at linking individual struggles with a critique of society, of institutional forms of inequality, and of modes of resistance and transformation. They were performing beyond par. And why? It was because they were finding meaning in the class they were in. They were positively engaged in their own education.

So, I thought, what else could be said, other than the obvious? I posed the question to some of the students themselves, and to their teacher as well. Here are some of their thoughts:

> Well, it's not as obvious as you think. I think that we realize now ... we kinda expect all of our classes to be like this, no? But then, we take all these classes that are completely the opposite! Like, we take classes in chemistry or biology or something, and nothing gets connected with our lives! Nothing!

> Ha-ha. That's true. And then, we take this class. And then, we wonder, wow, isn't this what it's supposed to be? How come we're experiencing this for the first time? And we're juniors already? That sucks.

> I wish classes were more like this, you know? Then, we'll all get As. Everybody will not think about it as going to class. Like, it's not going to be dragging our feet all the time, or worrying about tests and all that, struggling to wake up and go to school. Instead of all this, wow, we just go to our community! Everyone will just be happy to see each other and talk to each other. Like ... this is what learning is all about, ya? I wish school was like this ... every class ... and every classroom.

> I like that every day we go to this class, we are excited to be here. No pressure, you know? The only pressure, I guess, is to make sure you come prepared, that's all. But see, that's not even pressure for me. That's like ... it's your responsibility, you know. It's your responsibility to read and write, and keep up, and all. It's your contribution to the community. This class, for sure, makes us feel like this is our community. This is our ocean!

> TAVITA: I thought about that too, you know. When I was designing this class, I thought about all the classes I've been to. And then suddenly, I was

going to be responsible for teaching this. Man, I better make it good! Like, I better make it connect with the students, whether they were Pacific Islanders or not. I want everybody to connect. And to learn. And to get to know the ocean really well. And to live it too! I'm really inspired, Profe.

By the end of the quarter, as expected, there was yet another gathering in this class, a larger one to cap such a momentous set of community events. The last weeks of class were devoted to students' presentations, and I was invited to watch them. After the last group of students presented, a big round of applause thundered all across the hallways, right when Tavita was about to make his concluding remarks. He hadn't even begun to make his speech, but the students couldn't help but show their appreciation to their teacher as well as to themselves, as a collective of Pacific Islander learners. I saw both happy and sad faces as Tavita thanked everyone, motioning others—each and every student, one by one—to stand up and be acknowledged. He also expressed his gratitude toward us, the community guests from within and outside of the school, and, finally, he asked everyone to pray with him, to thank our families, our ancestors, and our "higher beings" for making all this possible.

A week passed, when I got a call from Tavita, who asked me, "How do you deal with grades for our class? I want to give everyone As. Everybody. Ya? Well, except those who didn't do much, you know? Like, those who just faded away?" "Well," I responded, "do as you wish! You're the teacher, Tavita." Assigning appropriate grades for classes like this, I thought, always posed challenges for teachers like us who thought and taught differently about the meanings of learning, the manners of considering the classroom as a community, and the standards by which students who found meaning in their classes were to be evaluated. Surely, the forms of learning my students and I undertook in these regards—from the "independent studies" of their work outside of the classrooms in the form of outreach and recruitment projects as well as studies abroad, to the "community work" they performed under the rubric of an actual college course—were not altogether new. All of these had been done before, in so many meaningful and successful ways to those who participated in them.[18] What was quite new to us was the infusion of Pacific Islander–themed ideas and practices of schooling that recognized, not pushed aside, a consciousness of the historical continuities of islander colonization that itself became a generative space for resisting the ravages of such a horrible past, for finding community in the ocean that was their school, and for searching for productive ways to be both a Pacific Islander and a student, as well as a teacher. These were indeed lessons on how school transformation, in the oceanic way, was enabled, configured, and engaged.

CONCLUSION
Transformative Schooling against Boundaries

It was an extraordinarily warm Saturday for the month of June, I remember thinking then. And it didn't help that we were wearing our thick and velvety college graduation outfits, looking so regal and official, and quite accomplished, yet dripping in sweat all over. It was more than warm; it was dry heat, we had another layer of clothing underneath our robe, and it was really, really hot. Whew! I couldn't even read my field notes for this particular day; there were ink stains all over, some small specks of dried-up dripped water (or sweat) here and there, and handwriting that was mostly unrecognizable even to me. But I do remember how my small office was abuzz with excitement with, say, six or seven graduating students, all Pacific Islanders, plus two hangers-on, and me, all of us squeezed tightly into an oddly shaped shoebox of an office space. Of course, for the students, this day was the culmination of many years of hard work, so it was definitely a day to prep for and be proud of. Everybody just kept fussing over themselves and one another. We were all giddy, but we were also quite anxious. Graduation speeches have routinely reminded graduates and guests that graduations are not the end, they are just the beginning, yeah, yeah, yeah; hence the admonition to refer to graduations instead as "commencement exercises" or beginnings. That was what was usually said. But for these students, part of their nervousness was manifested in questioning precisely that. Why do we have to start all over again? Who wants to begin anew? Can't we just simply move on from here? Can't we just continue our travels?

The reality of having to leave school once coursework was done was something I had seen many students face with excitement in the course of my professorship. But for those in this study, I had noticed how qualitatively different students' feelings were around this time of graduation or commencement. They were stressed, yes, as most students were so, as soon as they would be confronted with their impending and soon-to-be permanent participation (or not) in the job market. But they also did not want to leave school just yet. They were ready to work, as some of them had found jobs already, yet the thought of leaving behind a good part of their community—their ocean—was something that did not quite make sense to them, or something that they did not seem to desire. It was not as if time passed by just too quickly. And no, it was not about wanting to start all over again, or about extending the time left for finishing school. It was about continuing to make the school a space for themselves and for all those they counted as part of their communities. It was about wanting to preserve this practice of making school a meaningful location of what they thought constituted, even partly, who they were. It was about keeping the school within a place that had now been coextensive with and linked to every other spot in the vast seas of porous boundaries that organized and defined their lives.

Tavita, like almost all of the students whom I encountered in the course of this work, started out in college as an outsider, in the absolute sense of the word. He had never set foot on a university campus, he did not know anyone close who went to college, he practically did not think much about what college was all about! And when, indeed, he went to college, nobody knew him. For a while, nobody recognized him, and no one really took the time and care to know about him, until after he made friends with his dorm mates and until after he came up to one or two of his teachers to tell them he was a Pacific Islander undergraduate student. Tavita endured the agony of being in a place where his value as a human being, as a student of color, was mostly solely determined by the fact that he added one more number to the school's miniscule count of Pacific Islander students in attendance on campus. That was how he felt. And as he found himself in situations in which he was almost always perceived as an outsider, in social, cultural, and intellectual terms, there was no other recourse for him but to call on something that he knew best. This something was already a part of him, this he and I thought over and over; it was something that just needed to be shorn up and enhanced, and even transformed in this new place where he had landed. In fact, other than giving up, this was his only chance at survival in the alienating school that he attended.

"Is this islander thing something that is natural to you?" I asked Tavita once, over the phone, in one of the many long conversations we had over the years, even after he finished his degree at UW and moved on to graduate school, and then eventually obtained his PhD and became a college professor in California.

"Ooh, that's a trick question, huh," he smartly replied, paused, then continued:

Of course, I'm a Pacific Islander! I'm Polynesian. I'm Sāmoan. I was born on the islands, and I was raised in island ways. But yeah, I wouldn't call it just natural. I'd call it, I don't know, upbringing, maybe? To say it's natural kinda means it cannot be taught, yeah? Or it's something biological and essential. Or that you don't have to take care of it just because you have it. Inside of you. It can be taught. And yeah, you have to care for it, if you want to. Or else, it just . . . goes away, maybe?

"Then, why did you turn to your culture when you were in school? Why did you do this? To keep you from leaving college or make you do better in it? Why did you think about being a Pacific Islander?" I egged on.

"Because I was lonely," Tavita said.

We both paused, thinking of what he just said, me feeling a bit sad. I asked him to say a bit more, and he elaborated:

But it was not because my culture provided me with company, you know. Not that way, I think. I had to look for other people who were like me, I guess. I had to create community with other students like me. Who were like me, I thought. I looked for them. And then, what? Culture was something I thought we created among ourselves, for ourselves, using what we knew, what we inherited from home, what our parents taught us, or what we just observed from how we were brought up. It was just hard being alone. I had to look for others. Mind you, the first [islander] student I encountered was not even Sāmoan. He was Tongan! Someone [who was] thought of as the enemy of all Sāmoans, hah! Remember? Mafu? I saw him walking on the street, and we both did a double take. I pointed at him, and he pointed at me. And we both smiled. Ha-ha. I knew he was Tongan. And he knew I was Sāmoan. People think we [our people] don't get along. But then . . . what do you know? We did! We became friends right away. Of course, it's because we found things in common, but we found things that were also different [between the two of us]. But we worked on them along the way. We're besties 'til today, huh.

"So . . . what did you guys want? What did you want to do? Did you plan on doing things, like making a change on campus?" I asked.

We wanted some things to change, you know. We wanted community. We wanted to be present, to be visible, you know. We wanted to be known, to be accounted for, I think. Things cannot just be this way. The school needs to change. It needs to know us. It needs to change how it thinks about us, you know? It cannot just be the way it ignores us, or doesn't really know about us. Or thinks about us in stereotypes, you know? Like we were all football players. And I'm not! Schools need to learn too. And then, I . . . I think it wasn't just about the two of us as students, you know? It was for a whole lot of us, for our collective, for students like me and the future islander students who will be here after us. We wanted [to do] . . . something different for our community, for our people. And, of course, in a way, we wanted to do all these things for our school. So that it can be changed. For the better.

What motivates certain students to transform their school? What makes students choose "culture" as a fundamental element of such a transformation? In this book, we began with a reconsideration of conventional understandings of "success" and "failure" to calculate the extent to which Pacific Islander students and their allies pursued, negotiated, and offered their college campus communities a different approach to being a student, a different way of practicing school, even a different way of being and becoming. Rather than organizing student lives around the quest for the top grades (leading to eventual graduation and successful participation in the labor force afterward) or the mere fulfillment of requirements needed to earn a degree, and concomitantly demanding from them the usual virtues of hard work, sacrifice, and persistence that would supposedly make them garner the best marks, these students ordered their lives instead around the quest for meaningful schooling. They intentionally asked their school to assist them in such an effort by—the very same things we asked our students to do with their school and with their teachers—working hard, sacrificing, and persisting along with them, by listening to them, and by valuing who they were beyond the statistical numbers they represented in student demographic counts. In order to be successful at these, students here needed to do several things, sometimes one after the other, but oftentimes simultaneously and repeatedly, finding their way along through trials and mistakes.

They needed to transform themselves first. Or in more precise terms, these students thought they needed to first change their understanding of who they were as students of color and who they were in relationship to how their school perceived them. Once they had a clearer picture of how their identities and cultures mattered to their images and statuses as college students, the work of bringing their school to change its ways of treating them, as well as the ways in which their school treated other students who were similarly situated, became more manifest. They then thought about changing their school's cultures of teaching and dealing with students like them. This was how they paved their road to "success" in college.

I do not mean to abstract a well-defined and tried-and-tested recipe for school transformation here, now that we have reached the book's conclusion, where the expectation is for the author to mark coherences and offer relevant and practical applications. As I grapple with the intricacies of my academic thinking regarding school performance and student cultures vis-à-vis the voluminous records of student voices and interactions I have accumulated over the course of more than ten years of fieldwork, as well as the nuances and complexities, including the contradictions, of my subjects' thought processes and actions, I am careful to extrapolate on things that did not first appear as logical as they do now. And perhaps, the best way to approach such a project of analysis by hindsight is to invoke yet again the meanings of "the ocean in the school," the imagined and real totality—although not in a totalizing way—of the students' understanding of themselves and their school that named, undergirded, and defined this book's central theme of university transformation by Pacific Islander students and their allies. Let me recapitulate this.

If we follow, as the students did, Epeli Hauʻofa's (and also Teresia Teaiwa's and Albert Wendt's) invocation to think of the ocean as that which encompasses lands, instead of lands that are merely surrounded by ocean, then we can reimagine a kind of ocean that connects rather than separates.[1] For students who felt isolated from and alien to university schooling on the mainland, thinking this way enabled them not only to mitigate their distance from their island homelands in physical and temporal terms, but also to register their social estrangement from the dominant cultures of their school that treated them as if they were outsiders, incapable students, and, many times, even invisible beings. They invoked the ocean to understand their world. Of course, thinking this way did not have immediate effects, nor was it regarded as a straightforward cure-all for many student anxieties. Thinking and "practicing" a way of acting upon the ocean in the school was a daily but uneven and unstable process of working through, forgetting, reminding, doing again, engaging, and improving. It was something that had its highs and lows, sometimes clearly obvious, and sometimes tacit. The ocean in the school was lived experience; one of starts and stops, discovery and propagation, practice and change.

At the core of what had to occur for these students was learning how the ocean or how their school "navigated" them. What was the world like for a Pacific Islander student in college at that moment and place? For them, it was a world that dominated their existence, one that controlled their actions and determined their fates. School was about rigid rules, limited and limiting opportunities, and exclusionary spaces and attitudes. It was not that difficult to understand their university as the place that persistently reminded them of their colonized lives, the lives that they had already experienced way back before college, but only now appearing to them in much more palpable and precise ways because of a newly discovered language to designate it as such. This was how their ancestors were treated, and this was how their colonial masters continued to treat them. This world, they thought, was the past right in "front" of them. They were able to see it vividly—in the courses they took, in their interactions with their instructors, in the company of their classmates.[2] But going through nontraditional courses and reading what for them were new and alternative books that tackled issues such as racism, multiculturalism, and anti-imperialism in much more straightforward and critical ways than how they encountered them in high school (if they ever did), they began to learn and deploy a vocabulary that represented realities which before had no words attached to them. They also met teachers like me, and other students who thought and felt like them.

These students began to understand their treatment as outsiders not so much as an explanation of their being culturally different from the rest (as many were wont to convince them), but rather as an insidious practice of structural racism and sexism extending way back from their islands' colonization by the very nation they were a part of. They were treated as outsiders, but they soon started comprehending this experience as part of a larger context of an imperialist force whose historical stretches of white supremacy now encompassed their lives as students. It made sense that they were also seen as incapable, even unqualified to be called college students, and it was not because their teachers and classmates were not used to dealing with them or were simply misjudging them, they thought. It was because they were already imagined and assumed to be like that, way back before they entered the campus. And it became clearer day after day that the reason why so many people on campus were clueless about who they were as island people from the Pacific was not only because these people were stupid or unknowledgeable. It was also because, for them, islanders were not worth knowing. They were unimportant, these islander students surmised, and their value as people with no importance, even though their ancestors' labors were mercilessly exploited in wars and empire building, was again understood as all too distinctly yet another organic and sinister part of the colonial constellation of their people's conquest, deracination, and manipulation now materializing so garishly in this place called their university campus. This was, then, a part of the ocean that they had mixed feelings about, for it was their history and their reality. It was one that they were occupying right now. And it needed to be changed.

To be able, then, to start comprehending what the campus world was like for a Pacific Islander student at that time and place was to similarly know their location in a larger world and their relationship to that larger world. It was the same thing, or at least it amounted to one, as understanding that one was not simply an individual who was a Pacific Islander but, in true oceanic attitude, an individual who was connected with other Pacific Islanders, living and interacting in spaces related to and inseparable from each other. It was in this spirit that students such as Tavita and Migetu, Junior, Tanielu, Debbie, Kabru, and Apala, among so many others, yearned to find their community—or communities— with those others who came from familiar locations, both geographically and metaphorically, who experienced common conditions, and who shared similar histories and struggles. By word of mouth and happenstance, islander students got themselves connected and made attempts at organizing one another in small groups, recruiting even those who showed the slightest interest in making community with them, and, soon enough, coming to terms with a recognition of their mutual fates, attitudes, and desires. In their so doing, the work of school transformation was organically and intimately linked to this quest for community in the very same ocean they inhabited, for there could never be a separate or isolated set of spaces within the campus for these communities to exist if the practice of creating oceanic-related spaces were to flourish.

School/ocean transformation, for these students, meant reinforcing or oftentimes changing one's attitudes toward the self, the communities that one formed or associated with, and the campus that one had to contend with. Deploying an arsenal of cultural and ethical practices they learned at home and in the course of their migration experiences, islander students began a process of reaching in and casting out, educating themselves on their histories and conditions, teaching others about who they were through cultural presentations and workshops, leading recruitment efforts by outreaching to local high school islanders, and participating in campus student governance so that they had a place on certain tables of power. This also meant emphasizing to themselves and to others the values of respect for elders, for nature, and for religious be-liefs; the importance of community; and the paramount significance of taking care of one another in an ocean that was initially thought of as inhospitable. "Forming islander communities was not just for culture, not just to bring us together," Debbie once said to me. Forming communities, to her, was itself an expression of critique against a schooling environment that was not designed for islanders to succeed in. It was a way to reconstitute their world.[3]

A very small group of three students invited me to build a mentorship program that emphasized collaboration, support, and respect. This was one important step in the process for them. Instead of simply capitulating to the demands of their school to stay quiet and just be regular students, they envisioned a different set of possibilities. They wanted to do well in their school by studying together, keeping an eye out for one another while maintaining solid attachments to the virtues of caring, gratitude, and social responsibility that their families and communities taught them. Soon enough, this mentorship program flourished; it attracted a good number of committed participants and thereafter enlarged its reach to include students from other racial and ethnic groups. These students also focused on inviting high schoolers to come over—most of them setting foot on a college campus for the very first time in their lives, as the students did so before them—rather than visiting them in their high school campuses, which was the typical recruitment strategy in our university and in many other colleges. They recruited staff and a few interested faculty to join their on- and off-campus communities of support, to help them advocate for awareness, effective recruitment, and academic visibility. They brought community members into their campus to partake in their activities, in the learning and celebration of their cultures, and in intentionally narrowing the distances between campus and community lives. They considered learning their histories and cultures outside of their classrooms, even outside of their country. They discovered ways to engage issues of difference in these alternative sites, and then, when they returned to campus, they championed for the appreciation and acknowledgment of these differences, so that such differences became regarded as assets instead of deficits. They taught each other what they knew, and they in turn taught each other how to teach to others. And finally, they wanted their own class, so much so that a member of their community (who was a graduate student then) eventually designed and taught a course of their own, something that cohered and shared indigenous islander funds of knowledge and manners of teaching and learning that were rarely acknowledged and appreciated in almost all of the other courses they took in their college life. This class filled beyond capacity and later became regarded as a significant milestone for Pacific Islander history in the university. These students wanted their school to be relevant and accountable to them. They wanted their campus to be transformed along with them.

At the center of this transformation, I now have come to understand, was the practice of inclusive community building, of constructing, sustaining, and nurturing communities that were not so focused on boundaries of who can and cannot belong, and what can and cannot be done. It was something that was rarely mentioned out loud, but if there was one major matter that students longed for and *struggled* with, it was how to put this community of social relations into practice not only by them, but to be inclusive of everyone in the school who was interested and invested in the welfare of such a community. Students' idea of what a "community" was stressed its porous quality, its non-isolation, as well as its plurality. These qualities showed in their relative openness to members and program participants who were not specifically identified as Pacific Islander, in the conventional blood-determined way; in their refusal to segregate themselves, their organizations, and activities from the mainstream and centers of campus; and in their insistence on respecting the diverse elements of their own ethno-cultural and ethno-linguistic groups both within and outside of the Pacific Islander category. They desired communities in the plural. And they wanted their school to do the same.

In the end, these students wanted their school to recognize them, but only in ways that would respectfully engage with their cultures and communities. We almost always ask students to adapt to their school's standards in order to be successful. We require them to conform, to follow rules, to change their habits. And when they indeed obey, we reward them with outstanding marks and we hustle them into graduation and into the workforce right away. We do not want to keep them for long. Pacific Islander students who "fail" teach us a different lesson here, for their departure from school makes us realize that school models such as this unfairly privilege only those students who are willing to assimilate and conform, while disadvantaging others whose desires to learn and make meaning out of their schooling are differently configured when compared with the rest. These students left their school because they found it to be unwelcoming to those who took time to discover who and what they wanted to be, those who desired to integrate community work into their curricula, and those who considered school resources as holistically integrated with their family and community possessions. They considered themselves lifelong learners and alternative thinkers, but in quite violent though subtle ways, we have pushed them out, strictly policing the conventional boundaries of success and failure in our schools in our pursuit of narrowly calculating the limits of what can and cannot be. By the same token, we got to know students here who arrived at the university and were mostly thought of as "unprepared," yet they rarely heard any discourse on how schools were just as quite "unprepared" (or even completely so, as in many cases) to teach students like them. And for all the talk about dealing with "diverse" students such as the ones mentioned in this book, a good number of us educators and school caretakers have, over many years, barely set out efforts straight into making these students more "college ready" while rarely ever questioning how the ways we educate *all* of our students once they step into college have remained restrictively the same over so many years and across so many spaces. These "failed" students have a lot to teach us about the perils of uniformity, rigidity, and conformity in the ways we run our schools.

If the subjects of this book saw themselves transformed by the very school that appeared alien, neglectful, or hostile to them, they also witnessed parts of their school transformed institutionally because they prodded it to do so. The small and low-key PIPE mentorship program they started as a way to create a collective of learners who valued being a Pacific Islander *and* a student at the same time is now more than fifteen years old, and still running. These students asked their university to recognize their status as islanders, separate from their usual inclusion into the Asian American category, and so they have since been named and counted separately, and there's a student commission that is dedicated to addressing their group's specific needs and interests. At the school's Ethnic Cultural Center, Pacific Islander students and their allies mobilized in a rally to demand a separate function room for their community, and they got it. And during the last two years that I was writing and finishing this book, a minor in Oceania and Pacific Islander studies was launched, now housed in UW's Department of American Indian Studies. This academic program— hopefully, one that will become a major later, or even its own department in the future—was the brainchild of a group of students, faculty, staff, and community members, whose initial meeting was held twenty years earlier. Another incarnation of this group, created thirteen years later, and primarily led by Pacific Islander graduate students, committed that this program be implemented by the time they graduated, at the least. It was.

While this study did not directly measure the qualitative effects of Pacific Islander transformation projects upon the larger institution, many of its subjects were modestly proud of the difference they made—in whatever form or depth—on the lives of others while they were themselves on campus. Many of them also made it a point to visit their ocean after they left it, to see how things were going. A good sense of the collateral benefits of school/ocean transformation was something that was not talked about loud though. They were too discreet to do that, and some of them even thought it would have been so inappropriate to brag about something that was done without expectation to be praised for. I, on the other hand, tried to make sure that their due recognition was brought up whenever an opportunity to do so came. During the launch of the Oceania and Pacific Islander studies minor, I told the audience during my speech that a debt of gratitude should flow not to our school, the institution that now finally recognized Pacific Islander studies as a legitimate academic program, but to the students instead—especially those who fought for this program but were not here to take it. In their selfless and community-inspired ways, these students gave us gifts from their troves of oceanic knowledge and practice, which have now ended up as opportunities that will surely enrich the lives of so many others.

I can imagine these students telling educators that the boundaries we have erected between succeeding and failing in school, between what counts as knowledge and what does not, and between what constitutes respectful and inclusive schooling and what is undervalued or excluded, cannot hold sway for long if we are to make education more accessible and meaningful to our increasingly heterogeneous and multiple communities. Just as how Pacific Islander students and their allies constituted and sustained their own communities of care and respect, they also imagined and worked toward transforming their school—even a small part of it, they admitted—into a place that was more caring and respectful toward them. They changed their school or, more precisely, they changed their idea, imagination, and practice of their school, because they needed this place to matter to them, to connect with them, and they wanted to allow themselves and their communities to be constitutively woven into the very school that they sought to transform. In many ways, this "ocean in the school" became a more meaningful part of their world, their communities, their lives. And, as their university was transformed, they began to understand themselves in ways that exceeded their own individualities. They became larger than and more connected with the smaller communities they inhabited.

Each of the students I interacted with here, even those who chose not to graduate from their university, expressed to me in so many breathtaking ways how coming to school and attempting to change it mattered a great deal to them. It was like being a part of a larger history that was unfolding and mutating before their eyes. It was like slowly, then regularly, feeling as if they belonged and sensing that they were important. They found neither just a degree-granting elite institution nor a place to simply visit temporarily. They attempted to convert it instead into a set of spaces where discovery, family, and community could be enabled and nurtured. They uncovered meaning in linking knowledge with practice, they campaigned for appreciating the values and lessons of their histories and cultures, and they pursued what they thought was worth advocating for no matter how few or seemingly inconsequential they were. They thus saw themselves alive, important, and belonging in communities larger than themselves but profoundly and organically related to each and every one of them. Their university became connected with their wide and deep ocean. No wonder that during graduation, they did not want to leave it. Their school—their living ocean—was going to be a part of their lives forever.

INTRODUCTION

1   "Transforming schools" is a term I use loosely here for now, but it is widely articulated in the entire book. Within educational studies, it has a relatively recent origin as a term, it denotes multiple meanings, and it is referred to in different names and formulations, as well as applied to any or all levels of schooling. It may also include any or all schooling participants, curricula, teaching practices, and institutional policies. Edmund O'Sullivan, a principal advocate of the kind of transformative schooling I write about here, notes that "transformative education involves experiencing a deep structural shift in the basic premises of our thoughts, feelings and action. It is a shift of consciousness that dramatically and permanently alters our way of being in the world. Such a shift involves an understanding of ourselves and our self locations, our relations with other humans and with the natural world; an understanding of the relations of power in the interlocking structures of class, race, and gender; our body awareness; our visions of alternative approaches to living; and our sense of possibilities for social justice and peace and personal joy" ("The Project and Vision of Transformative Education," 11). While O'Sullivan privileges the transformation of the individual in his formulation, I instead pay greater attention to the transformation of the structure of the schooling institution in my deployment of the term. This would include primarily the transformation of the ways in which schools transact with their students as coproducers of knowledge, not just consumers of it. Applied to this study, transformative education is the antithesis to and a critique of a "neoliberal educational ethos, which remains oriented by prescriptive, market-driven, and reductionist ideologies" and practices that privilege, for example, through standardized curricula and testing, static models of efficiency in teaching and learning methods, and commodification of the entire schooling process over holistic and critical visions of education (Gardner and Kelly, *Narrating Transformative Learning in Education*, 1). Its philosophies and models run parallel to scholarship and practice emanating from feminist studies, ethnic studies, and studies in multicultural education. It is also allied with, and sometimes equally understood as, emancipatory, liberatory, critical, democratic, or holistic education.

See, for example, the works of Banks, *Multicultural Education, Transformative Knowledge, and Action*; Banks and McGee Banks, *Multicultural Education*; Freire, *Education for Critical Consciousness* and *Pedagogy of the Oppressed*; Giroux, *Pedagogy and the Politics of Hope*; and hooks, *Teaching to Transgress*.

2 I use the demographic category "Pacific Islander," like all the other categories mentioned after it, contingently, knowing and understanding that all such designations group people as if they were all the same or that the people identified under these categories can be different from each other in terms of race, ethnicity, class, age, gender, sexuality, religion, ability, or any other kind of social category. The differentiations across and within these categories are made more apparent in the rest of the book. For a discussion of Pacific Islander heterogeneity in U.S. and other settings, refer to Camacho, "Transoceanic Flows."

3 Sixty-five is the actual number of students who were closely observed and interviewed continuously, and whose responses were formally coded and analyzed. All of them are anonymously cited in this book, either as individuals or as composites. There were numerous other students, more than one hundred, who were informally observed and had casual conversations with me, and whose voices resonate with the main respondents in this ethnography. Unless specified, they are not directly cited in this ethnography.

4 For an actual and more recent study of UW undergraduate students as a whole, refer to Beyer, Gillmore, and Fisher, *Inside the Undergraduate Experience*, a study that was undertaken under the auspices of the UW's Center for Instructional Innovation and Assessment. It did not include Pacific Islander students.

5 Arguments regarding the benefits (or not) of having minorities in schools range from issues such as desegregation to funding priorities in both public and private school settings, and from student performance and curriculum transformation to overall institutional or systemic change in all levels of schooling. See, for example, Conchas, Gottfried, and Hinga, *Inequality, Power, and School Success*; Ferguson, *The Reorder of Things*, chap. 2, "The Proliferation of Minority Difference"; Hochschild and Scovronick, *The American Dream and the Public Schools*; and Tarca, "Colorblind in Control."

6 Refer to similar claims proposed by Darling-Hammond, "What Happens to a Dream Deferred?"; Tienda, "Diversity ≠ Inclusion"; and, collectively, the authors in McCarthy et al., *Race, Identity, and Representation in Education*. There are ample data that document these demographic changes, especially in terms of racial composition of students, in all levels of schooling and in both urban and rural schools. Studies that touch on these include Olson, "Children of Change"; Posey-Maddox, *Reconceptualizing the "Urban"*; and Suárez-Orozco and Suárez-Orozco, *Children of Immigration*. For primary data, consult the U.S. Department of Education, National Center for Education Statistics, *Digest of Education Statistics 2015*. The center's findings for data gathered from 1976 to 2012 show that "the percentage of American college students who are Hispanic, Asian/Pacific Islander, Black, and American Indian/ Alaska Native has been increasing (table 306.100). From 1976 to 2012, the percentage of Hispanic students rose from 4 percent to 15 percent, the percentage of Asian/

Pacific Islander students rose from 2 percent to 6 percent, the percentage of Black students rose from 10 percent to 15 percent, and the percentage of American Indian/ Alaska Native students rose from 0.7 to 0.9 percent. During the same period, the percentage of White students fell from 84 percent to 60 percent" (378). However, there is considerable variance in the data culled just from the last three years before 2013: the numbers of college students are actually decreasing (or stable, on average) for certain subpopulations of black and Asian groups, and specifically for Pacific Islanders and Native Americans. On the basis of SAT and ACT scores, and other benchmarks such as reading assessments, scores in mathematics and science subjects, and Advanced Placement exam scores, the pool for many college-eligible underrepresented high school minorities is also shrinking. The number of school-children of all races who live in poverty, except for white and select Asian students, is increasing. The number of faculty of color in postsecondary institutions was slightly over 21 percent of the total full-time faculty count in 2013. Adams, "SAT-ACT Performance for 2015 Graduates Called 'Disappointing,'" 6; Cole and Barber, *Increasing Faculty Diversity*, 5; multiple essays in Museus, Maramba, and Teranishi, *The Misrepresented Minority*; U.S. Department of Education, National Center for Education Statistics, *The Condition of Education 2016*, 223; U.S. Department of Education, National Center for Education Statistics, *Digest of Education Statistics 2015*, 30, 433; U.S. Department of Education, National Center for Education Statistics, *Status and Trends in the Education of Racial and Ethnic Groups 2010*, 17, 53.

7 Those who write about this particular history of U.S. education have long acknowledged the coupling of schooling (in all levels) with Americanization (otherwise referred to as "citizenship" or the process of "national integration"), specifically of immigrants and colonized subjects. See Carnoy, *Education as Cultural Imperialism*; Chatterjee and Maira, *The Imperial University*; Constantino, *The Miseducation of the Filipino*; del Moral, *Negotiating Empire*; Maramba and Bonus, *The "Other" Students*; Mercer, "Testing and Assessment Practices in Multiethnic Education"; and Racelis and Ick, *Bearers of Benevolence*.

8 In education studies, the key expression here is John U. Ogbu's "dual frame of reference" to denote those students whose schooling experiences are mediated by an exposure to at least two discrete countries or cultures of schooling, as a consequence of their relationship to and subjectification by the state. Ogbu, "Immigrant and Involuntary Minorities in Comparative Perspective." Elaborations can be found in Darling-Hammond, "What Happens to a Dream Deferred?"; Gándara and Contreras, *The Latino Education Crisis*; Gram, *Education at the Edge of Empire*; Matute-Bianchi, "Situational Ethnicity and Patterns of School Performance"; Museus, Maramba, and Teranishi, *The Misrepresented Minority*; Ochoa, *Academic Profiling*; Olneck, "Immigrants and Education in the United States"; Pitre et al., *Educating African American Students*; and Suárez-Orozco, "Immigrant Adaptation to Schooling."

9 Current U.S. colonies in the Pacific include the eastern part of Sāmoa (acquired in 1899 through a treaty between the United States, Great Britain, and Germany); Nuku Hiva in French Polynesia (colonized from 1813 to 1832); Guam (seized from Spain in 1898); several islands in Kiribati, the Marshall Islands (occupied in 1944);

Palau (captured from Japan in 1944); the Federated States of Micronesia (administered starting in 1947); the Northern Mariana Islands (invaded in 1944); and, at some point, Pukapuka and Rakahanga (claimed in 1856, but ceded to the Cook Islands in 1980). The Philippines was a U.S. colony from 1898 to 1946. Hawai'i, before statehood in 1959, was annexed in 1898. See Diaz, *Repositioning the Missionary*; Geiger, *Facing the Pacific*; Go, "'Racism' and Colonialism"; Isaac, *American Tropics*; and Trask, *From a Native Daughter*.

10 This relationship between U.S. imperialism—the exercise of U.S. political, economic, and cultural power over people and societies, including minorities from within the United States and its territories, often by force—and the university (or schooling in general and its disciplinary formations in particular) has been amplified in historical terms by scholars in the following works: del Moral, *Negotiating Empire*; Gram, *Education at the Edge of Empire*; Motha, *Race, Empire, and English Language Teaching*; Ng, "Knowledge for Empire"; Nugent, "Knowledge and Empire"; Stratton, *Education for Empire*; and the contributions in Altbach and Kelly, *Education and the Colonial Experience*, and Chatterjee and Maira, *The Imperial University*. Also see Giroux, "The Militarization of US Higher Education after 9/11," for connections with the U.S. military-industrial-prison complex, and Leonardo, *Race, Whiteness, and Education*, for discussions that include racism and white supremacy in the contexts of empire. From a more structural "global" angle, the role of the U.S. university in reproducing U.S. neocolonialism and global capitalism that extends the historical and contemporary formations of settler colonialism is most succinctly and insightfully discussed by Grace Kyungwon Hong in her review of two books on recent Asian migration to the United States. She writes, instructively, "Globalization as a cultural, political, and economic phenomenon demands that we reconceptualize disciplinary boundaries, objects of study, and methodologies as we shape the role of the university" ("Past Legacies, Future Projects," 118).

11 Neoliberalism is understood here to be the institutionalization of policies and practices that promote self-interest, privatization of social goods, and decreased government participation in the provision of social welfare. In schooling, neoliberalist practices may include high-stakes testing, school choice and competition, school corporatization and commercialization, the hiring of part-time and non-tenure-track faculty. See Newfield, *The Great Mistake*, and Williams, *Consuming Higher Education*.

12 This critique, that certain students are valued only as they indicate a number in the school's "diversity" count but are deeply ignored as racialized bodies at the same time, partly echoes the sentiments of the Korean American students who were the subjects of Nancy Abelmann's incisive ethnography, *The Intimate University*. She claims, "Asian Americans offer, by many counts, the one color that does not count. Even as Asian American students experience often troubling segregation, U.S. racial politics teach them that they are somehow different from other college students of color and thus undeserving of race-based programs and policies" (2). Korean American students, unlike Pacific Islanders, are stereotypically assumed to be overachievers and are perceived to be overrepresented in many campuses. Pacific Islanders are

counted, but ignored, because they are mostly assumed to be insignificant and their cultures are largely unknown or misunderstood. Hence, their critiques are similar to, but qualitatively different from, those put forth by Korean Americans in Abelmann's work. For parallel arguments, refer to Maramba and Museus, "The Utility of Using Mixed-Methods"; the chapters in Museus, Maramba, and Teranishi, *The Misrepresented Minority*; and Tienda, "Diversity ≠ Inclusion."

13 A good number of studies on minorities and schooling look at the identities and socioeconomic backgrounds of students to calculate connections between such individual or group descriptors and performance in educational institutions, including other elements such as school choice, degrees of participation in campus organizations, and places of employment after graduation. See, for example, Vivian Louie's *Compelled to Excel* for the ways in which class differences among Chinese Americans influence college track options, and Michael J. White and Jennifer E. Glick's *Achieving Anew: How New Immigrants Do in American Schools, Jobs, and Neighborhoods*, for a more general overview across different population groups. Other studies, such as *The Asian American Achievement Paradox*, by Jennifer Lee and Min Zhou, combine the effects of "culture" with laws and institutional support in analyzing the reasons why certain Asian Americans have higher rates of school achievement than other minorities. A version of this claim, which focuses instead on the high achievement of Dominican and Colombian young adults in U.S. schools, can be found in Louie's other book, *Keeping the Immigrant Bargain*. These works illustrate how the experiences of Pacific Islander students parallel those of other groups, at the same time as they differ from these groups. I am careful not to count Pacific Islanders within the category "Asian American," for this is an important critique that the subjects of my ethnography vehemently expressed. Studies of Asian Americans in education, especially those that engage with their stereotypical (or mythical) status as "model minorities," are works that intersect with, but are in contrast to, my study of Pacific Islanders in higher education. See Ching and Agbayani, *Asian Americans and Pacific Islanders in Higher Education*; Museus, Maramba, and Teranishi, *The Misrepresented Minority*; and Palaita, "Vāsā (Ocean)—the Space That Is Sacred."

14 "Student development theory" is a relatively large academic enterprise in the field of U.S. education studies. For an expansive summation and discussion, see Evans et al., *Student Development in College*. For a good overview of ethnic development with reference to Chicana and Chicano students, see Pizarro, *Chicanas and Chicanos in School*, 7–23. With reference to the illuminating connections between learning and identity for African American high school youth, see Na'ilah Suad Nasir's *Racialized Identities*. In contrast, studies that deal with what might be termed "school development theory" are rare and sometimes classified under historical studies of education or contemporary critiques of the American educational system. A few examples include Altbach, Berdahl, and Gumport, *American Higher Education in the Twenty-First Century*; Hurtado et al., *Enacting Diverse Learning Environments*; Newfield, *The Great Mistake*; O'Sullivan, *Academic Barbarism, Universities and Inequality*; Turner, *Racial and Ethnic Diversity in Higher Education*; and Williams, *Consuming Higher Education*.

15 In many studies of minorities in school, the campus is simply mentioned as "the setting." This is evident as well in most accounts of primary and secondary school experiences. With specific registers regarding the university itself, the preferred term is "organizational structure" or "institutional characteristics and behavior." See, for example, the reference to college characteristics in Braxton, "Reinvigorating Theory," 260–261, and Cole and Barber, *Increasing Faculty Diversity*, 20–29. "School characteristics" may include enrollment size, quality or selectivity, amount of money spent per student, type of training, and private versus state. Interestingly, Cole and Barber also state that most research finds such characteristics to have little influence on school outcomes (*Increasing Faculty Diversity*, 21). Another term that is used frequently is "campus climate" to encompass a range of variables—from institutional character and the behavior of people who inhabit the institution to curricula, policies, attitudes, and expectations—that collectively form a particular environment for the campus. On this, see Beyer, Gillmore, and Fisher, *Inside the Undergraduate Experience*; Maramba and Museus, "The Utility of Using Mixed-Methods"; and Yosso, *Critical Race Counterstories*.

16 Ferguson, *The Reorder of Things*, 213–214; Nelson, *No University Is an Island*, chap. 2.

17 Hauʻofa's *We Are the Ocean* is a collection of his important essays, interviews, stories, poetry, and artwork written and produced between 1975 and 2006. Integral to his writings was his linking of what would otherwise be the historically and politically separated areas of the Pacific Ocean identified as Micronesia, Melanesia, and Polynesia. Some of his ideas were known and, later, read by the students even before *We Are the Ocean* was published. They were drawn to Hauʻofa because they found in him a vocabulary of what and how they felt about their collective ocean-centered identities: "That the sea is as real as you and I, that it shapes the character of this planet, that it is a major source of our sustenance, that is something we all share in common wherever we are in Oceania—all are statements of fact. But above that level of everyday experience, the sea is our endless saga, the sea is our most powerful metaphor, the ocean is in us" (*We Are the Ocean*, 58). Of course, Hauʻofa has written about Oceania in this manner along with other writers such as Paul D'Arcy, Teresia Teaiwa, and Albert Wendt. It should be fair to say, however, that many students' attention to the ocean cannot be directly and only attributed to what they read. Rather, it was their intellectual exposure to the ocean's centrality in their lives, as it was made legible to them by Hauʻofa and others, that affirmed the connections they were already grappling with between their culture and the struggles they were experiencing in school. Also see such resonances in Wright and Balutski, "Understanding Pacific Islander Indigeneity."

18 Hauʻofa, *We Are the Ocean*. Also see the search for students' "home" in a study conducted by Goodwin in *Resilient Spirits*.

19 Hauʻofa, *We Are the Ocean*.

20 Refer to critiques of "decorative" diversity in Banks, *Multicultural Education, Transformative Knowledge, and Action*; Bowen and Bok, *The Shape of the River*; Bowen and Rudenstine, "Race-Sensitive Admissions"; McLaren, "White Terror and Oppositional Agency"; and Nieto, "From Brown Heroes and Holidays to Assimilationist Agendas."

21 Many educators refer to this set of strategies as bringing "funds of knowledge" or "cultural wealth" into the school. See González, Moll, and Amanti, *Funds of Knowledge*; Goodwin, *Resilient Spirits*; Valenzuela, *Subtractive Schooling*; and Yosso, "Whose Culture Has Capital?" The turn to "culture" as a resource for dealing with school struggles is not uncommon for minority students. It is interesting to note, however, that in many studies, students have "culture" but schools are simply "institutions" or possess "character," as mentioned above, as if schools, at least in terms of institutional behavior, do not follow, display, or practice a particular "culture."

22 Banks, *Multicultural Education, Transformative Knowledge, and Action*; Nieto, *Affirming Diversity*. Also see Au, *Rethinking Multicultural Education*; Howard, *We Can't Teach What We Don't Know*; Sleeter, *Multicultural Education as Social Activism*; Sleeter and Grant, *Making Choices for Multicultural Education*; and all the contributions in Banks and McGee Banks, *Handbook of Research on Multicultural Education*. Multicultural education research and practice extend into all levels of schooling experience, are varied in terms of strategy and application, and have their own share of criticisms and challenges. There is also a deep sense of its specificity to U.S. settings and a recognition that multiculturalism, as it is also advocated and practiced in many parts of the world where different population groups live together, has diverse historical roots and uneven inflections. See Early, "American Education," and Banks, *Diversity and Citizenship Education*.

23 For work on this specific area of inquiry, see Bowen, Schwartz, and Camp, *End of Academic Freedom*; Chatterjee and Maira, *The Imperial University*; Cole, *The Great American University*; Delbanco, *College*; and Ferguson, *The Reorder of Things*.

24 Studies that point to analyzing the wide achievement gaps among groups of students, and prescribing ways to narrow such gaps, abound in education studies. See Howard, *Why Race and Culture Matter in Schools*; Museus, Maramba, and Teranishi, *The Misrepresented Minority*; Rovai, Gallien, and Stiff-Williams, *Closing the African American Achievement Gap*; Singham, *The Achievement Gap in U.S. Education*; and Valencia, *Students of Color and the Achievement Gap*.

25 Enrollment numbers for Pacific Islander students at the UW Seattle campus have ranged from 159 (or 0.6 percent) in 2003 to 261 (or 0.9 percent) in 2012. Source: University of Washington, Office of Minority Affairs and Diversity, Assessment and Research Unit, *State of Diversity at UW—All Campuses*. National census data show that U.S. Pacific Islander adults are less likely than whites to hold a high school diploma or GED, have lower rates of college degree attainment, and, if admitted into college, are usually first-generation and likely unable to finish on time, if at all. In the state of Washington, 12 percent of Pacific Islanders have a bachelor's degree or higher, compared to 28 percent of the total population of state residents, or 24 percent of the entire U.S. population. Nationally, single-race Pacific Islanders are about half as likely as non-Hispanic whites to have at least a bachelor's degree (15 percent versus 30 percent). Sāmoans have the lowest percentage with a college degree. The graduation rate among the cohort of Pacific Islander students who entered UW Seattle in fall 2008 was 76 percent, one of the lowest rates among all U.S. racial groups. Sources: Asian Americans Advancing Justice, *A Community of Contrasts*; Commission

on Asian Pacific American Affairs, *The State of Asian Americans and Pacific Islanders in Washington*; National Commission on Asian American and Pacific Islander Research in Education, *Federal Higher Education Policy Priorities*; National Commission on Asian American and Pacific Islander Research in Education, *The Impact of Scholarships*; Pacific Island Women's Association, *Voices of Pacific Island Women Residing in the Pacific Northwest*; Takeuchi and Hune, *Growing Presence, Emerging Voices*; University of California, Los Angeles, Asian American Studies Center, "Pacific Islanders Lagging behind in Higher Educational Attainment"; and University of Washington, Office of Minority Affairs and Diversity, *State of Diversity at UW*.

26 See Kevin K. Kumashiro's excellent critique of the misuse of "common sense" in advocating for the narrowing of the achievement gap in education, in *The Seduction of Common Sense*.

27 Refer to the variety of explanations for student departure from colleges and universities in Braxton, *Reworking the Student Departure Puzzle*; Fleming, *Enhancing Minority Student Retention*; Tierney, "Power, Identity, and the Dilemma of College Student Departure"; and Tinto, *Leaving College*.

28 Tinto, *Leaving College*.

29 Tinto, *Leaving College*. Also, Nathan, *My Freshman Year*.

30 See a parallel argument made regarding Filipino Americans in the field of education, in Maramba and Bonus, *The "Other" Students*.

31 Many agree that racial and ethnic diversity is desirable, but how to achieve it is debatable. A most instructive summary of these arguments can be found in Cole and Barber, *Increasing Faculty Diversity*, chap. 1.

32 Even though some data show that many Filipinos who immigrated into the United States after 1965 were professional degree holders and were able to occupy highly skilled or professional jobs, the Filipino Americans in this study came from mostly working-class backgrounds. The parents of the Cambodian student in the study came in as refugees. National Commission on Asian American and Pacific Islander Research in Education, *Asian Americans and Pacific Islanders*.

33 See the arguments regarding intragroup diversity in U.S. group identities in Jiménez, Fields, and Schachter, "How Ethnoraciality Matters."

34 All the names specified in this book are aliases.

35 *Yəhawʔali* is a Lushootseed word that refers to a place where things begin or will happen. Lushootseed is the language spoken by the Duwamish people who are native to the Seattle area. *Ubuntu* is originally a Southern African Bantu word that, in contemporary applications, generally means to be a part of a collective or to think of one's self as interconnected with others. The original program was called BASIC PLAN, which stood for Black/African Students in Coalition, Peer Leadership, and Mentoring Program.

36 For a parallel argument regarding the exclusionary history of U.S. higher education and the reproduction of social inequality perpetuated by systems of higher education, see Stich, *Access to Inequality*.

37 The academic literature calculates these perspectives within the rubric of what has been termed a "cultural deficiency" model or theory, most heavily attributed to

the work of anthropologist Oscar Lewis. Although already widely problematized or even discredited by many scholars, numerous so-called "repair the individual" policies and programs continue their deep foothold in school systems at all levels. See Lewis, *Five Families*; Valenzuela, *Subtractive Schooling*; and Pizarro, *Chicanas and Chicanos in School*.

38 Valenzuela, *Subtractive Schooling*, 3.

39 Pizarro, *Chicanas and Chicanos in School*, 25 (italics in the original).

40 Winkle-Wagner and Locks, *Diversity and Inclusion on Campus*.

41 Winkle-Wagner and Locks, *Diversity and Inclusion on Campus*.

42 For specific suggestions on how schooling can be less restrictive and more inclusive, with a view toward achieving greater retention among students and deeper involvement in their schooling, see Astin, "Student Involvement"; Crosling, Thomas, and Heagney, "Conclusions and Curriculum-Based Approaches"; Fleming, *Enhancing Minority Student Retention*; Goodwin, *Resilient Spirits*; Howard, *Why Race and Culture Matter in Schools*; and Moxley, Najor-Durack, and Dumbrigue, *Keeping Students in Higher Education*.

43 Smith, *Decolonizing Methodologies*.

44 Smith, *Decolonizing Methodologies*. For other incisive discussions of the "politics" and limits of social science research methods, see Hau'ofa, *We Are the Ocean*; Law, *After Method*; Rosaldo, *Culture and Truth*; and Starbuck, *The Production of Knowledge*.

45 For inspiration regarding "prophetic criticism," see West, "The New Cultural Politics of Difference."

46 Morgan Gardner, a transformative education scholar, might similarly refer to this process of student-teacher interaction as a "pedagogy of movement." She writes: "In a pedagogy of movement, cohesion and continuity themselves become valued as movements. They, too, are part of the teaching and learning dance of 'certain uncertainties' and 'liquid' change." Gardner, "Transformative Learning," 28. Hau'ofa, *We Are the Ocean*.

CHAPTER 1. THE STUDENTS, THE SCHOOL, THE OCEAN

1 The literature on the presumed universality of schooling (or its particularities relative to specific societies) and its criticisms is quite robust. For the most pertinent examples, see Baker and LeTendre, *National Differences, Global Similarities*; Bowles and Gintis, *Schooling in Capitalist America*; and Young, *Knowledge and Control*.

2 To be sure, critiques of schooling that focus on the disconnect between student diversity and white-centered curricula along with conventional teaching practices abound in education studies. My main inspirations and sources of intellectual illumination for these include Abelmann, *The Intimate University*; Pizarro, *Chicanas and Chicanos in School*; and Valenzuela, *Subtractive Schooling*.

3 For a similar account, see Goodwin, *Resilient Spirits*.

4 García, *The Chicano Movement*; Hong, "Past Legacies, Future Projects"; Maeda, *Rethinking the Asian American Movement*; Rhoads, *Freedom's Web*; Wei, *The Asian American Movement*; Williamson-Lott, *Black Power on Campus*.

5   See Abelmann's *The Intimate University* for a similar study.

6   I should point out here that even though the students' perception of how U.S. empire manifests in their school appears to refer to a singular and unified colonial education project, the historical record shows that the imposition of U.S.-controlled schooling varied among the colonies. Solsiree del Moral, in *Negotiating Empire*, reminds us that

> while as students of US empire, race, and education we must acknowledge that the twin processes of national consolidation and empire building were interconnected, and while we can identify the individuals, institutions, and policies that wove the school projects together, we must not homogenize them. . . . [C]olonial peoples were not racially homogenized as the singular Other. Rather, US policy makers narrated differences in the racial construction of colonial others in the Caribbean and the Pacific. These different racial constructions, which were deeply classed and gendered, informed individual policy governance for each colony. For example, while the alleged amicable, friendly, and receptive "Porto Ricans" could be governed perpetually as members of an unincorporated territory, the wildly diverse and multiethnic brown and black tribal Filipinos could not. (36)

7   For an astute rendition of these historical connections between U.S. colonization and contemporary Pacific Islander student experiences, see Wright and Balutski, "Understanding Pacific Islander Indigeneity." They also point out that the most powerful expressions of colonization of the Pacific in the contemporary can be found in the continuing militarization of the islands and the ongoing struggles for sovereignty, cultural preservation, citizenship options, and control of indigenous lands and resources. For more of these Pacific Islander historical and contemporary "imperial" connections in general, see Camacho, "Transoceanic Flows"; Diaz and Kauanui, "Native Pacific Cultural Studies on the Edge"; Imada, *Aloha America*; Isaac, *American Tropics*; Labrador and Wright, "Engaging Indigeneity in Pacific Islander and Asian American Studies"; Silva, *Aloha Betrayed*; and Trask, *From a Native Daughter*. For a concise but brilliant exposé of and response to Pacific Islander belittlement as a product of imperial subjugation and control, see Hau'ofa, "Our Sea of Islands."

8   This reference to the ocean as a particular marker of experience and practice brings to mind French novelist Romain Rolland's coinage of the term "oceanic feeling," which, as Sigmund Freud would later write about in his work on the primitive ego, refers to a feeling of limitlessness and connection or oneness with the world. Freud, *Civilization and Its Discontents*.

9   All of these definitions and descriptions of the students' vasa were deeply inspired by Hau'ofa's writings, *We Are the Ocean*. Also see D'Arcy, *The People of the Sea*; Diaz, *Repositioning the Missionary*; Teaiwa, "Preparation for Deep Learning"; and Wilson, "Toward an Ecopoetics of Oceania."

10 For Sāmoan notions of self, see Mageo, *Theorizing Self in Sāmoa*.

11 For further ruminations by students on the vasa, see Palaita, *Matamai*, and Pacific Islander Studies Students et al., *Matamai 2*.

12 For the importance of community in college retention programs, see Moxley, Najor-Durack, and Dumbrigue, *Keeping Students in Higher Education*, pt. 3.

13 I do not mean to imply here that a static definition of islanders as sociocentric (as opposed to egocentric) is being proffered either by my respondents or by me. Rather, the notion that students and their family members imagine themselves as parts of larger social worlds is largely contextual, discursive, and in a dialectical relationship with their interior selves. For an ample discussion of this anthropological analytic, as applied to an ethnographic study of Sāmoans, see Mageo, *Theorizing Self in Sāmoa*, especially chap. 1.

14 U.S. Department of Veterans Affairs, Center for Minority Veterans, *Asian American and Pacific Islander Veterans Fact Sheet*.

15 Harris, Jones, and U.S. Census Bureau, *We the People: Pacific Islanders in the United States*; Kahn and Younger, *Pacific Voices*; Washington State Workforce Training and Education Coordinating Board, *Asians and Pacific Islanders*.

16 This claim is also made by many scholars in the field. Refer to the essays in Museus, Maramba, and Teranishi, *The Misrepresented Minority*.

17 University of Washington, Office of Minority Affairs and Diversity, Assessment Unit, *Diversity at the University of Washington—All Campuses*.

18 Occasionally, I also used "composites," or combinations of several subjects under one alias. The subjects' preference for anonymity is also the reason why there are no photographs of students in this book.

19 I define lower-middle-class status here as having family or household annual incomes between $40,000 and $100,000. Those with annual incomes of over $100,000 were considered to be of upper-middle-class status. It should be noted that class status, like other social categories, can be malleable. That is, household incomes and other measurements of wealth can change with each generation that passes. In this study, class status was self-reported by all the respondents. For a more elaborated history of Filipinos in Washington State, see Cordova and Filipino American National Historical Society, *Filipinos in Puget Sound*, and Fujita-Rony, *American Workers, Colonial Power*. For accounts of Filipino immigration to the United States in general, see Baldoz, *The Third Asiatic Invasion*, and Bonus, *Locating Filipino Americans*.

20 Washington State Workforce Training and Education Coordinating Board, *Asians and Pacific Islanders*; U.S. Department of Labor, *The Asian-American Labor Force in the Recovery*.

21 Baldoz, *The Third Asiatic Invasion*; Fujita-Rony, *American Workers, Colonial Power*; U.S. Census Bureau and Pew Hispanic Center, *The American Community—Asians*.

22 University of Washington, Office of Minority Affairs and Diversity, Assessment Unit, *Diversity at the University of Washington—All Campuses*.

23 For political linkages and interracial relationships among Filipinos and Mexicans, see Guevarra, *Becoming Mexipino*. For accounts of Mexican immigration into the Pacific Northwest in particular, see Gamboa, *Mexican Labor and World War II*; García and García, *Memory, Community and Activism*; and Sifuentez, *Of Forest and Fields*.

24 University of Washington, Office of Minority Affairs and Diversity, Assessment Unit, *Diversity at the University of Washington—All Campuses*.

25 For specific accounts of immigration by Africans to Washington State and their contemporary lives, see Chait, *Seeking Salaam*. For a comparative study of African and African American studies, see Sisay, "Together but Unequal." For a demographic profile of Native Americans in Washington State, see Washington State Workforce Training and Education Coordinating Board, *Native Americans*. Also consult Boyd, *Indians, Fire, and the Land in the Pacific Northwest*.

26 University of Washington, Office of Minority Affairs and Diversity, Assessment Unit, *Diversity at the University of Washington—All Campuses*.

27 There is a good amount of scholarship on the experiences of first-generation students in all school levels, including strategies on how to become successful as one. For a most incisive and intimate look into the experiences of one such group, see Braffith, *Breathing Stories 2 Life*. For a comparative study with non-first-generation students, see Davenport's "Examining Involvement as a Critical Factor." I also include in this category those students whose parents attended college outside the U.S. mainland and, thus, have very limited knowledge about and experience in local college attendance. Refer to Maramba's work, "Immigrant Families and the College Experience," in this regard.

28 See varied accounts of on-campus struggles especially as experienced by nontraditional minority students in Goodwin, *Resilient Spirits*; Lesage, *Making a Difference*; Pizarro, *Chicanas and Chicanos in School*; Rhoads, *Freedom's Web*; and Stockdill and Danico, *Transforming the Ivory Tower*.

29 This is a reminder of Amy E. Stich's argument about how universities are stratified; it matters where one goes to college, not if one goes to college. Stich, *Access to Inequality*, 7.

30 For an account of mostly traditional white students on campus, in comparison with others, see Beyer, Gillmore, and Fisher, *Inside the Undergraduate Experience*; Moore, *African Americans and Whites*; and Nathan, *My Freshman Year*.

31 Wills and Bolcer, *University of Washington*.

32 University of Washington, Office of Sponsored Programs and Grant and Contract Accounting, *Annual Report: Awards and Expenditures*.

33 Beyer, Gillmore, and Fisher, *Inside the Undergraduate Experience*; Wills and Bolcer, *University of Washington*.

34 Bonus, "Transforming the Place That Rewards and Oppresses Us."

35 For more on affirmative action cases and debates in university settings, see Dobbin, *Inventing Equal Opportunity*, and Kellough, *Understanding Affirmative Action*.

36 Sanders, "UW Strives for Diversity despite I-200."

37 Hau'ofa, *We Are the Ocean*. For an analysis of Oceania in the American public imagination, see, among others, Geiger, *Facing the Pacific*; Lyons, *American Pacificism*; and Wilson, *Reimagining the American Pacific*.

38 Of course, the experiences of first-generation college students depicted here are not unique among UW students. They parallel the experiences of similar students in many other universities across the United States. See Baldwin, *The First-Generation College Experience*; Pizarro, introduction to *Chicanas and Chicanos in School*; and the experiences of first-generation immigrant students in Goodwin, *Resilient Spirits*. For

experiences outside the United States, see Heagney, "Student Success and Student Diversity."

39 Matters of debt and obligation in connection with education usually appear in historical accounts of schooling in the context of colonization. See, for example, Joel H. Spring's brief history of the education of dominated cultures in *Deculturalization and the Struggle for Equality* and the classic *Pedagogy of the Oppressed*, by Paulo Freire. Colonization and education, as well as implicit debt in response to the "benefits" of formal schooling, also figure prominently in studies of Native American schooling, as in Gram's *Education at the Edge of Empire*, chaps. 4 and 5, and in studies of colonial education in the Philippines, such as Constantino, *The Miseducation of the Filipino*.

40 The links across colonization, education, and whiteness (or white power) and their production of attitudes and feelings of inferiority or "colonial mentality" among minoritized students have been the subjects of many studies in the education of students of color. See Constantino, *The Miseducation of the Filipino*; Ladson-Billings, "From Soweto to the South Bronx"; and the essays in Altbach and Kelly, *Education and the Colonial Experience*; Maramba and Bonus, *The "Other" Students*; and Racelis and Ick, *Bearers of Benevolence*. Also refer especially to chapter 3 of Leonardo's *Race, Whiteness, and Education*, in which he states that "stretching the conceptual tendons of orthodox Marxism makes it flexible in accommodating the subjective experience of students of color as they navigate through an educational system hostile to their worldview. Although Fanon was speaking of the decolonization struggle during the 1950s, his insights are valid today because internal colonies like ghettos, *barrios*, and reservations bear the material and psycho-cultural marks of colonial education within a nation that daily reminds their subjects of the rightness of whiteness" (49).

41 Freire, *Education for Critical Consciousness*; Goodwin, *Resilient Spirits*; Gregory, *The Academic Achievement of Minority Students*; hooks, *Teaching to Transgress*; Lesage, *Making a Difference*; Maramba, "Understanding Campus Climate"; Pizarro, *Chicanas and Chicanos in School*; Tinto, *Leaving College*; Valenzuela, *Subtractive Schooling*.

42 Ryan and Sackrey, *Strangers in Paradise*.

43 I have done a similar, though abbreviated, analysis for faculty of color like myself, in Bonus, "Transforming the Place That Rewards and Oppresses Us."

44 For similar accounts and analyses of student invisibility due to minority status, see Lesage, *Making a Difference*; Light, *Making the Most of College*; Maramba and Bonus, *The "Other" Students*; McLaren, "White Terror and Oppositional Agency"; and Watson, *How Minority Students Experience College*.

45 Diaz, "To 'P' or Not to 'P'?"; Kaplan and Pease, *Cultures of United States Imperialism*; Thompson and Frentzos, *The Routledge Handbook of American Military and Diplomatic History*.

46 An astute and concise reading of the connections across historical invisibility and imperialism in the academy can be found in Campomanes, "The Institutional Invisibility of American Imperialism, the Philippines and Filipino Americans."

47 Shame, in this context, is usually registered by educators and academics in general as *internalized oppression* or *colonial mentality*. I hesitate, for now, to impose such labels on this feeling, because most respondents disagreed with me when I said

so, although it will be mentioned later on as related to *internalized colonization*. Shame, as experienced here by students, was initially not seen as equal or similar to self-hatred, itself a representation of internalized oppression as it has usually been defined: "when members of targeted groups accept and incorporate negative images of themselves fostered by the dominant society." Bell, "Theoretical Foundations for Social Justice Education," 11. Numerous scholars and activists, such as Patricia Hill Collins, Frantz Fanon, Paolo Freire, Albert Memmi, and Malcolm X, have written about this. Nor was shame here simply equated with a sense of inferiority or a "desire to be more like the colonizers," as defined in Pyke, "What Is Internalized Racial Oppression and Why Don't We Study It?," 554. Rather, shame here was much more nuanced, itself a combination of feelings of belittlement, low self-esteem, as well as anger. It was also understood as a consequence of the interplays of historical subjugation and, thus, functioned as part of a critique rather than a fixed emotion. See Strobel, *Coming Full Circle*, for an extended discussion, specifically on the experiences of Filipino American students in this regard.

48 Strobel, *Coming Full Circle*.

49 This is in contrast to whites, who are perceived to have no culture, or no culture that can be displayed as "exotic." Bonilla-Silva, *Racism without Racists*. Ore, *The Social Construction of Difference and Inequality*.

50 Chin and Chan, "Racist Love."

51 Hula is a Polynesian dance form oftentimes accompanied by song or chant, or both. Haka, traditionally, refers to a war dance, chant, or cry practiced or performed by Māori people.

52 For an expansive review of diversity issues in college education, see the essays in Brown, Hinton, and Howard-Hamilton, *Unleashing Suppressed Voices on College Campuses*.

53 Brown, Hinton, and Howard-Hamilton, *Unleashing Suppressed Voices on College Campuses*.

54 Abelmann, in *The Intimate University*, discusses a similar phenomenon.

55 Maramba, "Understanding Campus Climate"; Pizarro, *Chicanas and Chicanos in School*; Watson, *How Minority Students Experience College*.

56 The practice of "riding the wave," within different contexts, abounds in Oceania scholarship: Camacho, "Transoceanic Flows"; Diaz, "To 'P' or Not to 'P'?"; Fermantez, "Between the Hui and Da Hui Inc."; Fuary, "Reading and Riding the Waves"; Hauʻofa, *We Are the Ocean*.

57 On the phenomenon of so-called overactive students who engage in campus politics, see Astin, "Student Involvement," and Light, *Making the Most of College*.

58 On more substantive appeals to "diversity" on campus, see Ferguson, *The Reorder of Things*; McCarthy et al., "Introduction: Transforming Contexts, Transforming Identities"; and Pizarro, *Chicanas and Chicanos in School*.

59 One of the documentaries is *Forward: A Story about Pacific Islanders*, produced and directed by Kapiʻolani Lee.

60 A concise, but well-explained, summary of such theories can be found in Calhoun, *Contemporary Sociological Theory*.

61 Calhoun, *Contemporary Sociological Theory.*

62 This series of events was documented in Lee, *Forward: A Story about Pacific Islanders.*

63 The question of whether or not Filipinos are Pacific Islanders is discussed in Rondilla, "The Filipino Question in Asia and the Pacific." Also see Diaz, "To 'P' or Not to 'P'?"

64 On the politics and "strategic" use of indigenous and modern dancing for Filipino American student organizations, see Kinoshita, "Revitalizing Identity Politics."

65 Goodwin, *Resilient Spirits*; Lesage, *Making a Difference.*

66 I discuss additional aspects of Poly Day in chapter 4.

CHAPTER 2. PIPE

1 The academic literature on the study of "culture" is immense and diverse, but I specifically subscribe to the precepts forwarded by Stuart Hall and others associated with Birmingham University's Centre for Contemporary Cultural Studies, that make a distinction between a static definition of culture as "the sum of the best that has been thought of and said" and a more dynamic rendition of culture as the expressive positioning (or enunciation) of ideas and practices as its preferred emphasis. Concurrent and later developments in the study of culture, particularly emanating from various fields such as anthropology, ethnic studies, and American studies, would also seriously consider the study of culture in relation to issues and practices of knowledge production, social formation, and power. See Hall, "Cultural Studies: Two Paradigms," 33. Hall also notes that in connection with "identity," culture is a matter of "'becoming' as well as of 'being.'" Hall, "Cultural Identity and Diaspora," 224. Also see the illuminating essay on studying culture in relationship to power and difference by Gupta and Ferguson, "Beyond 'Culture.'" For a historical discussion on the relationship between culture and education, see Spring's *Deculturalization and the Struggle for Equality.*

2 On the idea that culture is a social construction practiced within historical contexts of power relationships, see Hall, "Cultural Identity and Diaspora," 224–226.

3 This relationship between identities and schooling is most emphatically nuanced in a good deal of work in education theory that specifically tackles the dynamics of racialization and racism, both within and outside of classrooms, as they are experienced by students. Examples include Giroux, *Pedagogy and the Politics of Hope*; Leonardo and Grubb, *Education and Racism* (esp. chap. 3); Nasir, *Racialized Identities*; Sheets and Hollins, *Racial and Ethnic Identity in School Practices*; and Tatum, "Talking about Race, Learning about Racism."

4 On the histories, social construction, and practices of whiteness especially in relationship to racism, see Feagin and Vera, *White Racism*; Lipsitz, *The Possessive Investment in Whiteness*; McIntosh, "White Privilege"; and Roediger, *Towards the Abolition of Whiteness.*

5 For a more specific discussion of whiteness and schooling, see Castagno, *Educated in Whiteness*; Hawkins and Larabee, "Engaging Racial/Ethnic Minority Students"; Leonardo, *Race, Whiteness, and Education*; and Moore, *African Americans and Whites.*

Howard's *We Can't Teach What We Don't Know* and McLaren's "White Terror and Oppositional Agency" provide more thorough discussions of whiteness as it is engaged in pedagogical practice.

6   Mentorship as partnership is also the backbone of Pizarro's work with mostly high school students in *Chicanas and Chicanos in School*. For out-of-school mentorship, refer to Hawkins and Larabee's, "Engaging Racial/Ethnic Minority Students."

7   Pacific Islander students consistently rank lowest in the UW's rates of student retention and completion, similar to the national trend for K–12 and higher education. In a 2014 UW study, it was shown that Pacific Islanders had the lowest graduation rate among all racial groups, at 68 percent, compared with 82 percent for white and Asian American students. Beyer et al., *UW Undergraduate Retention and Graduation Study*, 16. This study analyzed demographic and academic undergraduate student data from 2005 to 2012, interviews with staff and administrators, and surveys of students. For a national picture, refer to Museus, antonio, and Kiang, "The State of Scholarship on Asian Americans and Pacific Islanders in Education."

8   One of our inspirations for creating this on-campus mentorship program was the Pin@y (Pinay/Pinoy) Educational Partnerships (PEP) program based in the Bay Area, founded by Allyson Tintiangco-Cubales and her students at San Francisco State University. The PEP program operates through a "partnership triangle" among universities, local public schools, and community organizations to implement what it calls a "transformative decolonizing curriculum and pedagogy" in all levels of schooling. Tintiangco-Cubales, *Pin@y Educational Partnerships*. Although we were not aware of it at the time of this study, a similar student-run program called Pacific Islander Education and Retention (PIER), focused on "youth empowerment and cultural relevance," was operating at UCLA. Its history is documented in Saelua et al., "Pacific Islander Education and Retention."

9   The Office of the President, the Department of American Ethnic Studies (my department), the Polynesian Student Alliance (PSA), and the Micronesian Islands Club (MIC) were also included as partners/supporters in this mentorship project.

10 My involvement in the establishment of the university's Diversity Minor program (which I headed later on) facilitated numerous conversations with many students, faculty, staff, and administrators.

11 On the critical importance and complexities of multicultural environments and perspectives that benefit both mainstream students and students of color, see Banks and McGee Banks, *Multicultural Education*, chap. 10, "Approaches to Multicultural Reform"; Castagno, *Educated in Whiteness*; Nathan, *My Freshman Year*; Nieto, *Affirming Diversity*; Sleeter, *Multicultural Education as Social Activism*; and the essays in Au, *Rethinking Multicultural Education*.

12 Vincent Tinto's primary explanation for student departure or retention highlights the importance of having students be effectively integrated or connected into the social and academic lives of the educational institution they are in. The less integrated they are, the more their chances of leaving the institution will increase. His studies suggest that "campus climate" affects how students connect or not with their school. Tinto, *Leaving College*. For similar studies and arguments regarding the

critical importance of campus climates or school environments, see Chang, *Compelling Interest*; Hurtado, Alvarado, and Guillermo-Wann, "Thinking about Race"; Hurtado et al., *Enacting Diverse Learning Environments*; and Singham, *The Achievement Gap in U.S. Education*. I examine the dynamics of student departure more deeply in chapter 3.

13 Vilsoni Hereniko's argument about "academic imperialism" states that schools usually "value the written word and marginalize indigenous ways of being." "Indigenous Knowledge and Academic Imperialism," 84.

14 Reynaldo I. Monzon demonstrates that for Filipino American students, and other students from collectively focused cultures, "the well-being of the family carries more weight than the happiness of the individual," so much so that "collective self-esteem is more relevant to academic performance than personal [or individualized] self-esteem." Having a sense of belonging to a family while in school, then, is important to these students. According to Monzon, this crucial difference between individual worthiness and collective well-being, usually conflated or unspecified in the term "self-esteem," is erroneously glossed over in many surveys that attempt to determine why students do well or not in school. Monzon, "Collective Self-Esteem and Perceptions of Family," 237, 256. On the importance of "family" for Native American cultures, see Ward, *Native Americans in the School System*.

15 On the significance of claiming public space for those who are underrepresented, see Bonus, *Locating Filipino Americans*.

16 See the critiques of capitalism in schooling as experienced by college students, in Nathan, *My Freshman Year*, 148–156; Spring, *Economization of Education*; and Stich, *Access to Inequality*.

17 Valenzuela, *Subtractive Schooling*.

18 Valenzuela, *Subtractive Schooling*.

19 For a comprehensive look into these outreach and retention strategies, including those designed for underrepresented students, see Cook and Rushton, *How to Recruit and Retain Higher Education Students*. Also see Kabuto and Martens, *Linking Families, Learning, and Schooling*.

20 To wit, "attending college is not an 'individual' activity, but rather a 'collective' one." Monzon, "Collective Self-Esteem and Perceptions of Family," 237.

21 The reliability of grades as indicators of student performance, among diverse college majors, male and female students, and racial/ethnic/class groups, is dealt with in Pennock-Román's *Prediction of College Grades*. Also see Nathan's *My Freshman Year*, for a discussion of "cultural codes" of college student performance that includes critical attitudes regarding course grading, especially in chap. 6.

22 Regarding significant examples of "quality" schooling beyond the reliance on grading as an indicator of school performance, an outstanding source is Valenzuela, *Subtractive Schooling*.

23 See Oppenheim, "Nelson Mandela and the Power of Ubuntu." Desmond Tutu has a different take on the word's meaning: "the essence of what it means to be human." Tutu, "Ubuntu," 23.

24 This argument is echoed from Valenzuela's *Subtractive Schooling*. Valenzuela's study approached the schooling experiences of high school students by critically reading

their differential treatment (as Mexican immigrants or U.S.-born Mexicans) as an instance of institutional racism. In such treatment, the tendency is to divest (or, from Valenzuela's book title, subtract) the cultures that certain students bring into the classrooms, removing especially from the low-performing students those knowledges and practices from their cultures that would have been instrumental in enabling them to succeed in school.

25 Students pronounced it as "ye-how-li." Bates, Hess, and Hilbert, *Lushootseed Dictionary*.

26 On the various practices of attempting a well-balanced college experience, see Braffith, *Breathing Stories 2 Life*; Goodwin, *Resilient Spirits*; Light, *Making the Most of College*; Moxley, Najor-Durack, and Dumbrigue, *Keeping Students in Higher Education*; and Nathan, *My Freshman Year*.

27 On "meaningful" schooling, see McGregor et al., *Re-imagining Schooling for Education*. In the Māori context, see Penetito, *What's Māori about Māori Education?* Relatedly, on the "democratization" of higher education through multicultural and other diversity-related projects, including especially its contradictions and paradoxes in reproducing exclusionary hierarchies, see Pollock, *Everyday Antiracism*, and Stich, *Access to Inequality*.

28 The seeming incongruities between capitalism and schooling have long been subjects of critiques in the field of education and beyond. See Bale and Knopp, *Education and Capitalism*; Bowles and Gintis, *Schooling in Capitalist America*; Castagno, *Educated in Whiteness*; Giroux, *Pedagogy and the Politics of Hope*; and Hursh, *The End of Public Schools*. For a review of responses to such incongruities, from the various perspectives of school transformation that this chapter reflects on, see the essays in Gardner and Kelly, *Narrating Transformative Learning in Education*.

29 Banks calls this multiculturalist strategy as "additive" or "contributionist." Banks, *Multicultural Education, Transformative Knowledge, and Action*. Also see Grant and Sleeter, *Doing Multicultural Education for Achievement and Equity*, and Sleeter, *Multicultural Education as Social Activism*.

CHAPTER 3. THOSE WHO LEFT

1 Pacific Islander students at UW Seattle were consistently less than 1 percent of the total undergraduate student population (between 150 and 260 of 25,000–28,000) over the years I worked on this ethnography. They were the lowest among all the major racial groups. University of Washington, Office of Minority Affairs and Diversity, *State of Diversity at UW*.

2 The most-cited U.S.-based scholar of student attrition is Vincent Tinto, whose book *Leaving College* has undergone two editions. He has also written numerous articles about this topic. I cite here only from the second edition of *Leaving College*, which contains additional data on population groups that were not covered in the first edition and includes some new analyses and theoretical revisions. While his studies have been critiqued for their methodological flaws and predictive limitations, I rely on him for his astutely holistic approach to recognizing attrition as both individual

and institutional failure. Significantly influenced by Émile Durkheim's theory of suicide, he argues that dropout occurs when a student is not sufficiently integrated into a school's life, similar to an individual committing (or attempting) suicide due to his or her lack of integration into society. For a school to effectively retain its students, he calls for a solid institutional commitment to its students and a willingness to implement meaningful learning communities that will assist in connecting students with their school.

3   For an example of a study that questions conventional meanings of student success as a way of designing more effective alternative college retention and completion programs, see Moxley, Najor-Durack, and Dumbrigue, *Keeping Students in Higher Education*. Also see Braxton, *Reworking the Student Departure Puzzle*, and Crosling, Thomas, and Heagney, *Improving Student Retention in Higher Education*.

4   In many surveys of student attrition, the reasons for leaving college are almost always framed as individually caused or determined. For example, in a 2014 Student Experience in the Research University (SERA) study, a national survey that the UW participated in, eleven out of the fourteen reasons for leaving college that were listed began with the word "I," providing a strong impression that the blame for leaving rested on the student, not the school. Beyer et al., *UW Undergraduate Retention and Graduation Study*, 48. Anecdotally, but similarly, parents, students, and teachers will almost always place the blame of dropping out or stopping on the students themselves, and even in cases when students do not do well in school. Whenever I explained this to my students, I always used my mom as an example, in that when I used to show her my grade report from school, and I had low grades that she did not expect to see, she always asked, "What happened to you?," instead of "What happened to the teacher who taught you this class?" See, as an example of this way of thinking, Gramling, "How Five Student Characteristics Accurately Predict For-Profit University Graduation Odds," which argues that institutional characteristics do not matter in rates of college graduation. There is a relatively meager amount of academic literature on student departures that instead focuses mainly on the effects of institutional factors (school environments, finances, resources) on student performance. Refer to Tinto's *Leaving College*.

5   Some scholars would claim that for most departures, leaving school may have little to do with the students' inability to meet formal academic requirements such as passing classes and taking appropriate courses. In general, it has been shown that those who drop out from higher education are often the ones who perform better academically than those who stay. Indeed, in many surveys, individuals who left voluntarily were the ones who achieved higher grade point averages and were found to be somewhat more committed and creative than the typical college "persister." In these cases, according to Tinto, the more accurate explanation is that "leaving appears to reflect, on one hand, significant differences in the intentions and commitments with which they enter college and, on the other, real differences in the character of individual integrative experiences in the formal and informal academic and social communities of the college. The latter experiences have been described here as relating to the problems of adjustment to college life, to the issue of congru-

ence between the individual and the institution, and to that of isolation from the life of the college." It is, technically, not about intelligence at all. Tinto, *Leaving College*, 82. Also see Bergman et al., "If Life Happened but a Degree Didn't," for a similar situation among older adult students, and Metzner and Bean, "The Estimation of a Conceptual Model of Nontraditional Undergraduate Student Attrition," for an analysis of institutional support that influences students' grades. In other words, a student's integration into the life of the institution appears to be the key in determining whether or not that student stays in and graduates from college. The question, at least for this study, is, who bears the burden and costs of integrating students into the school?

6   Specifically in terms of what and how students are taught, a more popular term for this phenomenon is "hidden curriculum," in which students are educated according to implicit expectations of what their class and social status dictate, so that different students are taught differently and social inequalities are effectively reproduced. Anyon, "Social Class and the Hidden Curriculum of Work"; Apple, *Ideology and Curriculum*; Bourdieu and Passeron, *Reproduction in Education, Society, and Culture*.

7   Abelmann, *The Intimate University*; Altbach, Berdahl, and Gumport, *American Higher Education in the Twenty-First Century*; Bale and Knopp, *Education and Capitalism*; Bowen and Bok, *The Shape of the River*.

8   This practice of creating meaningful relationships with faculty is resonant with Tinto's argument that "contact with faculty appears . . . to promote student development in ways that can be distinguished from other attributes of students that foster development." *Leaving College*, 70.

9   The reference to "the ocean as relations" is popularly attributed by many Pacific Islanders to Albert Wendt, a well-known Sāmoan poet and writer. For an astute overview of his work, see Teaiwa and Marsh, "Albert Wendt's Critical and Creative Legacy in Oceania." I am also deeply illuminated by Tēvita O. Kaʻili's work on *tauhi vā* (the combination of tauhi, meaning, "to take care," "to tend," or "to nurture," and vā, meaning "the space between people or things"), defined as the Tongan value and practice of keeping good relations with kin and friends across/between oceanic spaces. Tauhi vā is also thought of as a commitment to sustain harmonious social relations with kin and kin-like members. Kaʻili, "Tauhi vā: Nurturing Tongan Sociospatial Ties," 92.

10 According to a 2014 analysis of UW student demographic data from 2005 to 2012, the six-year graduation rate for Pacific Islanders was 68 percent, compared to 82 percent for white and Asian American students, 71 percent for African American students, 69 percent for Native American students, and 81 percent overall. The national rate for graduating within six years from a four-year institution was 59 percent, on average, from 2005 to 2009. The national rate for Pacific Islander students graduating from four-year institutions within six years after starting, and between 2005 to 2009, averaged 49 percent. From 1999 to 2003, Pacific Islander students' attrition rates at UW were 10 percent in the first year and 4 percent in the second year, which meant that 85 percent were retained after the second year. Beyer et al., *UW Undergraduate Retention and Graduation Study*, 16; National Commission on

Asian American and Pacific Islander Research in Education (CARE) and Asian and Pacific Islander American Scholarship Fund (APIASF), *Asian Americans and Pacific Islanders in the College Completion Agenda*, 16; National Center for Education Statistics, *Fast Facts: Graduation Rates*; Pitre et al., *University of Washington Study of Attrition and Retention*, 21.

11 Kava is a traditional ceremony or ritual practiced in many cultures of Oceania in which a beverage derived from the roots of the kava plant ('awa in Hawaiian, 'ava in Sāmoan) is imbibed by the participants.

12 The notion that choosing a career early on, or even going to college itself, to ensure a successful life is widely held among many, but this is a site of debate among scholars and policy makers in education. Altbach, Berdahl, and Gumport, *American Higher Education in the Twenty-First Century*. For this notion's connection to thinking about how college degree attainment among population groups may cumulatively lead to a reduction of poverty and inequality in society, and the complex and contradictory ideas surrounding this, see St. John and Bowman, "Conclusion: Education, Poverty, and Public Policy."

13 Many of those interviewed in a study by Light, *Making the Most of College*, had a similar view.

14 The mismatch between ideologies and practices of schooling among different student bodies, especially beginning at the time when minority students were entering college in greater numbers during the second half of the twentieth century, is dealt with in several works: Brint and Karabel, *The Diverted Dream*; Fass, *Outside In*; Lesage, *Making a Difference*; and Sleeter, *Multicultural Education as Social Activism*.

15 The annual Poly Day (short for Polynesia Day) event on campus featured workshops on college admission, teach-ins on Polynesian history and culture, and stage presentations of dances, chants, and songs. I go into greater detail about Poly Day in chapter 4.

16 Though the research is far from being universally tested and verified, it is apparent that the more students are involved in the social and intellectual life of a college, and the more frequently they make contact with faculty and other students about learning issues, especially outside the class, the more likely students are to learn, stay in, and eventually graduate from college. College "involvement" leads to an increased likelihood that students will continue to be involved in their own schooling and in the future of their educational process. Astin, "Student Involvement"; Tinto, *Leaving College*, 69.

17 On the notion of "funds of knowledge" or "community cultural capital," Tara Yosso's preferred term, see Moll and Gonzalez, "Engaging Life"; Valenzuela, *Subtractive Schooling*; and Yosso, "Whose Culture Has Capital?" Zeus Leonardo distinguishes cultural impoverishment (or deficit) from material poverty impoverishment at the level of ideology particularly in dealing with school reform. Leonardo, "Poverty in Education and the Social Sciences."

18 Tarca, "Colorblind in Control."

19 Similar claims are made in many works, such as Beyer et al., *UW Undergraduate Retention and Graduation Study*; Pitre et al., *University of Washington Study of Attrition and*

Retention; Reed and Marienau, *Linking Adults with Community*; and Rhoads, *Freedom's Web*.

20 The logic of collective property expressed by the students here may have originated from Pacific Islander practices of communal land ownership, as in the Sāmoan *fa'asamoa* (land ownership by family groups called *aiga*), and the existence of Hawaiian Crown–controlled lands before the Great Māhele (land division) in 1848. Lawson, *Tradition versus Democracy in the South Pacific*; Osorio, *Dismembering Lāhui*. At present, it is argued that "most land in the Pacific islands is not common property in either the sense of open access to all people, or equal access to all members of a particular community which claims ownership." Ward, "Changing Forms of Communal Tenure," 21. So, in this case, the students' idea and their practice of "collective property" are not exactly cultural identity claims per se, but are, rather, strategic signal distinctions they make between two different social systems' worldviews. On the deeper explanations of the reflexive ways these distinctions occur when there are different expectations on how to circulate resources between Sāmoans and others, see Gershon, *No Family Is an Island*. On related issues of extended kinship practices and the valuing of connections to place that may have to do with appropriating ideas of communal ownership, see Spickard, "Pacific Islander Americans and Multiethnicity," 47–52.

21 Two UW attrition studies reported that having to deal with finances was the most primary reason why students dropped out of school. Beyer et al., *UW Undergraduate Retention and Graduation Study*; Pitre et al., *University of Washington Study of Attrition and Retention*.

22 The Free Application for Federal Student Aid, or FAFSA, is a resource for determining eligibility to acquire student financial aid from the U.S. government.

23 Bowen, Schwartz, and Camp, *End of Academic Freedom*; Cole, *The Great American University*; Delbanco, *College*.

24 For a good summary of the relationships between structural inequalities, economics, and schooling in the United States, see Oakes, "Social Theory, Evidence, and Activism."

25 Ochoa, *Academic Profiling*; Yosso, *Critical Race Counterstories*; Young, *Knowledge and Control*.

CHAPTER 4. SCHOOLING OUTSIDE AND INSIDE

1 Examples include Bass, "Disrupting Ourselves"; Brownell and Swaner, *Five High-Impact Practices*; Kugler, *Innovative Voices in Education*; Kuh, *High-Impact Educational Practices*; Nieto, *Affirming Diversity*; and Paige, *The Learning Community Experience in Higher Education*.

2 Bass, "Disrupting Ourselves," 26.

3 Kuh, *High-Impact Educational Practices*, 2.

4 I use the term "extracurricular" as synonymous with "cocurricular." Randy Bass makes a similar claim in that even though university administrators tout the value of experiential types of courses for all the benefits that accrue to the students, and

for helping in fulfilling campus missions, such courses remain to be considered cocurricular and marginal to the center of learning that is the formal curriculum. "Disrupting Ourselves," 24.

5   My narrative of Poly Day here is a composite of over ten years of observing and participating in it.

6   On the notion of valuing "culture" in the school, see, for example, Hereniko, "Indigenous Knowledge and Academic Imperialism," 84; Teaiwa, "Preparation for Deep Learning"; Valenzuela, *Subtractive Schooling*; and Yosso, "Whose Culture Has Capital?"

7   The notion that one's culture, especially one's racialized identity, might be a constitutive part of the schooling process was theorized early on by Tatum, "Talking about Race, Learning about Racism."

8   According to some alumni, Poly Day at UW first started in 1999.

9   Lee, *Forward: A Story about Pacific Islanders.*

10 Hall, "Cultural Studies: Two Paradigms"; Storey, *Cultural Theory and Popular Culture*; Williams, *Keywords*. On the politics of Pacific Islander cultural production, representation, and appropriation, see Buck, *Paradise Remade*; Gonzalves, *The Day the Dancers Stayed*; Hezel, *Making Sense of Micronesia*; and Imada, *Aloha America*.

11 For an analysis of the gender aspects of the Taualuga, see Mageo, "Race, Gender, and 'Foreign Exchange.'" For some visual representations of it, see Mallon, *Sāmoan Art and Artists.*

12 On the integration of out-of-class activities into academic culture, similar to internship or community service credits, see Bass, "Disrupting Ourselves"; Jacoby, *Service-Learning in Higher Education*; and Paige, *The Learning Community Experience in Higher Education.*

13 Unauthored pamphlet, presumably written by a collective of PIONEER student founders.

14 This PIONEER solidarity clap has had different additions and subtractions over the years, but most parts of this particular version have been retained.

15 The letters and journal entries shared here were actually from three study abroad experiences that I organized and led in the Philippines in 2007, 2011, and 2013. The first one was held in collaboration with an organization called Tagalog On Site. The second and third ones were conducted in partnership with the Philippine Women's University. In both of these trips, I encouraged all the participants to interact with me and with their classmates regularly through letters exchanged with each other and journal entries that were shared among all the students and with me. I provide here selected excerpts of these interactions. A very different version of this section, using the same pool of sources, appears in Bonus, "Come Back Home Soon."

16 We had previously offered classes on Hawai'i's literatures and Filipino American history and culture, but this was the first time a class devoted to the teaching of Pacific Islander studies as a large category was offered within my department, American ethnic studies. It was called U.S. Pacific Islander Contemporary Culture, and it had an enrollment of fifty students (with an additional five who regularly attended without credit). Our campus's Department of Anthropology regularly taught Pacific

Islander studies courses because of the presence of faculty there who specialized in this field. This particular course was first taught in that department and was regularly cross-listed with my department.

17　Epeli Hau'ofa, in "Our Sea of Islands," wrote:

> The idea that the countries of Polynesia and Micronesia are too small, too poor and too isolated to develop any meaningful degree of autonomy, is an economistic and geographic deterministic view of a very narrow kind, that overlooks culture, history, and the contemporary process of what may be called "world enlargement" carried out by tens of thousands of ordinary Pacific Islanders right across the ocean from east to west and north to south, under the very noses of academic and consultancy experts, regional and international development agencies, bureaucratic planners and their advisers, and customs and immigration officials, making nonsense of all national and economic boundaries, borders that have been defined only recently, crisscrossing an ocean that had been boundless for ages before Captain Cook's apotheosis. . . . Do people in most of Oceania live in tiny confined spaces? The answer is "yes" if one believes in what certain social scientists are saying. But the idea of smallness is relative. . . . Smallness is a state of mind. (6–7)

18　See the expanse of alternative curricular work especially for minorities in the following examples: Brownell and Swaner, *Five High-Impact Practices*; Cook and Rushton, *How to Recruit and Retain Higher Education Students*; Richardson and Bender, *Fostering Minority Access and Achievement in Higher Education*; and Winkle-Wagner and Locks, *Diversity and Inclusion on Campus*.

CONCLUSION

1　Hau'ofa, *We Are the Ocean*; Teaiwa, "Preparation for Deep Learning"; Wendt, "Towards a New Oceania."

2　For a rendition of history that is located in the "front" for many Pacific Islanders, see Ka'ili, "Tauhi vā."

3　This reminds me of one of Adrienne Rich's often-quoted poems, "Natural Resources": "My heart is moved by all I cannot save: so much has been destroyed. I have to cast my lot with those who age after age, perversely, with no extraordinary power, reconstitute the world." *Collected Poems*, 506.

Abelmann, Nancy. *The Intimate University: Korean American Students and the Problems of Segregation*. Durham, NC: Duke University Press, 2009.

Adams, Caralee J. "SAT-ACT Performance for 2015 Graduates Called 'Disappointing.'" *Education Week* 35, no. 3 (September 9, 2015): 6.

Altbach, Philip G., Robert O. Berdahl, and Patricia J. Gumport, eds. *American Higher Education in the Twenty-First Century: Social, Political, and Economic Challenges*. 2nd ed. Baltimore: Johns Hopkins University Press, 2005.

Altbach, Philip G., and Gail P. Kelly, eds. *Education and the Colonial Experience*. New Brunswick, NJ: Transaction Books, 1984.

Anyon, Jean. "Social Class and the Hidden Curriculum of Work." *Journal of Education* 162, no. 1 (1980): 67–92.

Apple, Michael W. *Ideology and Curriculum*. Boston: Routledge and Kegan Paul, 1979.

Arum, Richard, and Josipa Roksa. *Academically Adrift: Limited Learning on College Campuses*. Chicago: University of Chicago Press, 2011.

Asian Americans Advancing Justice. *A Community of Contrasts: Asian Americans, Native Hawaiians and Pacific Islanders in the West*. Washington, DC: Asian Americans Advancing Justice, 2015.

Astin, Alexander. "Student Involvement: A Developmental Theory for Higher Education." *Journal of College Student Development* 40, no. 5 (1984): 518–529.

Au, Wayne, ed. *Rethinking Multicultural Education: Teaching for Racial and Cultural Justice*. Milwaukee: Rethinking Schools, 2009.

Baker, David P., and Gerald K. LeTendre. *National Differences, Global Similarities: World Culture and the Future of Schooling*. Stanford, CA: Stanford University Press, 2005.

Baldoz, Rick. *The Third Asiatic Invasion: Empire and Migration in Filipino America, 1898–1946*. New York: New York University Press, 2011.

Baldwin, Amy. *The First-Generation College Experience*. Boston: Pearson, 2012.

Bale, Jeff, and Sarah Knopp. *Education and Capitalism: Struggles for Learning and Liberation*. Chicago: Haymarket Books, 2012.

Banks, James A., ed. *Diversity and Citizenship Education: Global Perspectives*. San Francisco: Jossey-Bass, 2004.

———. *Education in the 80's: Multiethnic Education*. Washington, DC: National Education Association, 1981.

———. *Multicultural Education, Transformative Knowledge, and Action: Historical and Contemporary Perspectives*. New York: Teachers College Press, 1996.

Banks, James A., and Cherry A. McGee Banks, eds. *Handbook of Research on Multicultural Education*. 2nd ed. San Francisco: Jossey-Bass, 2004.

———. *Multicultural Education: Issues and Perspectives*. 4th ed. New York: Wiley, 2001.

Bartolome, Lilia T. "Beyond the Methods Fetish: Toward a Humanizing Pedagogy." *Harvard Educational Review* 64, no. 2 (1994): 173–194.

Bass, Randy. "Disrupting Ourselves: The Problem of Learning in Higher Education." *Educause Review*, March/April (2012): 23–33.

Bates, Dawn E., Thom Hess, and Vi Hilbert. *Lushootseed Dictionary*. Seattle: University of Washington Press, 1994.

Bell, Lee Anne. "Theoretical Foundations for Social Justice Education." In *Teaching for Diversity and Social Justice*, 2nd ed., ed. Marianne Adams, Lee Ann Bell, and Pat Griffin, 1–14. New York: Routledge, 2007.

Bergman, Mathew, Jacob P. K. Gross, Matt Berry, and Brad Shuck. "If Life Happened but a Degree Didn't: Examining Factors That Impact Adult Student Persistence." *Journal of Continuing Higher Education* 62, no. 2 (2014): 90–101.

Beyer, Catharine H., Angela Davis-Unger, Nana Lowell, Debbie McGhee, and Jon Peterson. *UW Undergraduate Retention and Graduation Study*. Seattle: University of Washington Office of Educational Assessment, 2014.

Beyer, Catharine H., Gerald M. Gillmore, and Andrew T. Fisher. *Inside the Undergraduate Experience: The University of Washington's Study of Undergraduate Learning*. San Francisco: Anker, 2007.

Bonilla-Silva, Eduardo. *Racism without Racists: Color-Blind Racism and the Persistence of Racial Inequality in the United States*. 3rd ed. Lanham, MD: Rowman and Littlefield, 2010.

Bonus, Rick. "'Come Back Home Soon': The Pleasures and Agonies of 'Homeland' Visits." In *Filipino Studies: Palimpsests of Nation and Diaspora*, ed. Martin F. Manalansan IV and Augusto F. Espiritu, 388–410. New York: New York University Press, 2016.

———. *Locating Filipino Americans: Ethnicity and the Cultural Politics of Space*. Philadelphia: Temple University Press, 2000.

———. "Transforming the Place That Rewards and Oppresses Us." In *Transforming the Ivory Tower: Challenging Racism, Sexism, and Homophobia in the Academy*, ed. Brett Stockdill and Mary Yu Danico, 31–52. Honolulu: University of Hawai'i Press, 2012.

Bourdieu, Pierre, and Jean-Claude Passeron. *Reproduction in Education, Society, and Culture*. Trans. Richard Nice. 2nd ed. London: Sage, 1990.

Bowen, William G., and Derek Bok. *The Shape of the River: Long-Term Consequences of Considering Race in College and University Admissions*. Princeton, NJ: Princeton University Press, 1998.

Bowen, William G., and Neil L. Rudenstine. "Race-Sensitive Admissions: Back to Basics." *Chronicle of Higher Education* 49, no. 22 (2003): B7–B10.

Bowen, William M., Michael Schwartz, and Lisa Camp. *End of Academic Freedom: The Coming Obliteration of the Core Purpose of the University*. Charlotte, NC: Information Age Publishing, 2014.

Bowles, Samuel, and Herbert Gintis. *Schooling in Capitalist America: Educational Reform and the Contradictions of Economic Life*. New York: Basic Books, 1977.

Boyd, Robert T., ed. *Indians, Fire, and the Land in the Pacific Northwest*. Corvallis: Oregon State University Press, 1999.

Braffith, Felix, ed. *Breathing Stories 2 Life: The Voices of Tacoma's First Generation College Students*. Olympia, WA: Evergreen State College, 2012.

Braxton, John M. "Reinvigorating Theory and Research on the Departure Puzzle." In *Reworking the Student Departure Puzzle*, ed. John M. Braxton, 257–274. Nashville: Vanderbilt University Press, 2000.

———, ed. *Reworking the Student Departure Puzzle*. Nashville: Vanderbilt University Press, 2000.

Brint, Steven G., and Jerome Karabel. *The Diverted Dream: Community Colleges and the Promise of Educational Opportunity in America, 1900–1985*. New York: Oxford University Press, 1989.

Brown, O. Gilbert, Kandace G. Hinton, and Mary F. Howard-Hamilton, eds. *Unleashing Suppressed Voices on College Campuses: Diversity Issues in Higher Education*. New York: Peter Lang, 2007.

Brownell, Jayne E., and Lynn E. Swaner. *Five High-Impact Practices: Research on Learning Outcomes, Completion, and Quality*. Washington, DC: Association of American Colleges and Universities, 2010.

Buck, Elizabeth Bentzel. *Paradise Remade: The Politics of Culture and History in Hawai'i*. Philadelphia: Temple University Press, 1993.

Calhoun, Craig J. *Contemporary Sociological Theory*. 3rd ed. Malden, MA: John Wiley and Sons, 2012.

Camacho, Keith L. "Transoceanic Flows: Pacific Islander Interventions across the American Empire." *Amerasia* 37, no. 3 (2011): ix–xxxiv.

Campomanes, Oscar. "The Institutional Invisibility of American Imperialism, the Philippines and Filipino Americans." Paper presented at the annual meeting of the Association for Asian Studies, Los Angeles, March 25, 1993.

Carnoy, Martin. *Education as Cultural Imperialism*. New York: D. McKay, 1974.

Castagno, Angelina E. *Educated in Whiteness: Good Intentions and Diversity in Schools*. Minneapolis: University of Minnesota Press, 2014.

Chait, Sandra M. *Seeking Salaam: Ethiopians, Eritreans, and Somalis in the Pacific Northwest*. Seattle: University of Washington Press, 2011.

Chang, Mitchell J. *Compelling Interest: Examining the Evidence on Racial Dynamics in Colleges and Universities*. Stanford, CA: Stanford University Press, 2003.

Chatterjee, Piya, and Sunaina Maira, eds. *The Imperial University: Academic Repression and Scholarly Dissent*. Minneapolis: University of Minnesota Press, 2014.

Chin, Frank, and Jeffery Paul Chan. "Racist Love." In *Seeing through Shuck*, ed. Richard Kostelanetz, 65–79. New York: Ballantine, 1972.

Ching, Doris M., and Amefil Agbayani. *Asian Americans and Pacific Islanders in Higher Education: Research and Perspectives on Identity, Leadership, and Success*. Washington, DC: NASPA–Student Affairs Administrators in Higher Education, 2012.

Chuh, Kandice. *Imagine Otherwise: On Asian Americanist Critique*. Durham, NC: Duke University Press, 2003.

Cole, Jonathan R. *The Great American University: Its Rise to Preeminence, Its Indispensable National Role, and Why It Must Be Protected*. New York: Public Affairs, 2009.

Cole, Stephen, and Elinor Barber. *Increasing Faculty Diversity: The Occupational Choices of High-Achieving Minority Students*. Cambridge, MA: Harvard University Press, 2003.

Commission on Asian Pacific American Affairs. *The State of Asian Americans and Pacific Islanders in Washington*. Olympia: Washington State Commission on Asian Pacific American Affairs, 2010.

Conchas, Gilberto Q., Michael A. Gottfried, and Briana M. Hinga, eds. *Inequality, Power, and School Success: Case Studies on Racial Disparity and Opportunity in Education*. New York: Routledge, 2015.

Constantino, Renato. *The Miseducation of the Filipino*. Quezon City, Philippines: Foundation for Nationalist Studies, 1982.

Cook, Anthony E., and Brian S. Rushton. *How to Recruit and Retain Higher Education Students: A Handbook of Good Practice*. New York: Routledge, 2009.

Cordova, Dorothy Laigo, and Filipino American National Historical Society. *Filipinos in Puget Sound*. Charleston, SC: Arcadia, 2009.

Crosling, Glenda, Liz Thomas, and Margaret Heagney. "Conclusions and Curriculum-Based Approaches: Some Suggestions for Future Action." In *Improving Student Retention in Higher Education: The Role of Teaching and Learning*, ed. Glenda Crosling, Liz Thomas, and Margaret Heagney, 166–182. London: Routledge, 2008.

D'Arcy, Paul. *The People of the Sea: Environment, Identity, and History in Oceania*. Honolulu: University of Hawai'i Press, 2006.

Darling-Hammond, Linda. "What Happens to a Dream Deferred? The Continuing Quest for Equal Educational Opportunity." In *Handbook of Research on Multicultural Education*, 2nd ed., ed. James A. Banks and Cherry A. McGee Banks, 607–630. San Francisco: Jossey-Bass, 2004.

Darling-Hammond, Linda, and John Bransford, eds. *Preparing Teachers for a Changing World: What Teachers Should Learn and Be Able to Do*. San Francisco: Jossey-Bass, 2005.

Davenport, Mona Yvette. "Examining Involvement as a Critical Factor: Perceptions from First Generation and Non-first Generation College Students." PhD diss., Illinois State University, 2010.

del Moral, Solsiree. *Negotiating Empire: The Cultural Politics of Schools in Puerto Rico, 1898–1952*. Madison: University of Wisconsin Press, 2013.

Delbanco, Andrew. *College: What It Was, Is, and Should Be*. Princeton, NJ: Princeton University Press, 2012.

Diaz, Vicente M. *Repositioning the Missionary: Rewriting the Histories of Colonialism, Native Catholicism, and Indigeneity in Guam*. Honolulu: University of Hawai'i Press, 2010.

———. "To 'P' or Not to 'P'?: Marking the Territory between Pacific Islander and Asian American Studies." *Journal of Asian American Studies* 7, no. 3 (2004): 1–26.

Diaz, Vicente M., and J. Kēhaulani Kauanui. "Native Pacific Cultural Studies on the Edge." *Contemporary Pacific* 13, no. 2 (2001): 315–342.

Dobbin, Frank. *Inventing Equal Opportunity*. Princeton, NJ: Princeton University Press, 2009.

Domina, Thurston. "What Works in College Outreach: Assessing Targeted and School-wide Interventions for Disadvantaged Students." *Educational Evaluation and Policy Analysis* 31, no. 2 (2009): 127–152.

Early, Gerald. "American Education and the Postmodernist Impulse." *American Quarterly* 45, no. 2 (1993): 220–229.

Evans, Nancy J., Deanna S. Forney, Florence M. Guido, Lori D. Patton, and Kristen A. Renn. *Student Development in College: Theory, Research, and Practice.* 2nd ed. San Francisco: Jossey-Bass, 2010.

Fass, Paula S. *Outside In: Minorities and the Transformation of American Education.* New York: Oxford University Press, 1989.

Feagin, Joe R., and Hernán Vera. *White Racism: The Basics.* New York: Routledge, 1995.

Ferguson, Roderick A. *The Reorder of Things: The University and Its Pedagogies of Minority Difference.* Minneapolis: University of Minnesota Press, 2012.

Fermantez, Kali. "Between the Hui and Da Hui Inc.: Incorporating N-oceans of Native Hawaiian Resistance in Oceanic Cultural Studies." In *Indigenous Encounters: Reflections on Relations between People in the Pacific,* ed. Katerina Martina Teaiwa, 85–99. Honolulu: Center for Pacific Islands Studies, School of Hawaiian, Asian, and Pacific Studies, University of Hawai'i at Mānoa, 2007.

Fleming, Jacqueline. *Enhancing Minority Student Retention and Academic Performance.* San Francisco: Jossey-Bass, 2012.

Freire, Paulo. *Education for Critical Consciousness.* New York: Continuum, 2008.

——. *Pedagogy of the Oppressed.* New York: Continuum, 1993.

Freud, Sigmund. *Civilization and Its Discontents.* New York: W. W. Norton, 1962.

Fuary, Maureen. "Reading and Riding the Waves: The Sea as a Known Universe in Torres Strait." *Historic Environment* 22, no. 1 (2009): 32–37.

Fujita-Rony, Dorothy B. *American Workers, Colonial Power: Philippine Seattle and the Transpacific West, 1919–1941.* Berkeley: University of California Press, 2003.

Gamboa, Erasmo. *Mexican Labor and World War II: Braceros in the Pacific Northwest, 1942–1947.* Seattle: University of Washington Press, 2000.

Gándara, Patricia C., and Frances Contreras. *The Latino Education Crisis: The Consequences of Failed Social Policies.* Cambridge, MA: Harvard University Press, 2009.

García, Jerry, and Gilberto García. *Memory, Community and Activism: Mexican Migration and Labor in the Pacific Northwest.* East Lansing: Michigan State University Press, 2005.

García, Mario T., ed. *The Chicano Movement: Perspectives from the Twenty-First Century.* New York: Routledge, 2014.

Gardner, Morgan. "Transformative Learning as a Pedagogy of Movement." In *Narrating Transformative Learning in Education,* ed. Morgan Gardner and Ursula A. Kelly, 11–30. New York: Palgrave Macmillan, 2008.

Gardner, Morgan, and Ursula A. Kelly, eds. *Narrating Transformative Learning in Education.* New York: Palgrave Macmillan, 2008.

Geiger, Jeffrey. *Facing the Pacific: Polynesia and the U.S. Imperial Imagination.* Honolulu: University of Hawai'i Press, 2007.

Gershon, Ilana. *No Family Is an Island: Cultural Expertise among Samoāns in Diaspora.* Ithaca, NY: Cornell University Press, 2012.

Giroux, Henry A. "The Militarization of US Higher Education after 9/11." *Theory, Culture and Society* 25, no. 5 (2008): 56–82.

———. *Pedagogy and the Politics of Hope: Theory, Culture, and Schooling; A Critical Reader*. New York: Westview, 2008.

Go, Julian. "'Racism' and Colonialism: Meanings of Difference and Ruling Practices in America's Pacific Empire." *Qualitative Sociology* 27, no. 1 (2004): 35–58.

González, Norma, Luis C. Moll, and Cathy Amanti, eds. *Funds of Knowledge: Theorizing Practices in Households, Communities, and Classrooms*. Mahwah, NJ: Lawrence Erlbaum Associates, 2005.

Gonzalves, Theodore S. *The Day the Dancers Stayed: Performing in the Filipino/American Diaspora*. Philadelphia: Temple University Press, 2010.

Goodwin, Latty Lee. *Resilient Spirits: Disadvantaged Students Making It at an Elite University*. New York: RoutledgeFalmer, 2002.

Gram, John R. *Education at the Edge of Empire: Negotiating Pueblo Identity in New Mexico's Indian Boarding Schools*. Seattle: University of Washington Press, 2015.

Gramling, Tim. "How Five Student Characteristics Accurately Predict For-Profit University Graduation Odds." *SAGE Open* 3, no. 3 (2013).

Grant, Carl A., and Christine E. Sleeter. *Doing Multicultural Education for Achievement and Equity*. 2nd ed. New York: Routledge, 2011.

Gregory, Sheila T., ed. *The Academic Achievement of Minority Students: Perspectives, Practices, and Prescriptions*. Lanham, MD: University Press of America, 2000.

Guevarra, Rudy. *Becoming Mexipino: Multiethnic Identities and Communities in San Diego*. New Brunswick, NJ: Rutgers University Press, 2012.

Gupta, Akhil, and James Ferguson. "Beyond 'Culture': Space, Identity, and the Politics of Difference." *Cultural Anthropology* 7, no. 1 (February 1992): 6–23.

Hall, Stuart. "Cultural Identity and Diaspora." In *Identity: Community, Culture, Difference*, ed. John Rutherford, 222–237. London: Lawrence and Wishart, 1990.

———. "Cultural Studies: Two Paradigms." In *What Is Cultural Studies? A Reader*, ed. John Storey, 31–48. London: Arnold, 1996.

Harris, Philip M., Nicholas A. Jones, and U.S. Census Bureau. *We the People: Pacific Islanders in the United States*. Washington, DC: U.S. Census Bureau, 2005.

Hau'ofa, Epeli. "Our Sea of Islands." *Contemporary Pacific* 6, no. 1 (1994): 147–161.

———. *We Are the Ocean: Selected Works*. Honolulu: University of Hawai'i Press, 2007.

Hawkins, Viannda M., and Heather J. Larabee. "Engaging Racial/Ethnic Minority Students in Out-of-Class Activities on Predominantly White Campuses." In *Student Engagement in Higher Education*, ed. Shaun R. Harper and Stephen John Quaye, 179–197. New York: Routledge, 2009.

Heagney, Margaret. "Student Success and Student Diversity." In *Improving Student Retention in Higher Education: The Role of Teaching and Learning*, ed. Glenda Crosling, Liz Thomas, and Margaret Heagney, 17–28. London: Routledge, 2008.

Hereniko, Vilsoni. "Indigenous Knowledge and Academic Imperialism." In *Remembrance of Pacific Pasts: An Invitation to Remake History*, ed. Robert Borofsky, 78–91. Honolulu: University of Hawai'i Press, 2000.

Hezel, Francis X. *Making Sense of Micronesia: The Logic of Pacific Island Culture*. Honolulu: University of Hawai'i Press, 2013.

Hochschild, Jennifer, and Nathan Scovronick. *The American Dream and the Public Schools.* New York: Oxford University Press, 2003.

Hong, Grace Kyungwon. "Past Legacies, Future Projects: Asian Migration and the Role of the University under Globalization." *Diaspora: A Journal of Transnational Studies* 10, no. 1 (2001): 117–127.

hooks, bell. *Teaching to Transgress: Education as the Practice of Freedom.* New York: Routledge, 1994.

Howard, Gary R. *We Can't Teach What We Don't Know: White Teachers, Multiracial Schools.* 2nd ed. New York: Teachers College Press, 2006.

Howard, Tyrone C. *Why Race and Culture Matter in Schools: Closing the Achievement Gap in America's Classrooms.* New York: Teachers College Press, 2010.

Hune, Shirley. *Asian Pacific American Women in Higher Education: Claiming Visibility and Voice.* Washington, DC: Association of American Colleges and Universities, Program on the Status and Education of Women, 1998.

Hursh, David W. *The End of Public Schools: The Corporate Reform Agenda to Privatize Education.* New York: Routledge, 2016.

Hurtado, Sylvia, Adriana Ruiz Alvarado, and Chelsea Guillermo-Wann. "Thinking about Race: The Salience of Racial Identity at Two-and Four-Year Colleges and the Climate for Diversity." *Journal of Higher Education* 86, no. 1 (2015): 127–155.

Hurtado, Sylvia, Jeffrey Milem, Alma Clayton-Pedersen, and Walter Allen. *Enacting Diverse Learning Environments: Improving the Climate for Racial/Ethnic Diversity in Higher Education.* ASHE-ERIC Higher Education Report, vol. 26, no. 8. Washington, DC: George Washington University Graduate School of Education and Human Development, 1999.

Imada, Adria L. *Aloha America: Hula Circuits through the U.S. Empire.* Durham, NC: Duke University Press, 2012.

Isaac, Allan Punzalan. *American Tropics: Articulating Filipino America.* Minneapolis: University of Minnesota Press, 2006.

Jacoby, Barbara. *Service-Learning in Higher Education: Concepts and Practices.* San Francisco: Jossey-Bass, 1996.

Jencks, Christopher, and Riesman, David. *The Academic Revolution.* Garden City, NY: Doubleday, 1968.

Jiménez, Tomás R., Corey D. Fields, and Ariela Schachter. "How Ethnoraciality Matters: Looking inside Ethnoracial 'Groups.'" *Social Currents* 2, no. 2 (2015): 107–115.

Kabuto, Bobbie, and Prisca Martens. *Linking Families, Learning, and Schooling: Parent-Research Perspectives.* New York: Routledge, 2014.

Kahn, Miriam, and Erin Younger, eds. *Pacific Voices: Keeping Our Cultures Alive.* Seattle: University of Washington Press in association with Burke Museum of Natural History and Culture, 2005.

Kaʻili, Tēvita O. "Tauhi vā: Nurturing Tongan Sociospatial Ties in Maui and Beyond." *Contemporary Pacific* 17, no. 1 (2005): 83–114.

Kaplan, Amy, and Donald E. Pease, eds. *Cultures of United States Imperialism.* Durham, NC: Duke University Press, 1993.

Kellner, Douglas. "Globalization and New Social Movements: Lessons for Critical Theory and Pedagogy." In *Globalization and Education: Critical Perspectives,* ed.

Nicholas C. Burbules and Carlos Alberto Torres, 299–322. New York: Routledge, 1999.

Kellough, J. Edward. *Understanding Affirmative Action: Politics, Discrimination, and the Search for Justice*. Washington, DC: Georgetown University Press, 2006.

Kinoshita, Akira. "Revitalizing Identity Politics: Filipino American College Students and Folk Dance." *Nanzan Review of American Studies* 36 (2014): 25–43.

Kugler, Eileen Gale. *Innovative Voices in Education: Engaging Diverse Communities*. Lanham, MD: Rowman and Littlefield, 2012.

Kuh, George. *High-Impact Educational Practices: What They Are, Who Has Access to Them, and Why They Matter*. Washington, DC: Association of American Colleges and Universities, 2008.

Kumashiro, Kevin K. *The Seduction of Common Sense: How the Right Has Framed the Debate on America's Schools*. New York: Teachers College Press, 2008.

Labrador, Roderick N., and Erin Kahunawaika'ala Wright. "Engaging Indigeneity in Pacific Islander and Asian American Studies." *Amerasia* 37, no. 3 (2011): 135–148.

Ladson-Billings, Gloria. "From Soweto to the South Bronx: African Americans and Colonial Education in the United States." In *Sociology of Education: Emerging Perspectives*, ed. Carlos Alberto Torres and Theodore R. Mitchell, 247–264. Albany: State University of New York Press, 1998.

Law, John. *After Method: Mess in Social Science Research*. New York: Routledge, 2004.

Lawson, Stephanie. *Tradition versus Democracy in the South Pacific: Fiji, Tonga, and Western Sāmoa*. Cambridge, MA: Cambridge University Press, 1996.

Lee, Jennifer, and Min Zhou. *The Asian American Achievement Paradox*. New York: Russell Sage Foundation, 2015.

Lee, Kapi'olani, dir. *Forward: A Story about Pacific Islanders*. Seattle: University of Washington Native Voices, 2003. VHS.

Leonardo, Zeus. "Poverty in Education and the Social Sciences: Three Definitions." In *Rethinking Education and Poverty*, ed. William G. Tierney, 77–96. Baltimore: Johns Hopkins University Press, 2015.

——. *Race, Whiteness, and Education*. New York: Routledge, 2009.

Leonardo, Zeus, and W. Norton Grubb. *Education and Racism: A Primer on Issues and Dilemmas*. New York: Routledge, 2014.

Lesage, Julia. *Making a Difference: University Students of Color Speak Out*. Lanham, MD: Rowman and Littlefield, 2002.

Lewis, Oscar. *Five Families: Mexican Case Studies in the Culture of Poverty*. New York: New American Library, 1959.

Light, Richard J. *Making the Most of College: Students Speak Their Minds*. Cambridge, MA: Harvard University Press, 2001.

Lipsitz, George. *The Possessive Investment in Whiteness: How White People Profit from Identity Politics*. Philadelphia: Temple University Press, 1998.

Louie, Vivian. *Compelled to Excel: Immigration, Education, and Opportunity among Chinese Americans*. Stanford, CA: Stanford University Press, 2004.

——. *Keeping the Immigrant Bargain: The Costs and Rewards of Success in America*. New York: Russell Sage, 2012.

Lyons, Paul. *American Pacificism: Oceania in the U.S. Imagination*. New York: Routledge, 2006.

Maeda, Daryl J. *Rethinking the Asian American Movement*. New York: Routledge, 2012.

Mageo, Jeannette. "Race, Gender, and 'Foreign Exchange' in Sāmoan Performing Arts." *Anthropological Forum* 20, no. 3 (2010): 269–289.

———. *Theorizing Self in Sāmoa: Emotions, Genders, and Sexualities*. Ann Arbor: University of Michigan Press, 1998.

Mallon, Sean. *Sāmoan Art and Artists: O Measina a Sāmoa*. Honolulu: University of Hawai'i Press, 2002.

Maramba, Dina C. 2008. "Immigrant Families and the College Experience: Perspectives of Filipina Americans." *Journal of College Student Development* 49, no. 4 (2008): 336–350.

———. "Understanding Campus Climate through the Voices of Filipino/a American College Students." *College Student Journal* 42, no. 4 (2008): 1045–1060.

Maramba, Dina C., and Rick Bonus, eds. *The "Other" Students: Filipino Americans, Education, and Power*. Charlotte, NC: Information Age Publishing, 2013.

Maramba, Dina C., and Samuel D. Museus. "The Utility of Using Mixed-Methods and Intersectionality Approaches in Conducting Research on Filipino American Students' Experiences with the Campus Climate and on Sense of Belonging." In *Using Mixed Methods to Study Intersectionality in Higher Education*, ed. Kimberly A. Griffin and Samuel D. Museus, 92–101. San Francisco: Jossey-Bass, 2011.

Matute-Bianchi, Maria Eugenia. "Situational Ethnicity and Patterns of School Performance among Immigrant and Nonimmigrant Mexican-Descent Students." In *Minority Status and Schooling: A Comparative Study of Immigrant and Involuntary Minorities*, ed. Margaret A. Gibson and John U. Ogbu, 205–247. New York: Garland, 1991.

McCarthy, Cameron, Warren Crichlow, Greg Dimitriadis, and Nadine Dolby. "Introduction: Transforming Contexts, Transforming Identities: Race and Education in the New Millennium." In *Race, Identity, and Representation in Education*, 2nd ed., ed. Cameron McCarthy, Warren Crichlow, Greg Dimitriadis, and Nadine Dolby, xv–xxix. New York: Routledge, 2013.

———, eds. *Race, Identity, and Representation in Education*. 2nd ed. New York: Routledge, 2013.

McGregor, Glenda, Martin Mills, Kitty te Riele, Aspa Baroutsis, and Debra Hayes. *Re-imagining Schooling for Education: Socially Just Alternatives*. London: Palgrave Macmillan, 2017.

McIntosh, Peggy. "White Privilege: Unpacking the Invisible Knapsack." *Peace and Freedom*, July/August (1989): 10–12.

McLaren, Peter. "White Terror and Oppositional Agency: Towards a Critical Multiculturalism." In *Multicultural Education, Critical Pedagogy, and the Politics of Difference*, ed. Christine E. Sleeter and Peter McLaren, 33–70. Albany: State University of New York Press, 1995.

Mercer, Jane R. "Testing and Assessment Practices in Multiethnic Education." In *Education in the 80's: Multiethnic Education*, ed. James A. Banks, 93–104. Washington, DC: National Education Association, 1981.

Metzner, Barbara S., and John P. Bean. "The Estimation of a Conceptual Model of Nontraditional Undergraduate Student Attrition." *Research in Higher Education* 27, no. 1 (1987): 15–38.

Moll, Luis C., and Norma Gonzalez. "Engaging Life: A Funds-of-Knowledge Approach to Multicultural Education." In *Handbook of Research on Multicultural Education*, 2nd ed., ed. James A. Banks and Cherry A. McGee Banks, 699–715. San Francisco: Jossey-Bass, 2004.

Monzon, Reynaldo I. "Collective Self-Esteem and Perceptions of Family and Campus Environments among Filipino American College Students." In *The "Other" Students: Filipino Americans, Education, and Power*, ed. Dina C. Maramba and Rick Bonus, 237–258. Charlotte, NC: Information Age Publishing, 2013.

Moore, Robert M., ed. *African Americans and Whites: Changing Relationships on College Campuses*. Lanham, MD: University Press of America, 2006.

Motha, Suhanthie. *Race, Empire, and English Language Teaching: Creating Responsible and Ethical Anti-Racist Practice*. New York: Teachers College Press, 2014.

Moxley, David P., Anwar Najor-Durack, and Cecille Dumbrigue. *Keeping Students in Higher Education: Successful Practices and Strategies for Retention*. London: Kogan Page, 2001.

Museus, Samuel D., anthony lising antonio, and Peter Nien-Chu Kiang. "The State of Scholarship on Asian Americans and Pacific Islanders in Education: Anti-Essentialism, Inequity, Context, and Relevance." In *Focusing on the Underserved: Immigrant, Refugee, and Indigenous Asian American and Pacific Islanders in Higher Education*, ed. Sam D. Museus, Amefil Agbayani, and Doris M. Ching, 1–51. Charlotte, NC: Information Age Publishing, 2017.

Museus, Samuel D., Dina C. Maramba, and Robert T. Teranishi, eds. *The Misrepresented Minority: New Insights on Asian Americans and Pacific Islanders, and the Implications for Higher Education*. Sterling, VA: Stylus, 2013.

Nasir, Na'ilah Suad. *Racialized Identities: Race and Achievement among African American Youth*. Stanford, CA: Stanford University Press, 2012.

Nathan, Rebekah. *My Freshman Year: What a Professor Learned by Becoming a Student*. New York: Penguin, 2006.

National Center for Education Statistics. *Fast Facts: Graduation Rates*. 2017. Accessed August 18, 2017. https://nces.ed.gov/fastfacts/display.asp?id=40.

National Commission on Asian American and Pacific Islander Research in Education (CARE). *Asian Americans and Pacific Islanders: Facts, Not Fiction—Setting the Record Straight*. New York: College Board, 2008.

———. *Federal Higher Education Policy Priorities and the Asian American and Pacific Islander Community*. Washington, DC: National Commission on Asian American and Pacific Islander Research in Education, 2008.

———. *The Impact of Scholarships for Asian American and Pacific Islander Community College Students: Findings from an Experimental Design Study*. Washington, DC: Partnership for Equity in Education Through Research, 2015.

National Commission on Asian American and Pacific Islander Research in Education (CARE) and Asian and Pacific Islander American Scholarship Fund (APIASF). *The*

Relevance of Asian Americans and Pacific Islanders in the College Completion Agenda. Washington, DC: National Commission on Asian American and Pacific Islander Research in Education, 2015.

Nelson, Cary. *No University Is an Island: Saving Academic Freedom*. New York: New York University Press, 2010.

Newfield, Christopher. *The Great Mistake: How We Wrecked Public Universities and How We Can Fix Them*. Baltimore: Johns Hopkins University Press, 2016.

Ng, Franklin. "Knowledge for Empire: Academics and Universities in the Service of Imperialism." In *On Cultural Ground: Essays in International History*, ed. David Robert Johnson, 123–146. Chicago: Imprint Publications, 1994.

Nieto, Sonia. *Affirming Diversity: The Sociopolitical Context of Multicultural Education*. 2nd ed. White Plains, NY: Longman, 1996.

———. "From Brown Heroes and Holidays to Assimilationist Agendas: Reconsidering the Critiques of Multicultural Education." In *Multicultural Education, Critical Pedagogy, and the Politics of Difference*, ed. Christine E. Sleeter, and Peter McLaren, 191–220. Albany: State University of New York Press, 1995.

Nugent, David. "Knowledge and Empire: The Social Sciences and United States Imperial Expansion." *Identities: Global Studies in Culture and Power* 17, no. 1 (2010): 2–44.

Oakes, Jeannie. "Social Theory, Evidence, and Activism: Challenging Education Inequality in an Unequal Society." In *Rethinking Education and Poverty*, ed. William G. Tierney, 117–136. Baltimore: Johns Hopkins University Press, 2015.

Ochoa, Gilda L. *Academic Profiling: Latinos, Asian Americans, and the Achievement Gap*. Minneapolis: University of Minnesota Press, 2013.

Ogbu, John U. "Immigrant and Involuntary Minorities in Comparative Perspective." In *Minority Status and Schooling: A Comparative Study of Immigrant and Involuntary Minorities*, ed. Margaret A. Gibson and John U. Ogbu, 3–33. New York: Garland, 1991.

Olneck, Michael R. "Immigrants and Education in the United States." In *Handbook of Research on Multicultural Education*, 2nd ed., ed. James A. Banks and Cherry A. McGee Banks, 381–403. San Francisco: Jossey-Bass, 2004.

Olson, Lynn. "Children of Change: The Changing Face of American Schools." *Education Week* 20, no. 4 (2000): 30–41.

Ong, Aihwa. *Buddha Is Hiding: Refugees, Citizenship, the New America*. Berkeley: University of California Press, 2003.

Oppenheim, Claire E. "Nelson Mandela and the Power of Ubuntu." *Religions* 3, no. 2 (2012): 369–388.

Ore, Tracy E. *The Social Construction of Difference and Inequality: Race, Class, Gender, and Sexuality*. 3rd ed. Boston: McGraw-Hill, 2006.

Osorio, Jonathan Kamakawiwoʻole. *Dismembering Lāhui: A History of the Hawaiian Nation to 1887*. Honolulu: University of Hawaiʻi Press, 2002.

O'Sullivan, Edmund. "The Project and Vision of Transformative Education: Integral Transformative Learning." In *Expanding the Boundaries of Transformative Learning: Essays on Theory and Praxis*, ed. Edmund O'Sullivan, Amish Morrell, and Mary Ann O'Connor, 1–12. New York: Palgrave, 2002.

O'Sullivan, Michael. *Academic Barbarism, Universities and Inequality*. New York: Palgrave Macmillan, 2016.

Pacific Island Women's Association. *Voices of Pacific Island Women Residing in the Pacific Northwest: Reflections on Health, Economics, Education, and More*. Seattle: Pacific Island Women's Association, 2006.

Pacific Islander Studies Students, Kerri Ann Borja-Navarro, Richard Benigno Cantora, Andrew Fatilua Tunai Tuala, and David Ga'oupu Palaita, eds. *Matamai 2: Intersecting Knowledge across the Diaspora*. North Charleston, SC: CreateSpace, 2012.

Paige, Susan Mary. *The Learning Community Experience in Higher Education: High-Impact Practice for Student Retention*. New York: Routledge, 2017.

Palaita, David Ga'oupu, ed. *Matamai: The Vasa in Us*. El Cerrito, CA: Achiote, 2011.

———. "Vāsā (Ocean)—the Space That Is Sacred: Pacific Islanders in Higher Education." PhD diss., University of California, Berkeley, 2015. ProQuest.

Penetito, Wally. *What's Māori about Māori Education? The Struggle for a Meaningful Context*. Wellington: Victoria University Press, 2011.

Pennock-Román, María. *College Major and Gender Differences in the Prediction of College Grades*. New York: College Entrance Examination Board, 1994.

Pitre, Abul, Esrom Pitre, Ruth Ray, and Twana Hilton-Pitre, eds. *Educating African American Students: Foundations, Curriculum, and Experiences*. Lanham, MD: Rowman and Littlefield, 2009.

Pitre, Emile, Catharine H. Beyer, Sebastian Lemire, and Cyndy Snyder. *University of Washington Study of Attrition and Retention*. Seattle: University of Washington Office of Educational Assessment, 2006.

Pizarro, Marcos. *Chicanas and Chicanos in School: Racial Profiling, Identity Battles, and Empowerment*. Austin: University of Texas Press, 2005.

Poblete-Cross, JoAnna. "Bridging Indigenous and Immigrant Struggles: A Case Study of American Sāmoa." *American Quarterly* 62, no. 3 (2010): 501–522.

Pollock, Mica, ed. *Everyday Antiracism: Getting Real about Race in School*. New York: New Press, 2008.

Posey-Maddox, Linn. *Reconceptualizing the "Urban": Examining Race, Class, and Demographic Change in Cities and Their Public Schools*. Chicago: University of Chicago Press, 2014.

Pyke, Karen D. "What Is Internalized Racial Oppression and Why Don't We Study It? Acknowledging Racism's Hidden Injuries." *Sociological Perspectives* 53, no. 4 (2010): 551–572.

Racelis, Mary, and Judy Celine Ick, eds. *Bearers of Benevolence: The Thomasites and Public Education in the Philippines*. Pasig City, Philippines: Anvil, 2001.

Reed, Susan C., and Catherine Marienau. *Linking Adults with Community: Promoting Civic Engagement through Community Based Learning*. San Francisco: Jossey-Bass, 2008.

Rhoads, Robert A. *Freedom's Web: Student Activism in an Age of Cultural Diversity*. Baltimore: Johns Hopkins University Press, 1998.

Rich, Adrienne. *Collected Poems: 1950–2012*. Ed. Pablo Conrad. With an introduction by Claudia Rankin. New York: W. W. Norton, 2016.

Richardson, Richard C., Jr., and Louis W. Bender. *Fostering Minority Access and Achievement in Higher Education*. San Francisco: Jossey-Bass, 1987.

Roediger, David. *Towards the Abolition of Whiteness: Essays on Race, Politics, and Working Class History*. London: Verso, 1994.

Rondilla, Joanne L. "The Filipino Question in Asia and the Pacific: Rethinking Regional Origins in the Diaspora." In *Pacific Diaspora: Island Peoples in the United States and across the Pacific*, ed. Paul Spickard, Joanne L. Rondilla, and Debbie Hippolite Wright, 56–68. Honolulu: University of Hawai'i Press, 2002.

Rosaldo, Renato. *Culture and Truth: The Remaking of Social Analysis*. Boston: Beacon, 1989.

Rovai, Alfred P., Louis B. Gallien, and Helen R. Stiff-Williams. *Closing the African American Achievement Gap in Higher Education*. New York: Teachers College Press, 2007.

Ryan, Jake, and Charles Sackrey. *Strangers in Paradise: Academics from the Working Class*. Lanham, MD: University Press of America, 1996.

Saelua, Natasha, Erin Kahunawaika'ala Wright, Keali'i Troy Kukahiko, Meg Malpaya Thornton, and Iosefa (Sefa) Aina. "Pacific Islander Education and Retention: The Development of a Student-Initiated, Student-Run Outreach Program for Pacific Islanders." In *Focusing on the Underserved: Immigrant, Refugee, and Indigenous Asian American and Pacific Islanders in Higher Education*, ed. Sam D. Museus, Amefil Agbayani, and Doris M. Ching, 121–137. Charlotte, NC: Information Age Publishing, 2017.

Sanders, Al. "UW Strives for Diversity despite I-200: Recruiting Program Reaches out to 'Underrepresented' Students." *Skanner* 9, no. 33 (November 15, 2000): 1.

Sheets, Rosa Hernández, and Etta R. Hollins. *Racial and Ethnic Identity in School Practices: Aspects of Human Development*. Mahwah, NJ: Lawrence Erlbaum Associates, 1999.

Sifuentez, Mario Jimenez. *Of Forest and Fields: Mexican Labor in the Pacific Northwest*. New Brunswick, NJ: Rutgers University Press, 2016.

Silva, Noenoe K. *Aloha Betrayed: Native Hawaiian Resistance to American Colonialism*. Durham, NC: Duke University Press, 2004.

Singham, Mano. *The Achievement Gap in U.S. Education: Canaries in the Mine*. Lanham, MD: Rowman and Littlefield, 2005.

Sisay, Brukab. "Together but Unequal: Contemporary College Experiences of African and African American Students." *Ronald E. McNair Fellowship Journal* (University of Washington, Seattle) (2011).

Sleeter, Christine E. *Multicultural Education as Social Activism*. Albany: State University of New York Press, 1996.

Sleeter, Christine E., and Carl A. Grant. *Making Choices for Multicultural Education: Five Approaches to Race, Class, and Gender*. 4th ed. New York: Wiley, 2003.

Smith, Linda Tuhiwai. *Decolonizing Methodologies: Research and Indigenous Peoples*. New York: Zed Books, 1999.

Spickard, Paul. "Pacific Islander Americans and Multiethnicity: A Vision of America's Future?" In *Pacific Diaspora: Island Peoples in the United States and across the Pacific*, ed. Paul Spickard, Joanne L. Rondilla, and Debbie Hippolite Wright, 40–55. Honolulu: University of Hawai'i Press, 2002.

Spickard, Paul, Joanne L. Rondilla, and Debbie Hippolite Wright, eds. *Pacific Diaspora: Island Peoples in the United States and across the Pacific*. Honolulu: University of Hawai'i Press, 2002.

Spring, Joel H. *Deculturalization and the Struggle for Equality: A Brief History of the Education of Dominated Cultures in the United States.* 7th ed. New York: McGraw-Hill, 2013.

———. *Economization of Education: Human Capital, Global Corporations, Skills-Based Schooling.* New York: Routledge, 2015.

St. John, Edward P., and Phillip Bowman. "Conclusion: Education, Poverty, and Public Policy." In *Rethinking Education and Poverty,* ed. William G. Tierney, 259–262. Baltimore: Johns Hopkins University Press, 2015.

Starbuck, William H. *The Production of Knowledge: The Challenge of Social Science Research.* Oxford: Oxford University Press, 2006.

Stich, Amy E. *Access to Inequality: Reconsidering Class, Knowledge, and Capital in Higher Education.* Lanham, MD: Lexington Books, 2012.

Stockdill, Brett, and Mary Yu Danico, eds. *Transforming the Ivory Tower: Challenging Racism, Sexism, and Homophobia in the Academy.* Honolulu: University of Hawai'i Press, 2012.

Storey, John, ed. *Cultural Theory and Popular Culture: An Introduction.* 5th ed. New York: Pearson Longman, 2009.

Stratton, Clif. *Education for Empire: American Schools, Race, and the Paths of Good Citizenship.* Oakland: University of California Press, 2016.

Strobel, Leny Mendoza. *Coming Full Circle: The Process of Decolonization among Post-1965 Filipino Americans.* Quezon City, Philippines: Giraffe Books, 2001.

Stuart, Reginald. "Setting a New Standard." *Diverse: Issues in Higher Education* 26, no. 9 (2009): 16–18.

Suárez-Orozco, Carola, and Marcelo M. Suárez-Orozco. *Children of Immigration.* Cambridge, MA: Harvard University Press, 2001.

Suárez-Orozco, Marcelo M. "Immigrant Adaptation to Schooling: A Hispanic Case." In *Minority Status and Schooling: A Comparative Study of Immigrant and Involuntary Minorities,* ed. Margaret A. Gibson and John U. Ogbu, 37–61. New York: Garland, 1991.

Takeuchi, David T., and Shirley Hune. *Growing Presence, Emerging Voices: Pacific Islanders and Academic Achievement in Washington.* Report submitted to the Washington State Commission on Asian Pacific American Affairs. Seattle: University of Washington, 2008.

Tarca, Katherine. "Colorblind in Control: The Risks of Resisting Difference amid Demographic Change." *Educational Studies: A Journal of the American Educational Studies Association* 38, no. 2 (2005): 99–120.

Tatum, Beverly Daniel. "Talking about Race, Learning about Racism: The Application of Racial Identity Development Theory in the Classroom." *Harvard Educational Review* 62, no. 1 (Spring 1992): 1–24.

Teaiwa, Teresia. "Preparation for Deep Learning: A Reflection on 'Teaching' Pacific Studies in the Pacific." *Journal of Pacific History* 46, no. 2 (2011): 214–220.

Teaiwa, Teresia, and Selina Marsh. "Albert Wendt's Critical and Creative Legacy in Oceania: An Introduction." *Contemporary Pacific* 22, no. 2 (2010): 233–248.

Thompson, Antonio S., and Christos G. Frentzos, eds. *The Routledge Handbook of American Military and Diplomatic History, 1865 to the Present.* New York: Routledge, 2013.

Tienda, Marta. "Diversity ≠ Inclusion: Promoting Integration in Higher Education." *Educational Researcher* 42, no. 9 (2013): 467–475.

Tierney, William G. "Power, Identity, and the Dilemma of College Student Departure." In *Reworking the Student Departure Puzzle*, ed. John M. Braxton, 213–234. Nashville: Vanderbilt University Press, 2000.

Tintiangco-Cubales, Allyson. *Pin@y Educational Partnerships: A Filipina/o American Studies Sourcebook*. Vol. 1. Santa Clara, CA: Phoenix Publishing House, 2007.

Tinto, Vincent. *Leaving College: Rethinking the Causes and Cures of Student Attrition*. 2nd ed. Chicago: University of Chicago Press, 2012.

Trask, Haunani-Kay. *From a Native Daughter: Colonialism and Sovereignty in Hawai'i*. Honolulu: University of Hawai'i Press, 1999.

Treston, Helen. "Peer Mentoring: Making a Difference at James Cook University, Cairns—It's Moments like These You Need Mentors." *Innovations in Education and Training International* 36, no. 3 (1999): 236–243.

Turner, Caroline Sotello Viernes, ed. *Racial and Ethnic Diversity in Higher Education*. 2nd ed. Boston: Pearson, 2002.

Tutu, Desmond. "Ubuntu." *Amnesty International* 37, no. 4 (2010): 23.

University of California, Los Angeles, Asian American Studies Center. "Pacific Islanders Lagging behind in Higher Educational Attainment." Los Angeles: University of California, Los Angeles, Asian Pacific American Legal Center, 2006.

University of Washington, Office of Minority Affairs and Diversity. *State of Diversity at UW*. Accessed August 23, 2017. https://www.washington.edu/diversity/files/2016/03/2016-02-11-State-of-Diversity-report-New-Template.pdf.

University of Washington, Office of Minority Affairs and Diversity, Assessment and Research Unit. *State of Diversity at UW—All Campuses*. February 11, 2016.

University of Washington, Office of Minority Affairs and Diversity, Assessment Unit. *Diversity at the University of Washington—All Campuses*. October 2011. http://www.washington.edu/diversity/files/2013/04/diversitystats2011.pdf.

University of Washington, Office of Sponsored Programs and Grant and Contract Accounting. *Annual Report: Awards and Expenditures Related to Research, Training, Fellowships, and Other Sponsored Programs*. 2008.

U.S. Census Bureau and Pew Hispanic Center. *The American Community—Asians: 2004*. American Community Survey Reports, ACS-05. U.S. Census Bureau and Pew Hispanic Center, 2007. https://www2.census.gov/library/publications/2007/acs/acs-05.pdf.

U.S. Department of Education, National Center for Education Statistics. *The Condition of Education 2016*. NCES 2016–144.

———. *Digest of Education Statistics 2015*. NCES 2015-011.

———. *Status and Trends in the Education of Racial and Ethnic Groups 2010*. NCES 2010-015.

U.S. Department of Labor. *The Asian-American Labor Force in the Recovery, 2011*. Washington, DC: U.S. Department of Labor.

U.S. Department of Veterans Affairs, Center for Minority Veterans. *Asian American and Pacific Islander Veterans Fact Sheet*. November 2013. https://www.va.gov/centerforminorityveterans/docs/factSheetAanhpiInDepth.pdf.

Valencia, Richard R. *Students of Color and the Achievement Gap: Systemic Challenges, Systemic Transformations*. New York: Routledge, 2015.

Valenzuela, Angela. *Subtractive Schooling: U.S.-Mexican Youth and the Politics of Caring.* Albany: State University of New York Press, 1999.

Ward, Carol Jane. *Native Americans in the School System: Family, Community, and Academic Achievement.* Lanham, MD: AltaMira, 2005.

Ward, R. Gerard. "Changing Forms of Communal Tenure." In *The Governance of Common Property in the Pacific Region*, ed. Peter Larmour, 19–32. Canberra: Australian National University E Press, 2013.

Washington State Workforce Training and Education Coordinating Board. *Asians and Pacific Islanders: Workforce Focus.* Olympia: Washington State Workforce Training and Education Coordinating Board, 2005.

———. *Native Americans: Workforce Focus.* Olympia: Washington State Workforce Training and Education Coordinating Board, 2005.

Watson, Lemuel W. *How Minority Students Experience College: Implications for Planning and Policy.* Sterling, VA: Stylus, 2002.

Wei, William. *The Asian American Movement.* Philadelphia: Temple University Press, 1993.

Wendt, Albert. *Pouliuli.* Honolulu: University of Hawai'i Press, 1980.

———. "Towards a New Oceania." In *Writers in East-West Encounter: New Cultural Bearings*, ed. Guy Amirthanayagam, 202–215. London: Macmillan, 1982.

West, Cornel. "The New Cultural Politics of Difference." In *Out There: Marginalization and Contemporary Cultures*, ed. Russell Ferguson, 19–36. New York: New Museum of Contemporary Art, 1990.

White, Michael J., and Jennifer E. Glick. *Achieving Anew: How New Immigrants Do in American Schools, Jobs, and Neighborhoods.* New York: Russell Sage, 2009.

Williams, Joanna. *Consuming Higher Education: Why Learning Can't Be Bought.* New York: Bloomsbury Academic, 2013.

Williams, Raymond. *Keywords: A Vocabulary of Culture and Society.* London: Fontana, 1988.

Williamson-Lott, Joy Ann. *Black Power on Campus: The University of Illinois, 1965–75.* Urbana: University of Illinois Press, 2003.

Wills, Antoinette, and John D. Bolcer. *University of Washington.* The Campus History Series. Charleston, SC: Arcadia, 2014.

Wilson, Rob. *Reimagining the American Pacific: From "South Pacific" to Bamboo Ridge and Beyond.* Durham, NC: Duke University Press, 2000.

———. "Toward an Ecopoetics of Oceania: Worlding the Asia-Pacific Region as Space-Time Ecumene." In *American Studies as Transnational Practice: Turning toward the Transpacific*, ed. Yuan Shu and Donald E. Pease, 213–236. Hanover, NH: Dartmouth College Press, 2015.

Winkle-Wagner, Rachelle, and Angela M. Locks. *Diversity and Inclusion on Campus: Supporting Racially and Ethnically Underrepresented Students.* New York: Routledge, 2014.

Wright, Debbie Hippolite, and Paul Spickard. "Pacific Islander Americans and Asian American Identity." In *Contemporary Asian American Communities: Intersections and Divergences*, ed. Linda Trinh Võ and Rick Bonus, 105–119. Philadelphia: Temple University Press, 2002.

Wright, Erin Kahunawaika'ala, and Brandi Jean Nalani Balutski. "The Role of Context, Critical Theory, and Counter-Narratives in Understanding Pacific Islander Indigeneity." In *The Misrepresented Minority: New Insights on Asian Americans and Pacific Islanders, and the Implications for Higher Education*, ed. Samuel D. Museus, Dina C. Maramba, and Robert T. Teranishi, 140–157. Sterling, VA: Stylus, 2013.

Yee, Jennifer A. "Ways of Knowing, Feeling, Being, and Doing: Toward an Asian American and Pacific Islander Feminist Epistemology." *Amerasia Journal* 35, no. 2 (2009): 49–64.

Yosso, Tara. *Critical Race Counterstories along the Chicana/o Educational Pipeline.* New York: Routledge, 2006.

———. "Whose Culture Has Capital? A Critical Race Theory Discussion of Community Cultural Wealth." *Race, Ethnicity, and Education* 8, no. 1 (2005): 69–91.

Young, Michael F. D. *Knowledge and Control: New Directions for the Sociology of Education.* London: Collier-Macmillan, 1971.